Wailua Falls

MAUI TRAILBLAZER
Where to Hike, Snorkel, Surf, Drive
fourth edition
written by Jerry Sprout
photographs, art direction, production by Janine Sprout
technical advisor: Michael Sagues

For Thomas Mobius and Sara Emmaline Sagues, Carmen Frances and Lucia Jane Sagues, Lea Alexandra Butler, and Kylan Solei and Bodin Sprout

ISBN10: 0-9829919-1-6
ISBN13: 978-0-9829919-8-5
Library of Congress Catalog Card Number: 2001127203

Diamond Valley Company, Publishers
89 Lower Manzanita Drive, Markleeville, CA 96120
P.O. Box 422, Kilauea, HI 96754
www.trailblazertravelbooks.com
www.trailblazerhawaii.com
trailblazertravelbooks@gmail.com

Copyright ©2002, 2003, 2004, 2005, 2006, 2007, 2008, 2009, 2010, 2012
by Jerry and Janine Sprout

Mahalo Nui to our Trailblazer ohana:

The Hyde family, Mark, Vicki, Blair and Spencer; Paula Pennington and Jimmy Dunn; John and Patty Brissenden; John and Suzanne Barr; Gail and Brian Butler; Deanne Hawkins; Brian and Sue Kanegai; Matthew and Amy Sagues; Georgia Sagues; Michael and Cynthia Sagues; Jack and Sandy Lewin; Carol Mallory and Jim Rowley; Rich and Kate Harvey; Greg Hayes and Joan Wright; John Manzolati and Linda Kearney; Ellen Scott and Joe Stroud; Rob, Nancy, Kate and Sarah Moser; Judy Farnsworth, Barbara and Gary Howard; Margaret Daniels.

Marsha Wienert, Maui Visitors Bureau; Lucienne de Naie, Maui Tomorrow; Alan Bradbury, Vadra Doser, Garden of Eden; Larry Rodrigues and friends, Baldwin Beach; Gary Kaufman, Pacific Whale Foundation; Tom Vrbensky, Yarrow Flower at Kapalua; Kaleo Amadeo; Christopher and Caroline from Germany; Marian Feenstra, Department of Parks and Recreation; Steve Knight, Island Marine; Bob Chambers, Dave Castles, and Captain Rae, Maui Dive Shop; Stacey, Wailuku Main Street Assn.; Mike Townsend, Haleakala National Park; Lahaina Restoration Foundation; Maui Historical Society; Robert at Hotel Lanai; Dexter Tom, Carol Sh'e, Hattie, and Chris, Department of Land and Natural Resources; Becky and others at Haleakala National Park; Sarah from Kai Pali Place; Jerry and Claire, Hawaiian Islands National Humpback Whale Sanctuary; Melissa Kirkendall, State Historic Preservation Division; Rosalyn Baker, Leanne, Office of Economic Development; Russell Sparks, Division of Aquatic Resources; Brittney Dinson, Anuhea Rodrigues Auld, Debi and Dan Strick; Kate Zolezzi, Liz Smith, and Jonathan Hultquist, Maui Ocean Center; June Friewald, Pacific Whale Foundation; Polly Rhodes, Maui Eco-Adventures; Kaau Abraham and Patty Miller, Humpback Marine Sanctuary; Meiling Rossi, Hana Cultural Center; Jason Coloma, Kim Gaines, Swinging Bridges; Alii Chang, Maui Kula Lavender; Paula Heggle and Tara, Tedeschi Vineyard; Sandy and Tammy Hueu from Keanae; Leimomi, Hotel Hana Maui; Leslie, Ben, and J.D. Wyatt, Hawaii Nature Center; Linda Domen and Kahena at Kaupo Store; Roslyn Lightfoot, Maui Historical Society; Toni and Margo, Maui Natural History Association; Kamaui from Kahanu Gardens; Malia Carvalho from Keanae, surfer Dan Moore, and photographer Frank Quirarte.

Proofreader: Greg Hayes
Cover photo: Jaws

Baldwin Beach

MAUI TRAILBLAZER is an offering to these islands, to all their plants and animals and living things in the sea, and to all persons who dedicate their lives to fulfilling the promise of Aloha.

Iao Needle

MAUI

Trailblazer

WHERE TO
HIKE, SNORKEL, SURF, DRIVE

JERRY AND JANINE SPROUT

DIAMOND VALLEY COMPANY

MARKLEEVILLE, CALIFORNIA • KILAUEA, HAWAII

PUBLISHERS

TABLE OF CONTENTS

INTRODUCING MAUI

Aficionados of Hawaii debate which is the favorite among the islands, a discussion akin to picking the most charming rock star in a universally beloved band. People on this island have an expression meant to cut the friendly rivalry short—*Maui No Ka Oi,* Maui Is The Best.

With some eighty beaches, more than any other island, Maui will make converts of those whose primary quest is for sand, sun, and surf. The entire west coast—from Kapalua, Ka'anapali and Lahaina in the north to Kihei, Wailea and Makena in the south—is a run of beaches and coves, all with usually safe swimming. As an added bonus, offshore are enticing views of the sister islands that make up Maui County—Molokai, Lanai, Molokini, and Kahoolawe.

West Maui beaches (the island is hour-glass shaped, connected by an isthmus) will fulfill most people's fantasy of a Polynesian vacation: resorts with coco palms shading white sand and warm aquamarine waters, while inland loom dark green valleys and ridges 5,000-feet high. This side of Maui is about two-million years old, twice the age of East Maui, giving nature time to add shape and nuance.

The beaches of Kihei and Wailea, sometimes called the Gold Coast, lie at the foot of Haleakala, a 10,000-foot high active volcano that rises into another dimension on East Maui. In the lee of the volcano, this coast is more arid and sunnier, although gardens and parks add greenery to the coastline. South of the resorts, Makena State Park and the Ahihi-Kinau Reserve are natural areas, with beaches and lava peninsulas that serve up pristine snorkeling and coastal hiking.

Having explored these areas, beachcombers will just be beginning. Maui's windward east coast has rain forests, an arid wilderness coast, and more coco palms and white sand beaches—along with red, black, and yellow sand beaches. Add in as well, remote boulder bays, pastoral bluffs, and lava reefs fringed by forests.

Along this windward side is Paia, the world capital of windsurfing, and just south of that is Jaws, where some of the biggest waves draw surfers from all over the world. And if surf's not up here, try Honolua Bay just north of Kapalua, another five-star wave ride. For tamer water sports like snorkeling and scuba, Maui offers dozens of coral reefs, including several Marine Life Conservation Districts. Molokini Island, just offshore, is considered one of the best dive spots in the world.

For all these reasons—the mind reels at the scope—beach lovers may well agree that *Maui No Ka Oi*. But beaches are only part of the the story. Hikers will be drawn to West Maui's tropical mountains and streams, like Iao Valley and Waihe'e Ridge. The north coast is an undeveloped series of bluffs and bays, made for whale-and-wave watching, or hiking grasslands toward the jungly interior.

Kamaole III Beach Park

The road to Hana zigzags over fifty-plus one-lane bridges, penetrating rain forest that is one of the wettest spots on earth. The highway is a world-class attraction, and driving it sets heads gimbaling and eyes popping. The coast is wild, where waves meet cliffs. A new waterfall appears at every turn, punctuated by tropical flora literally too copious to comprehend. Visitors can pause at several arboretum and garden hikes, and take side trips to villages where Old Hawaii lives on.

It's a tall order not to be an anticlimax after such a highway, but Hana has the charm to pull it off. History and pastoral scenery overlay the town, set beside a pleasantly diverse coast that ranges from sculpted lava bluffs, to red-cinder coves, to a white-sand beach at Hamoa.

The pilgrimage to Hana ends down the road, at the Pools of Oheo, which are the lower section of Haleakala National Park. Nature's bathtubs await in a stream, while a trail inland ascends to towering waterfalls in a subtropical forest and bamboo grove.

The upper part of Haleakala National Park bears no resemblance to the lower—or to anywhere else. The crater at the summit, some 19 square miles, draws millions of visitors each year—Maui's main event in an all-star array of attractions. Bike down it, hike within it on miles of trails past cinder cones and mysterious lava caves, or stroll from roadside turnouts to sky-high overlooks. The drive to the top is the steepest in the world, and along Haleakala's slopes are eight biological zones, designated as an International Biosphere Reserve.

All these charms have made readers of national travel magazines tout Maui as the "World's Best Island" for several years running. Visitors can choose from a range

Kepaniwai Heritage Gardens, Iao Valley

Haleakala from Sliding Sands Trail

of accommodations—rustic beach cottages, wilderness camping, country bed-and-breakfast cottages, beachside condos, and the destination resort strips at Kaʻanapali and Wailea. Maui's fine restaurants and art galleries are numerous.

Even considering all these glitzy superlatives, the most surprising aspect of the island is its wealth of cultural sites and archeological ruins. Some are well preserved, like the Halekiʻi-Pihana Heiaus State Historical Monument in Kahului and the Piʻilanihale Heiau near Hana. Others are overgrown and uncharted, like many along the Kaupo coast, Kipahulu, and the interior valleys of West Maui. Here are reminders of the Hawaiian culture and geographical wonders. For many visitors, these intrigues will overshadow the island's allure as a vacation wonderland.

GETTING TO AND AROUND ON MAUI

AIRLINES
Most flights to Kahului Airport in Maui include a stopover and change of terminals in Honolulu. Most international airlines service Honolulu. Some airlines have non-stop flights to Maui: From Los Angeles, check with American, Delta, and United. From San Francisco try United, and from Seattle, give Hawaiian a call. Hawaiian has fewer length-of-stay restrictions and the most flights.

Hawaiian and Go! airlines are the major inter-island carriers. Several small airlines travel to Lanai and Molokai, as do passenger ferries. See *Resource Links* for all telephone numbers.

CAR RENTAL
All the major companies, plus a few local companies, service Maui. Book early and phone around to get the best deals. Some companies, such as Avis, offer mini-leases, if you're planning to stay longer. Numbers are in *Resource Links*.

Most highways and streets have bike lanes, and it's possible to navigate by bicycle as a means of transportation. But most roadways also have traffic, and dedicated bike paths and quiet rural thoroughfares are uncommon. A public bus services Kihei and the Lahaina-Ka'anapali Coast. Tour companies and shuttle taxis are widely available. For independent travelers, a car is essential.

WHEN TO COME
High season is when school's out during the summer, and also briefly around Christmas and New Year's. Maui visitation doesn't drop off much during any month. But if you'd like a slack time, early autumn and mid-to-late winter are the best bets. Room occupancy rates vary from 60 to 80 percent.

See *Driving Tours* at the start of each trailhead section for specific road descriptions. Also see *Free Advice & Opinion* for driving conditions and tips.

KAHULUI AIRPORT TO:	KA'ANAPALI TO:
Hana 55 mi., 2.5 hr.	Lahaina 4 mi., 10 min.
Wailuku, 5 mi., 10 min.	Kihei 25 mi., 50 min.
Ma'alaea 14 mi., 30 min.	Haleakala summit 65 mi., 2.5 hr.
Lahaina 28 mi., 40 min.	Hana 83 mi., 3.5 hr.
Ka'anapali 32 mi., 50 min.	
Kapalua 39 mi., 1 hr.	KIHEI TO:
Kihei, 10 mi., 20 min.	Haleakala summit 45 mi., 2 hr.
Wailea, 15 mi., 30 min.	Hana 62 mi., 3 hr.
Makena, 20 mi., 45 min.	Lahaina 25 mi., 50 min.

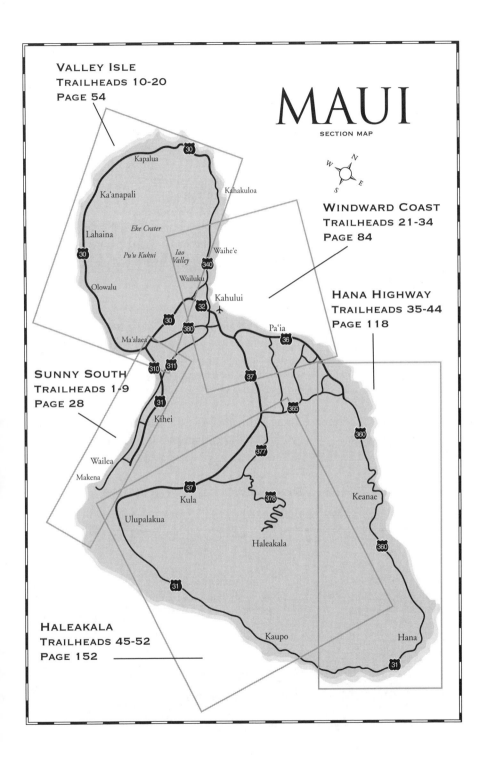

MAUI

SECTION MAP

VALLEY ISLE
TRAILHEADS 10-20
PAGE 54

WINDWARD COAST
TRAILHEADS 21-34
PAGE 84

HANA HIGHWAY
TRAILHEADS 35-44
PAGE 118

SUNNY SOUTH
TRAILHEADS 1-9
PAGE 28

HALEAKALA
TRAILHEADS 45-52
PAGE 152

Kapalua

Ka'anapali

Kahakuloa

Lahaina

Eke Crater

Pu'u Kukui

Iao Valley

Waihe'e

Wailuku

Olowalu

Kahului

Pa'ia

Ma'alaea

Kihei

Wailea

Makena

Kula

Keanae

Ulupalakua

Haleakala

Kaupo

Hana

30

340

32

30

380

310

311

31

37

365

360

377

37

378

31

360

31

HOW TO USE THIS BOOK

Use the INDEX to locate a trail or place that you've already heard about. Use the TABLE OF CONTENTS and MASTER MAP to find a part of the island you'd like to explore. Then use the TRAILHEAD MAP for each region to focus on a particular spot, and go to the descriptions to pick out a hike or other activity that looks good to you. Each trailhead contains hikes of varying lengths, and most have water sports. Use the Activities Banner in the TRAILHEAD DIRECTORY to see which recreational opportunities are available and where. Go to the BEST OF section to locate a hike or other activity that suits your interests, mood, and the day.

Use RESOURCE LINKS to find listings and phone numbers for public agencies and organizations, museums and attractions, tours and outfitters, accommodations and restaurants, and all other visitor information. For advice on obtaining SUPPLEMEN-TAL MAPS, see page 232 in Resource Links.

CALCULATING HIKE TIMES

Hikers in average condition will cover about 2 mph, including stops. Groups and slower-movers will make about 1.5 mph, or less. Well-conditioned hikers can cover 3-to-3.5 mph. Everyone should add about 30 minutes for each 800 feet of elevation gain. Also add 60 minutes to daylong hikes, for a margin of error, and just because this is Maui—trails are not generally easy, and people tend to look around more.

To check your rate of speed: 65 average-length steps per minute, equals about 2 mph; 80 steps per minute, about 2.5 mph; 95 average steps per minute, about 3 mph.

KEY TO READING TRAILHEAD DESCRIPTIONS

23. TRAILHEAD NAME   **ACTIVITIES BANNER**

WHAT'S BEST:
PARKING:

HIKE: Hike Destination (distance, elevation)

Hike descriptions.   (SAMPLE)
Talk Story:
Be Aware:
More Stuff:
SNORKEL: SURF:
Snorkeling, Surfing descriptions.

"23." TRAILHEAD NUMBER: These correspond to the numbers shown on the five Trailhead Maps, plus the three outer islands. Numbers begin with Map 1, Sunny South, continue to Map 5, Haleakala, and conclude with the three outer islands. In most cases, trailhead numbers that are close together numerically will be close geographically. There are 55 trailheads, listed sequentially in the text of the book. When looking for a particular trailhead, "TH23" for example, you may find it easier to flip through the text rather than look up the page number in the Trailhead Directory.

TRAILHEAD NAME: Each trailhead offers one or more of the activities—hiking, snorkeling, and surfing. Some trailheads have one parking place and a single activity. Other trailheads have several parking places, all close together, and several recreational activities. Some trailheads take a whole day, or more, to explore, while others can be combined with other nearby trailheads to fill out a day of adventuring.

ACTIVITIES BANNER: This shows which of the three recreational activities are available at this trailhead. Activities are always listed in the same order.

HIKE:	Hikes, ranging from long treks to easy strolls.
SNORKEL:	Snorkeling and swimming, including freshwater pools.
SURF:	Surfing, with boards, boogie boards, and bodies.
	Also includes windsurfing and kiteboarding.

WHAT'S BEST: A brief description of what to expect when visiting this trailhead.

PARKING: Gives specific directions from the nearest highway to the parking spot for the trailhead's primary hike destination, which will be listed first in the descriptions that follow. Secondary parking directions are also given for nearby hikes that follow in order. Additional parking directions are always *noted*, in italics.

HIKE: The first paragraph after the **HIKE:** symbol lists each **Hike Destination** available at the trailhead, followed by the (distance, and elevation gain) for each hike, in parentheses. Distances are given to the nearest .25-mile. Only elevation gains of 100 feet or greater are noted. All hiking distances in parentheses are ROUND TRIP.

The second paragraph after the **HIKE:** symbol often gives background and history for the trailhead (*Talk Story*). Following paragraphs give trail descriptions. The first reference to a **Hike Destination** is boldfaced. Trail descriptions include junctions with other trails, the type of terrain and walking surface, as well as elevation changes and landmarks along the way. **Second Destinations** follow in subsequent paragraphs, boldfaced and described in the order they are listed in the first **HIKE:** paragraph.

Talk Story: Gives historical or other background information. Rooted in the islands' oral traditions, 'talk story' is the term locals use for reminiscing about the old days.

Be Aware: Notes special precautions and difficulties associated with a hike or other activity. Also read *Free Advice & Opinion* for listings of rules and hazards that apply to adventuring on Maui.

More Stuff: Gives other hikes and activities available at this trailhead that are not among the primary listings. Normally these are out-of-the-way spots, sometimes with difficult access and terrain. Fewer visitors will be at these places.

SNORKEL: SURF: Descriptions for snorkeling and surfing follow, in order, after the hike paragraphs. Descriptions include where to go for these water sports, as well as notations for precautions. Parking directions for these activities will be included in the descriptions—unless they have already been listed in the parking directions or hike descriptions above. For example, parking directions for a snorkel or surf spot will most often be among those already given for a beach walk. **Snorkel** and **Surf** locations are boldfaced. One trailhead may have several locations for each activity.

Kahului, Windward Coast

WHAT NOT TO MISS ON MAUI

Everything in this book is recommended, but these places are among Hawaii's best. Lists are in ascending order of trailhead numbers.
TH = trailhead

HIKES

Pools of Oheo

SURFING

WINDSURFING-KITEBOARDING

KAYAKING

PICNIC SPOTS

Kanaha

TRAILHEAD DIRECTORY

HIKE: HIKING, STROLLING
SNORKEL: SNORKELING, SWIMMING
SURF: SURFING, BODYBOARDING, WIND SPORTS

Twin Falls

WINDWARD COAST - Trailheads 21 through 34

HANA HIGHWAY - Trailheads 35 through 44

HALEAKALA - Trailheads 45 through 52

OUTER ISLANDS - Trailheads 53 through 55

Big Beach, Makena State Park

SUNNY SOUTH

You'll need fingers and toes to count all the beaches along the twenty-plus mile coast from La Perouse Bay to Ma'alaea. Take a survey on this snorkeling safari. Although sun, sand, and surf remain constants, the settings range from the rugged lava wilderness of the King's Trail, to swank destination resorts with poolside gardens, to neighborhood beach parks with lawns and coco palms, and finally to a harbor where the tour boats return and nearby cliffs are perches to watch whales.

DRIVING TOUR
PICKING THE RIGHT DAY

This is called the Sunny South—and also Maui's Gold Coast—for a reason: In the lee of the trade winds and the rain-shadow of Haleakala, the southwest coast has reliable beach-going weather—320 days a year of sunshine. The isthmus, a land bridge between West and East Maui, moderates ocean currents. You may want to save this tour for a day when weather is inclement elsewhere. Beach parks and local's beaches, in the middle section of the tour, will see more action on the weekends. For a quieter time, pick a weekday.

THE ROADS

From Makena State Park to La Perouse, the road is narrow and bumpy in places, but easily navigated. From Makena north, the roads are all good, but traffic can be a problem. By starting in the south in the morning, you will avoid the slow going on Highway 31 that occurs in the afternoons. South Kihei Road, fronted by condos and small malls, has pedestrians and cross traffic. But a slow pace is compatible with sightseeing—you could miss things even going the speed limit.

THE COURSE

Follow along on the Sunny South map, page 28. Refer to trailhead descriptions beginning on page 29 for more details.

EARLY MORNING. BEGIN LA PEROUSE BAY. Snorkelers hit the water early at La Perouse Bay, which is also the best time to venture on the sun-baked lava fields for a look back to ancient times on the King's Trail. Then return to the present with a refreshing a dip in the bay, or move up the road a short distance and get in the water at Ahihi Cove. The drive takes you across the flow of Maui's most recent eruption, several hundred years ago, and the likely spot for Haleakala's next blow, which will occur ... sometime in the future.

Wailea Resort

MID-MORNING. Move north to the main parking area for Makena State Park. A short beach walk leads to the point separating Big Beach from Little Beach. You can also take the scamper up Puʻu Olai for a great view, beginning here, or from the trail at Black Sand Beach. Then get back in the car, and, past the Maui Prince Hotel, head to Makena Landing. Meander the shade and gardens of Keawalai Church, and then take the road north, hugging the coast past Chang's Point, as well as Poʻolenalena and Palauea beaches. Locals will be here as soon as it warms up on the weekends.

NOON. North of Palauea Beach, you'll come to the parking for Polo Beach Park. Here is the south end of the Wailea Coast Walk, a promenade past several beaches and opulent resorts. You can opt for an out-and-back on part of this paved path—or a driver can drop off walkers and then drive north around the resorts to pick up the walkers at Keawakapu Beach. For lunch, choose a plate lunch or deli sandwich from among the many choices in Kihei, and hang around the Kamaole Beach Parks. If you want beverages and snacks for sunset, pick them up here also.

Kamaole III, Kings Trail, Wailea

AFTERNOON. Continue north on Kihei Road. On weekends you might find some big doings at Kalama Park, or a race finale at the Kihei Canoe Club. You'll want to stop in at the Humpback Whale National Marine Sanctuary, where you can also visit the ancient fishpond. Birdwatchers can stop off at the Kealia Pond National Wildlife Sanctuary and stroll the boardwalk on the north end near the beach. Save the late afternoon for a visit to the Maui Ocean Center in Maʻalaea Bay.

SUNSET. Head out to the wharf at Maʻalaea Bay and watch the tour boats and fishermen returning from a day at the ocean. Or head to McGregor Point, on the west end of the bay, or Papawai Point, and watch the sun take a dive (an maybe spot a whale) from a higher elevation.

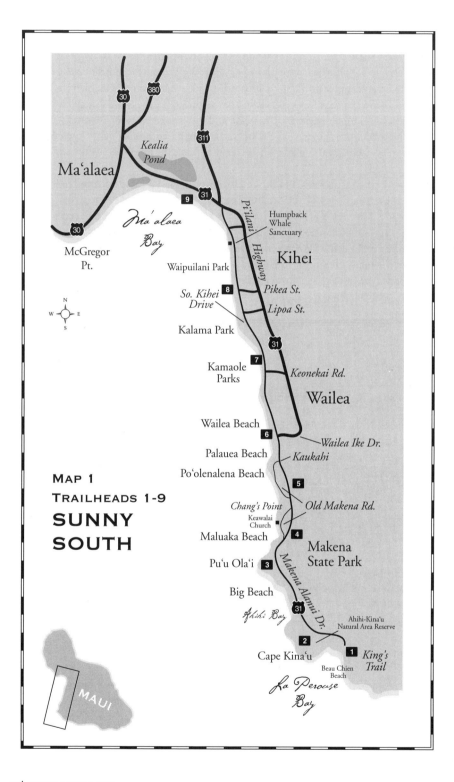

Map 1

Trailheads 1-9

SUNNY SOUTH

Ma'alaea

Kealia Pond

Ma'alaea Bay

McGregor Pt.

Kihei

Waipuilani Park

Humpback Whale Sanctuary

So. Kihei Drive

Pikea St.

Lipoa St.

Kalama Park

Kamaole Parks

Keonekai Rd.

Wailea

Wailea Beach

Wailea Ike Dr.

Palauea Beach

Kaukahi

Po'olenalena Beach

Chang's Point

Old Makena Rd.

Keawalai Church

Maluaka Beach

Makena State Park

Pu'u Ola'i

Makena Alanui Dr.

Big Beach

Ahihi Bay

Ahihi-Kina'u Natural Area Reserve

Cape Kina'u

Beau Chien Beach

King's Trail

La Perouse Bay

MAUI

Pi'ilani Highway

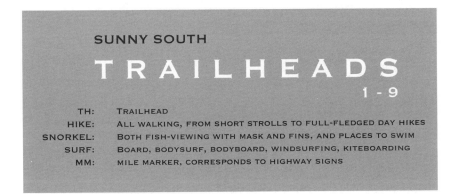

SUNNY SOUTH

TRAILHEADS
1 - 9

TH:	TRAILHEAD
HIKE:	ALL WALKING, FROM SHORT STROLLS TO FULL-FLEDGED DAY HIKES
SNORKEL:	BOTH FISH-VIEWING WITH MASK AND FINS, AND PLACES TO SWIM
SURF:	BOARD, BODYSURF, BODYBOARD, WINDSURFING, KITEBOARDING
MM:	MILE MARKER, CORRESPONDS TO HIGHWAY SIGNS

All hiking distances in parentheses are ROUND TRIP.
Elevation gains of 100 feet or more are noted.

1. LA PEROUSE BAY   HIKE, SNORKEL

WHAT'S BEST: The ancient King's Trail runs through historic ruins and jumbled lava fields to a remote bay. Return to snorkel in one of Maui's pristine locales.

PARKING: Take Hwy. 31 (the Pi'ilani Hwy.) south to Wailea. Continue south on Wailea Alanui for 8 mi., as the route becomes Makena Alanui and then So. Makena Rd. Road narrows and ends at La Perouse Monument, about 2 mi. after entering the Ahihi-Kinau Natural Area. Park on right in unimproved lot at the shore. *Be Aware:* No parking or hiking access on the road through the natural area. Scheduled to reopen in 2012.

HIKE: King's Trail to: Oasis Beach (4 mi., 150 ft.) or (Kanaio Beach (5.5 mi., 200 ft.); Cape Hanamanioa (3.25 mi.)

Talk Story: The parking area is within Keoneoio Village, a 65-acre historic district. Some of the lava-rock ruins date back about 500 years. The bay is named for French Admiral Compte de la Perouse, who thought this a "dismal coast" when he laid anchor in 1786, the first documented landing by Europeans on Maui. Historians long believed that four years after La Perouse's departure a wave of lava three-miles wide swept down from above—the most recent flow of Maui's million years of volcanic activity. New charcoal dating by volcanologists suggest this eruption may have occurred 300 years earlier—and La Perouse simply had not included the flow on his map. Captain George Vancouver mapped the Cape Kinau flow in 1793, spawning the notion that the eruption had taken place between the two visits. *Be Aware:* Take care not to distrub any ruins. Bring plenty of water and sun protection.

For the **King's Trail to Oasis (Kaunahana) Beach and Kanaio Beach**, walk the coastal trail through the village site, to the left as you face the ocean. You'll come to a grove of large kiawe trees and then reach an open area with a small sandy shore, called Beau

Ahihi-Kinau Natural Area Reserve

Chien (Pretty Dog) Beach. Just past the trees, about .5-mile from the parking, go left, departing the shore road and pass through an opening in a wire fence. Turn right on the wide, lava-stone trail, and you'll soon come to a large trailhead sign, noting the Hoapili Trail—named for Maui's governor in the early 1800s who improved the roads built by King Pi'ilani and his son, Kiha, in the early 1500s. It's also called the King's Highway, the alaloa, literally "long road" that encircled Maui—metaphorically, the path of life that we all travel from birth to death.

The 8-foot-wide paved trail leads gradually upward for a mile from the trailhead sign, reaching a rise. **For Oasis Beach,** look for coastal greenery as you descend from the rise. Leave the main trail and stay left of a rock enclosure at the beginning. The going is rough and the trail sketchy as you circle left of kiawe trees and then drop right to the (somewhat) sandy beach, which lies at the base of Cape Hanamanioa. **To continue to Kanaio Beach,** the former site of Kamanamana village, stay on the main trail as it descends for a mile from the rise and reaches the welcome shade of kiawe trees at the shore. White sand and coral among the black rocks will interest beachcombers, as will ancient rock enclosures located at the southern end of the little bay. *Note:* For more on this area, contact Project Kaeo; see *Resource Links*, page 234. *More Stuff:* The King's (Hoapili) Trail continues for another 10 miles across no-man's-land, although the footing is rougher and the trail is less defined and more overgrown after Kanaio Beach. See Manwainui, TH49, page 166 for access from other side.

To reach **Cape Hanamanioa,** the light beacon at the southern end of La Perouse Bay, follow the trail at water's edge to Beau Chien Beach. Keep right on the road closest to the water—passing two short connector trails that lead to the King's Trail. Follow the rough road to your right as it climbs briefly onto the cape. You'll get views of the bay and also inland toward the lava flow. The beacon is at the tip of the cape.

SNORKEL: The **north side of La Perouse Bay** is one of Maui's four marine preserves. From the parking area, head to your right, passing the haggard, barbed-wire fence. Land access is prohibited but it's okay to enter the water. You'll find a few smooth spots to sit down, but this rocky area is tough for tenderfoots. Booties will help. Swim across the sandy-bottomed bay, and then out the lava fingers of Cape Kinau, which forms the northern border of the bay. More adventurous snorkelers can try the **Beau Chien Beach**. To get there, see directions for the King's Trail. Look for a sandy channel just as you reach the greenery of the beach. *Be Aware:* Feeding fish is not allowed.

2.   AHIHI-KINAU NATURAL AREA RESERVE   HIKE, SNORKEL

WHAT'S BEST: Rugged trails lead across jagged lava to sacred fishponds, a hidden beach, and a rugged coast. The reserve offers some of the best the snorkeling on Maui.

PARKING: Take Hwy. 31 (the Pi'ilani Hwy.) south to Wailea. Continue south on Wailea Alanui for about 4 mi., as route becomes Makena Alanui and then So. Makena Rd. The Ahihi-Kinau boundary sign is about 1 mi. past last entry to Makena State Park, after the road narrows. *For Dumps Coast:* About .3-mile from the reserve boundary, just beyond where the road comes close to houses and the shore of Ahihi Cove, you'll see a large trailhead parking on your right. An information booth is manned by the Maui Wildlife Fund. *Kalaeloa Cove (Aquarium)-Halua Pond:* Drive across the barren lava of Cape Kinau—about 2 miles from the reserve boundary—to road's end at the La Perouse Monument (same parking as previous trailhead). *Be Aware:* No parking or hiking access on the road between Dumps and La Perouse. Scheduled to reopen in 2012 after 3 years of environmental study. Access to the hikes below may be limited. Heed signs.

HIKE: Dumps Coast (1.25 mi.); Kalaeloa Cove (Aquarium)-Halua Pond (2 mi.)

For the Dumps Coast hike, which follows the northern end of the natural area and reaches a small pond, take the well-trod path from the parking area to the coast. You continue left around the southern lip of Ahihi Bay and reach a sign noting "end of trail" at a small kiawe grove. Cut left inland at the sign on a trail marked by coral chunks and smoother rocks. You'll reach the shore again and find passage along black boulders that skirt the edge of the rougher a'a lava heaps. The shore transitions to coral chunks, a beach of sorts, with scrub kiawe at the backshore. After that is the pond, roughly 100 by 30 feet, with a squiggly shore. Fresh water and sea water surface and mingle near shore to form these ponds.

For Kalaeloa Cove (Aquarium)-Halua Pond, walk the road back about one-tenth mile from the La Perouse Monument parking. The trailhead is just after a walled and gated driveway, marked by a round mirror. The trailhead sign may not be present, but step over a low pile of rocks and take the sandy trail along the fence line, under

Aihi-Kinau Natural Area Reserve

the shade of kiawe trees. After a couple hundred feet you break into the open. **For Halua Pond**, keep right at an obscure junction, following the direction of the fence, avoiding options that lead left toward La Perouse Bay (and Kalaeloa Cove). The trail meanders over broken tabletops of lava. You'll come to the first pond, Kauhioaiakini, with greenery at its banks. (Some of the greenery is the rare Makaloa sedge, coveted by ancient chiefs for the supple weavings it can make.) Go right—avoiding another left-bearing option—keeping the pond on your left. You'll reach a black-cinder trail above the pond that continues due west toward the ocean. Halua Pond will be visible from the low ridge. Sitting close to the sea, this is one of several brackish ponds in the lava fields where ancient Hawaiians raised large mullet. Stay to the left of the pond and make your way down to the small bay that lies just beyond. This bay is marked by a good-sized kiawe tree, casting precious shade upon a rare patch of sand, a perfect spot to plant the fanny. *Be Aware:* This route is seldom used and hard to follow.

For Kalaeloa Cove (Aquarium), stay left on the trail as you leave the fence line, heading toward La Perouse Bay. On lava gravel, you'll head seaward along the bayshore and reach a little pond. Continue along water's edge. You'll reach a second pond, with orange-tinted shores. Keep this pond to your right. Climb a low bluff and negotiate a rocky chute—the route's roughest section—and then reach a more defined route that ends at the cove. (White spray paint will mark the way in confusing sections.) The lava shore of the cove is tricky to walk. Stay left for the easier going. *Be Aware:* Double back to a known spot if you find yourself lost. This area is subject to closure.

SNORKEL: Dumps is the best snorkeling in the reserve, and some of the best on Maui. You'll find a good entry spot at the far end of the lava shore, backed by shade trees. Waters are pristine and current normally calm. **Ahihi Cove** also offers very good snorkeling with easy access, located just .1-mile from the boundary sign. Parking at the inlet has been restricted, so you may want to park at Dumps and walk back to the cove. The best entry is on the north side of the cove, via a smooth submerged rock. Access to the cove and to Dumps was not changed by the environmental closure.

Kalaeloa Cove, also known as the **Aquarium**, offers excellent snorkeling, although considering the rough trail to get there, its popularity, and the difficult entry, you might conclude that it is overrated. See the hiking description above. Low surf and clean lava make for great visibility, and the fish are bountiful. *Be Aware:* Don't feed fish in this natural area. This area is subject to closure, due to environmental impacts.

3.   MAKENA STATE PARK   HIKE, SNORKEL, SURF

WHAT'S BEST: People watching, wave-play, sunning, scenery, and snorkeling: Makena (Big Beach) is one of Hawaii's superstar natural beaches. You can also take a short hike to a Maui landmark with a view of geographical significance.

PARKING: Take Hwy. 31 (the Pi'ilani Hwy.) south to Wailea. Continue south on Wailea Alanui, which becomes Makena Alanui. Pass the entrance to Maui Prince Hotel and a jct. with a spur of Makena Rd. Four access points: *For Oneuli (Black Sand) Beach*, go .2-mi. past the Makena Rd. jct. and look for pipe gate (closed evening hours) and a rutted dirt road. (Access to the nearby Pu'u Olai Wetlands may be limited.) *Big Beach has three access points and two parking lots;* the first lot is .4-mi. past the Makena Rd. jct. and is usually more crowded since it is closest to Little Beach; the second lot is less than .2-mi. beyond the first. After the second lot are roadside turnouts where you can can easily access the less-crowed, far end of Big Beach. *Note:* A parking fee of around $5 may be charged at some of the state park lots.

Makena State Park

HIKE: Pu'u Olai (1 mi., 350 ft.); Big and Little Beach (up to 1.5 mi.)

Known variously as Hill of Earthquakes, Round Mountain, and Red Hill, **Pu'u Olai** is the volcanic hillock that is prominent from many viewpoints on the west side of Maui. To reach the summit, turn toward Oneuli Beach, the first access described above. A rutted, .25-mile dirt road leads to an unimproved lot. From the lot, backtrack a short distance from the beach and head up through the trees, near a signpost that holds multiple messages. After a short, steep burst, you'll reach a trail that heads directly to the top of the north side of the pu'u. Once there you'll see that the top is a crater, overgrown with greenery. Head to your left along the rim. Once at the south side of the crater, the trail circumnavigates the rim, and you'll wind up making a loop.

Talk Story: According to local lore, Pu'u Olai was near the epicenter of an earthquake in the last century. A fishing shrine, or heiau, once adorned its summit. On a clear day you'll see Mauna Loa and Mauna Kea on the Big Island.

For the **Big and Little Beach** stroll, turn in at the first Big Beach access described above. A short path leads through trees from the lot to the northern end of the beach. *Note:* This parking lot fills up first; if arriving later on a weekend, try the second lot or use roadside parking where the road narrows. From the first lot access, the wide sand beach extends about .5-mile to the left, or south. Big Beach is officially called Oneloa Beach, and is also known as Makena Beach.

To walk to Little Beach head to your right along a path that skirts the sand, toward the point that marks the north end of Big Beach. You'll reach a short sand-and-rock connector trail that takes you up and over to Little Beach. You'll also want to walk out through trees to the point, a lava terrace with sunset views and tide pools. *Be Aware:* Although nudity is unlawful and not part of Hawaiian culture, Little Beach has become a popular clothing-optional beach. It's normally way more crowded than Big Beach.

SNORKEL: The south end of **Oneuli Beach**, or **Black Sand Beach**—see first access parking—attracts snorkeling and scuba tours. Swim out along the base of Pu'u Olai. Lack of freshwater runoff creates clear waters here when the surf is low. The reef has good snorkeling, with occasional turtle sightings. At **Big Beach**, go the the far north end and snorkel the calmer waters below the point, where the trail leads up to Little Beach.

Snorkelers will also like pretty **Kanahena Cove**, a Shoreline Public Access .3-mile south of the second Makena parking lot. You can park at a turnout marked by a "speed bump" sign or along a lava wall that extends from the turnout. The access is via an opening the wall, just past address 6900. A sand channel leads out to the right of the small sand beach, although wave action can make entry difficult. Fish viewing is excellent.

Little Beach

SURF: Bodysurfers are drawn to **Little Beach**, although the shore break can be hazardous. Keep a lookout for spinner dolphin, who like to play offshore of Puʻu Olai. Surfers and boogie boarders like the south end of **Big Beach**, particularly in the summer when the Kona surf is up. Pass all park entrances, and park along the road for the easiest board access. In the winter, skim-boarders ride the down-sloping wet sands of Big Beach and ride up the shorebreak—an entertaining sight.

4. MAKENA LANDING   HIKE, SNORKEL, SURF

WHAT'S BEST: Snorkeling, beachcombing, and historical sites combine for a full day of fun at this less visited coastline.

PARKING: Take Hwy. 31 (the Piʻilani Hwy.) south to Wailea. Continue south on Wailea Alanui, about 2 mi. The road becomes Makena Alanui past Kaukahi St. Pass first Makena Rd. (and Makena Surf) and turn right on second Makena Rd. *For Chang's Point,* continue for less than .25-mi. to a Shoreline Public Access, located between high-end homes before ascending a hill. *For Maluaka Beach Loop,* continue over the hill, pass Makena Landing Co. Park and Honoiki St. Park at the lot across from Keawalai Church.

HIKE: Chang's Point (.25-mi); Maluaka Beach loop (up to 1.25 mi.)

For the **Chang's Point** stroll, walk out a low lava wall and look for graves to your left—remnants from the 1800s when Chinese emigrants had a settlement on this coast below their larger villages in Kula. (We'll see what Chang's spirits have to say about the impolite encroachment of the new homes.) Continue out to water's edge and make your way a short distance to the end—its formal name is Nahuna Point.

The **Maluaka Beach loop** is a stroll along the sands below the Maui Prince Hotel, one of Maui's underrated beaches. Start by exploring the pleasant gardens and Hawaiiana around the Keawalai Church, built in 1832 using coral rocks (memorable services are held Sunday mornings at 7:30 and 10). Then continue walking a short distance down the road to where a parking turnout provides access to the beach. Walk the tree-fringed swath of sand, which is sometimes confusingly called Makena Beach Park.

At the end of the beach, you can skirt the golf course and new large homes to Maluaka Point, with its view of Pu'u Olai. Then backtrack, cutting inland at the south end of the beach toward the Maui Prince. A flagstone path runs through rolling lawn and gardens, between the hotel and the beach. *More Stuff:* You can also access Maluaka Beach, and the south end of the paved path, by driving past the Maui Prince entrance on Makena Alanui and, about .6-mile later, making a hairpin right on Makena Road. This short spur of the old road leads to a big parking lot, less frequented by beachgoers, but also the locale of a large beach villa development. At the shore is a superlative picnic area on treed terraces.

SNORKEL: **Five Graves**, also known as **Turtle Town** and **Five Caves**, is destination for snorkeling tour boats, which anchor a couple hundred feet offshore. You can swim here from the shore using two access points: The easiest entry, but longer swim, is at **Makena Landing County Park**, just over the hill from Chang's Point. Swim from the sandy landing entry to your right, a few hundred yards, out to the point. After the swim, you'll find a small sunning beach just around the shore from the county park.

Keawalai Church

Maluaka Beach, Turtle Town resident

The five caves, accessible only by experienced scuba divers, are underwater off the north side of the point. *Talk Story:* From 1850 to the early 1900s, Makena was Maui's busiest port, used to ship sugar and also to send cattle to a large ranch on Kahoolawe.

The second access to explore Turtle Town/Five Caves is from **Chang's Point**, as per the hike description above. Look for a small black-rock cove set in from the point. You'll have to do less swimming from this entry. Sea turtles commonly swim just off the point. *Be Aware:* Surf and rocks can make entry at Chang's Point tricky. Also, if swimming a distance off the point, watch out for boat traffic.

SURF: **Maluaka Beach** has a good bodysurfing break during summer swells.

---

5.   **PO'OLENALENA BEACHES**   HIKE, SNORKEL, SURF

WHAT'S BEST: In spite of new development, you'll find solitude on weekdays at these local's beaches, made for strolling, surfing, snorkeling, or just hanging out.

PARKING: Take Hwy. 31 (the Pi'ilani Hwy.) south to Wailea. Continue south on Wailea Alanui. After 1 mi., turn right on Kaukahi St., just past the Fairmont Kea Lani Hotel. At the bottom of the hill, turn left on Makena Rd. Three access points: *For Palauea Beach,* continue .25-mi. to unimproved parking amid shade trees across from new homes. *For Po'olenalena Beach,* continue on Makena Rd. another .5-mi. until it loops back out to Makena Alanui. Turn right and then turn right immediately on short access road to a signed, gated parking lot. *For Chang's Cove,* stay on Wailea Alanui, which becomes Makena Alanui past Kaukahi St. Pass the first Makena Rd. jct. Just before second Makena Rd. jct., turn right at a Shoreline Access sign (which may be missing) into Makena Surf condos into improved lot with a half-dozen spaces.

HIKE: Palauea to Poʻolenalena Beach walk (up to 2.25 mi.)

Talk Story: Off the main road—between the Wailea resorts on the north and the Makena beaches on the south—this mile-long run of sandy beaches interrupted by lava points is a longtime local's favorite. New homes have put the Poʻolenalena Beaches on the map, but not to the point of detracting from their serene nature. You'll find shade trees, swaths of sand, safe swimming, with views of Molokini and Kahoolawe. Unsigned ancient ruins are scattered in nearby kiawe groves, including a prominent site to the left as you drive down Kaukahi Street, on land owned by the University of Hawaii.

To walk from **Palauea Beach to Poʻolenalena Beach**, make your way to the beach through the shaded backshore and head left, or south. You'll soon run out of sand and have to climb up and around the low-lying Haloa Point. Look for a fishing shrine, or heiau, on the point. In ancient times, this coast was a fruitful net-fishing area. You drop down from Haloa Point and reach the north end, called Little Poʻolenalena Beach. After crossing the first stretch of sand, you top a small point and reach the south portion of the beach, which runs for nearly .5-mile before hitting the rugged point on which the Makena Surf condos are situated. *More Stuff:* For a shorter walk that avoids rock hopping, follow the directions in *Parking* above to Poʻolenalena. The beach runs mainly to the south from this access but—hot tip—you can also go right, or north, over a low point to reach the hidden Little Poʻolenalena Beach.

SNORKEL: Haloa Point, which is at the south end of Palauea Beach, has a reef offshore, but it's known more as a scuba zone. Although condo dwellers sun here, **Chang's Cove** is a secret among tourists and can be an ideal little snorkeling stop. From the lot described in parking directions above, walk the brick path down through buildings to the small, sort-of-sandy cove. Surf can be an issue here, but on calm days you'll have plenty of fish habitat in which to float. A marker for Hale Waʻa, an ancient canoe site, sits above the cove; to the left is a pathway to Chang's Point. **Poʻolenalena** and **Palauea beaches** both offer good swimming for a day at the beach.

SURF: Poʻolenalena and **Palauea** draw wave riders in the summer. Board and bodysurfers gather, along with the occasional windsurfer.

6.   WAILEA RESORTS COAST   HIKE, SNORKEL, SURF

WHAT'S BEST: A paved path runs beside five beaches and the gardens of luxury resorts and beach villas. People-watch, take a swim, and treat yourself to a luxury lunch.

PARKING: Take Hwy. 31 (the Piʻilani Hwy.) south to Wailea. Continue to the end, turn right on Wailea Ike Dr. *To Polo Beach (south access, primary hike description):* At the stop light, turn left on Wailea Alanui. After about 1 mi., turn right on Kaukahi St., just past the Farimont Kea Lani, and follow signs to Polo Beach Shoreline Access. *To Keawakapu Beach (north access):* Turn right at the stop light on Wailea Alanui. Turn left

Wailea Resorts Coast

on Okolani Dr., go downhill, and make a hairpin left at a "Wailea" sign on on an extension of So. Kihei Rd. Follow .25-mi. to beach access parking. *Note:* Direct access to the middle beaches is given below in *Snorkel.*

HIKE: Wailea Coast Walk (up to 4.25 mi.)

Talk Story: The five beaches of the Wailea are all curves of golden sand (which is sometimes depleted by storm surf) ranging from less than .25-mile to almost .5-mile in length, separated by low lava fingers, and flanked inland by the lawns, gardens, and poolside paraphernalia of destination resorts. Offshore, Kahoolawe is the island view, although West Maui to the north appears to be the separate island it once was. Picking your favorite among the beaches is like trying to select the cutest among quintuplets. Why bother?

Begin the **Wailea Coast Walk** on the lawn and picnic area of Polo Beach Park and head to your right on the paved path. Above Polo Beach are the gleaming turrets Fairmont Kea Lani Resort. After Polo, the path rounds Wailea Point, a lava shelf with a viewing area amid a native Hawaiian plants garden. After 15 minutes, you'll cross a bridge and come to Wailea Beach, which is shared by the tastefully appointed Four Seasons and Grand Wailea Resort. With a fantasy pool complete with caverns and waterfalls, the Grand Wailea is well worth a saunter. Check out its fourth-story plaza that dwarfs huge Botero bronze statues and a lake-sized fountain surrounding a bar. Outside are the serene lawns of the chapel, with more statuary, a fountain, and royal palms. Off the front portico is another garden hosting a large Kamehameha Statue.

After Wailea Beach, the path crosses the lawns above the lava at the Marriott and then drops alongside sweet Ulua Beach. The path peters out as you reach the next beach north, Mokapu Beach, which fronts the Renaissance Wailea Beach Resort. Mokapu Beach blends with Keawakapu Beach, which is the longest run of sand on the walk. *More Stuff:* For hoity-toity shopping (Gucci, Vuitton, Fendi, etc.) local art, and dining, try the Shops at Wailea—off Wailea Alanui Drive, near the light at Wailea Ike Dr.

SNORKEL: For all the Wailea beaches, snorkeling can be very good, although wave action can create turbidity and erode sand. **Polo Beach** has two entry points: At the left, or south, end of the beach near the beach club, which is a shorter swim; and to the right, or north, at Wailea Point, where you need to swim out a little farther but are rewarded with more colorful coral. At **Wailea Beach**, you want to go to the left, or south, to Wailea Point and flipper out around the lava. Some of the best coral on this coast awaits. *To Wailea Beach direct access,* head south on Wailea Alanui from Wailea Ike Drive. Pass the entrances to the Grand Wailea Resort and look for a Wailea Beach sign; drive down a short distance to a large parking lot.

Another good snorkeling spot is the lava point at north end of **Ulua Beach**, which is also the south end of **Mokapu Beach**. *For direct access to these pretty beaches,* turn north, or right, on Wailea Alanui from Wailea Ike Drive. Look for an access sign and road on your left, across from Hale Aliʻi Place; the access is just south of the Renaissance Wailea Resort. Ulua Beach will be just left from the beach facilities, and Mokapu is just to the right. The point is a good spot for novice snorkelers. **Keawakapu Beach** offers a long run of resort-free sand, gentle surf, and offshore views. It's the locals' choice for hanging out. *Note:* Shoreline Public Access to the north end of Keawakapu is a lot near 2980 South Kihei Road.

SURF: Bodysurfers and bodyboarders head to **Polo Beach** and **Ulua Beach** to catch the shore break. Afternoons are the best bet, and surf is usually bigger in the summer. During the summer, **Wailea Beach** is the site for the windsurfer race to Molokai, a spectacle you'll want to behold.

7. KAMAOLE BEACH PARKS   HIKE, SNORKEL, SURF

WHAT'S BEST: Four beach parks offer excellent swimming, spacious lawns, a coastal trail, and shaded picnic spots—combining to make Maui's best family beach scene.

PARKING: *North-end access:* Take Hwy. 31 (the Piʻilani Hwy.) south toward Kihei and Wailea. About 2.25 mi. south of jct. with Hwy 311, turn right on Lipoa St. Continue to South Kihei Rd. Turn left, continue for 1 mi.(passing Kalama Beach Park and a bridge) and veer right on Iliʻili Rd., at Cove Park. Go to the end and park at the corner of Iliʻili and Kaiau Pl. *South-end access:* Take Hwy. 31 about 4 mi. south of the jct. with Hwy 311. Turn right on Keonekai Rd. Continue and turn left at South Kihei Rd. Park at a lot for Kamaole III Beach Park. *Notes:* Hiking description starts at north access. On busy days, use the big lot at the Kihei Boat Ramp, which is just south of Kamaole III.

HIKE: Kamaole Beach walk to Eddie Pu Trail (up to 2.5 mi.)

Talk Story: These pleasant beach parks are across a busy street from oodles of mid-range hotel and condo resorts, local-style eateries, souvenir and sundries stores, kayak rentals, and dive shops. Kihei is abuzz with the sandy-footed and sunburned, playing hard and living the good life on their Maui vacation. On weekends, local families join the fray. While not quaint, Kihei exemplifies fun-in-the-sun Maui. Each beach has lifeguards on duty until late afternoon. At sunset, bring a picnic dinner and thank yourself for having the good sense to be in Hawaii. Park facilities were refurbished in 2008.

The **Kamaole Beach walk** begins at tiny Charley Young Beach Park, set on a palmy terrace that affords a postcard look south toward Kamaole I. Head down to the sand and walk to your left. After less than .5-mile, you'll run out of beach and need to cross the broad grassy bench in front of a large hotel. Then descend again to the sands of Kamaole II. Stroll the palm-fringed shores before ascending once again, to the point that is the north boundary of Kamaole III, and home to the lifeguard office. Walk the grassy bluff or the beach at the south end of Kam III, where you pick up the wood-chip

Kamaole Beach walk

pathway that is the new Eddie Pu Trail. Benches and interpretive signs line the trail, which continues through the Kihei Boat Ramp and then through shade trees and along the outer lawn of the Kihei Surfside Resort. From here you can continue to Keawakapu Beach and along the Wailea Resorts path. *Talk Story:* Local consevationist Eddie Pu used his time off every year for 25 years to walk the entire shoreline of Maui.

SNORKEL: The best snorkeling is off the rocky point that separates **Kamaole II** from **Kamaole III**. Park at Kam III. Begin either at the north end of the sand at Kam

III and snorkel toward the point, or start at the south end of Kam II and stroke out the same point. At Kamaole III, you can also snorkel closer to the shore on the south end of the beach—heading toward the bluff at the Kihei Boat Ramp. At **Kamaole I**, dip your mask on the south end of the sand, out and around the lava rocks in front of the Royal Mauian Hotel; or try the north end, off the steps at **Charley Young Park**. Unless the surf is up, which is rare, the waters along the beach parks are safe for beginning snorkelers.

SURF: Body surfers and boogie borders ride the shore break, mostly during summer, at all three **Kamaole beaches**, but this shore is not known for wave sports.

8.   **NORTH KIHEI**   HIKE, SNORKEL, SURF

WHAT'S BEST: Beach parks and historic sites are often missed by visitors to this section of the sunny coast. And for whale watchers, this trailhead is a must.

PARKING: Drive to the junction of Hwy. 31 (the Pi'ilani Hwy.) and Hwy. 311 (Mokulele Hwy.). At traffic signal where these highways join, go south on South Kihei Rd. *Note:* Further directions follow, starting north and proceeding south.

HIKE: Vancouver Monument to Sugar Beach (2 mi.); Hawaiian Islands Humpback Whale Sanctuary (.25-mi.); Waipuilani Park (.75-mi.); Cove Park to Kalama Park (.75-mi.)

Talk Story: The 4-mile coastline of north Kihei—featuring narrow sand strips, shallow waters, and rocky embankments—was in ancient times home to many of Maui's saltwater fishponds. Today, this coast is mostly a State Beach Reserve, buffeted by mid-range resorts, condos, and quiet neighborhoods. A stop-and-go, driving lollygag is the best way to visit.

For the **Vancouver Monument to Sugar Beach** walk, park at Mai Poina 'Oe Iau Beach Park, which is just south of the junction with Highway 311. The modest monument is less than .5-mile down the beach (at mile marker 1). Walk to your left as you face the water and look for a patch of coco palms. You will find a totem pole erected in 1968 to commemorate Captain George Vancouver, the famed British explorer who visited in 1793 and is credited with fostering peace among the warring Hawaiians. From the monument, double back northward, to walk the fine sands of Sugar Beach. Less than .5-mile north of the beach park, you'll pass the remnants of Kihei Wharf, where Henry Baldwin's men shipped sugar in the late 1800s, and today paddlers of the Kihei Canoe Club put in. North of here is the long sweep of Ma'alaea Bay.

The **Hawaiian Islands Humpback Whale National Marine Sanctuary** is at 726 South Kihei Road, about .25-mile south of the monument. The center is a living classroom, where interpretive displays and knowledgeable docents teach the history and ecology of the seagoing mammals. New meeting facilities were built in 2007. Nearby, on the water is the center's administrative office, set in a historic building with a whale-watching deck, complete with complimentary binoculars. And next door is small Kalepolepo Beach Park, home to the ancient Koieie Loko Ia Fishpond. Today, the nonprofit Association of Fishponds in Maui is restoring the large semicircle of lava stone at the shore, which, centuries ago, were handed down in a human chain of workers from the uplands miles away.

Waipuilani Park, for some reason, is absent from most maps. To get there, turn right on Waipuilani Road at mile marker 2, less than a mile south of Kalepolepo Beach Park. Drive a short distance to road's end. The park offers a wide expanse of lawn spreading to the north toward low-key resorts. This strip of sand with shallow waters is a peaceful beach walk in Kihei and a prime sunset stroll. Ancient fishpond ruins are offshore.

For the stroll from **Cove Park to Kalama Park**, continue on South Kihei Road. Turn right into Kalama Park, just past Waimahaihai Street, before mile marker 4. On weekends, the grassy expanses of the park are often the site of community festivities. Not to be missed is Pacific Whale Foundation's Whale Day, usually held in mid-February and featuring Grammy-winning entertainment, local-style food, booths by nonprofit organizations, and artwork. Continue southward from Kalama to a roadway bridge, across which is cozy Cove Park, a safe swimming and surfing spot.

SNORKEL: Kalepolepo Beach Park's **Koieie Loko Ia Fishpond** is a safe place for the keikis to take a dip. Good-sized fish breach the rock walls at high tide and have to hang around inside, an inviting circumstance for snorkelers. Volunteers continue to make improvements to the fishpond, bolstered in 2005 by a grant—but hampered by a 2007 flash flood.

SURF: **Cove Park**, with a modest break at the mouth of the cove, is Maui's best place for beginning board surfers. Just north, at **Kalama Park**, boarders ride the 4- to 9-foot summer swells, breaking both left and right. Body and board surfing is fairly good at **Mai Poina 'Oe Iau Beach Park**, but the real action there is for windsurfers in the summer when the Kona surf arrives.

9.   MA'ALAEA BAY   HIKE, SNORKEL, SURF

WHAT'S BEST: Birdwatchers, exercise walkers, and joggers can roam free at Maui's longest beach and largest wildlife ponds. Then stop in at the harbor for seagoing shops and a visit to the Maui Ocean Center.
PARKING: *For Ma'alea Bay-Wetlands Boardwalk:* Take Hwy. 31, which is North Kihei Rd., north from Kihei; or take Hwy. 31 south from its jct. with Hwy. 30 (Honoapi'ilani Hwy.) Park at the boardwalk parking lot, west of Kealia Pond and near mm2. *For Kealia*

Maalaea Bay

Pond: Take Hwy. 311 (Mokulele Hwy.) north from north Kihei. At mm6—be alert—make a left across the divided highway toward the the signed refuge gate. *For Ma'alea Harbor-Maui Ocean Center:* Take Hwy. 30 west (toward Lahaina) from its jct. with Hwy. 31. The harbor is with on the left within a mile.

HIKE: Ma'alaea Beach (up to 5.5 mi.) or Wetlands Boardwalk (1.25 mi.); Kealia Pond Wildlife Refuge (.75-mi); Ma'alaea Harbor-Maui Ocean Center (.75-mi.)

After crossing the dunes at the parking area, you will be about in the middle of **Ma'alaea Beach**. To your left is a 1.5-mile run of sand, near the highway, that gets you to Sugar Beach. Headed to your right, you can look forward to 1.75 miles of open sand, with coastal wetlands and a large cane field as an inland buffer. The beach ends at Haycraft Park, near Ma'alaea Harbor. *Talk Story:* At night, from July through December, beachgoers include hawksbill turtles, who come ashore to lay eggs at the high-tide line; watch out for the egg pits in the sand of these endangered reptiles. In the late 1700s, King Kalaniopu'u of the Big Island used these shores to invade Maui, and 800 of his elite warriors were annihilated in the Battle of the Sand Hills. In 1944 the U.S. Marines came ashore here in preparation for the taking of Iwo Jima.

For **Wetlands Boardwalk**, opened in 2005, go right from the parking area. An eight-foot wide, railed deck meanders along coastal mudflats and a good-sized pond, which is a gathering places for both shorebirds and waterfowl. Among the dozens of species to be seen here are Hawaiian ducks and stilts. Golden plovers, ruddy turnstones, and

*Wetlands Boardwalk, Humpback Whale Marine Sanctuary, stingray at
Maui Ocean Center, North Kihei windsurfer, Kihei Canoe Club*

wandering tattlers—migrating here from more than 2,000 miles away in Alaska and Canada—will be among the shorebirds.

Devout birders may like **Kealia Pond National Wildlife Refuge**. It's not really a tourist place. The U.S. Fish and Wildlife offices are about .5-mile from the highway. Levees between rectangular fishponds provide raised trails around the water. In the 1600s, villagers dug a channel through the dunes, creating a pond for shore-dwelling fish. Kealia Pond was also the island's salt source. *Note:* Visitors should check in at the office. Hours are weekdays, 9 to 4:30.

At **Ma'alaea Harbor**, your first stop should be the **Maui Ocean Center**, featuring the largest tropical aquarium in America. Whale life, ocean ecology, and Hawaiian culture exhibits are evocative as well as educational. The aquarium's sea tunnel makes you feel like you're snorkeling without getting wet, and the shark tank makes you glad you're not. Plenty of staff are on hand to personalize your visit, and local art vendors sometimes set up inside. Sea turtles and a living reef highlight outdoor exhibits, along with a new home for hammerhead and tiger sharks. *Note:* Admission is about $24 for adults and $17 for kids. Weekly passes save money.

Highlighting the shopping center next door to the center is the Pacific Whale Foundation, offering non-touristy ocean tours and a wealth of nature-related gift ideas. Below the complex is the Ma'alaea Harbor Village, and behind that is the Ma'alaea Small Boat Harbor. Take a saunter out the wharf to view the comings and goings of whale-watching vessels and fishing boats. The Lanai Expeditions ferry operates here, as well as from Lahaina.

SNORKEL: To reach **Haycraft Beach Park**, drive inland .5-mile from the harbor village on Hauoli Street. Pass all the condos to the end, at the Ma'alaea Community Garden. Haycraft, a less-used starting point for beach walkers, has a shower, tables, and a pretty beach with a winning view toward Haleakala, Molokini, and Kahoolawe. The fish are few, but the swimming is good. This park is not on many maps.

SURF: During the summer, **Ma'alaea Bay** brings the board heads running. There are three spots: **Mud Flats**, offshore in the middle of the bay, is a right-breaking 3- to 10-foot swell; watch out for the reef at low tide. **Breakwater**, accessible from the harbor, features a larger right break with long rides. The breakwater is a good place to view surfers under the right conditions. Big waves sometimes wash the parking lot.

The third spot, **Kapoli Beach Park**, is tough to find: Head toward Lahaina from Ma'alaea Harbor, pass Ma'alaea Bay Place, and look for an unsigned left turn, leading down a rugged road. Sometimes called Little Cape St. Francis, this spot offers long right-breaking tubes in the summer. Windsurfers, usually in the summer, can be seen offshore of **Haycraft Beach Park**. You'll also see windsurfers taking off from the middle of Ma'alaea Beach.

Valley Isle

Ukumehame Valley

VALLEY ISLE

West Maui is almost two million years old, twice the age of Haleakala, but the years have been kind. Nature—rain, wind, waves, erosion—has cleaved 3,000-foot deep valleys into the old volcano and adorned them with tropical greenery. From the west side, you view these classic green chasms opening inland from a coast that is almost continuous beach. As you go north, the coast becomes a series of bays and bluffs, and the tropical forests encroach the road. Finally, on the north, the coast is mainly steep cliffs, more arid here, with grassy upslopes that give way to forested ridgelines.

Resort beaches and coves are plentiful, and Lahaina is Maui's best strolling town for history buffs and window-shoppers. Take your pick from several wave-watcher's walks along sea-sculpted bluffs, hike into the forest, and turnouts with panoramic views. You can afford to be fickle in the Valley Isle trailhead section, since the distance between being a beach potato or hardcore eco-adventurist is not far, in terms of miles.

Driving Tour
PICKING THE RIGHT DAY

Get an early start to the north shore, and you'll feel like you're discovering the place. But don't go during or just after big rains: You'll get a discomforting look at erosion in progress, as mud and rocks wash into the roadway. In the winter, weather hits from Kapalua north. As you go south, sun is more likely. From Ka'anapali down to Olowalu will often be in the sunny lee of minor storms, giving a view of the weather in the West Maui Mountains while you bask in the sun.

THE ROADS

From McGregor Point to Lahaina, traffic often flows in a steady stream from midmorning to nightfall. You move along fine, but merging and getting across the highway can be exasperating—although a new road is planned (or at least talked about a lot) to bypass the coast, which would ease the congestion. This driving tour has you going south during that period to minimize the hassle. Traffic bogs down in Lahaina, and Ka'anapali, especially since several beach parks front the road. But then it's normally smooth sailing on Highway 30 going north, since this newer road bypasses the condo coast at Kahana.

North of Kapalua, the scenery shifts dramatically. The highway becomes a nicely swerving view road for the next dozen miles along the north shore—until the abyss at Kahakuloa. Here, the road takes a several-mile dive through the valley, and you might grip the steering wheel like the reins on a wayward steed. Traction and clearance are no problem—four-wheel drive is not needed—but a two-foot wide car would be helpful. Cars tend to wait for others oncoming, and then drive through in small caravans. After Kahakuloa, where the route becomes Highway 340, you encounter more one-lane spots, but they are shorter in length. This tour takes you down to Kahakuloa and back again, without circumnavigating West Maui.

THE COURSE

Follow along on the Valley Isle map, page 54. Refer to trailhead descriptions beginning on page 55 for more details.

BEGIN EARLY MORNING. TAKE HIGHWAY 30 NORTH TO KAHAKULOA VILLAGE. Get a cup of java to go and breakfast in a bag, and drive in the morning light. This tour plans for stops on the way back. Make your first stop Kahakuloa Head, the "Tall Lord" of a mountain that anchors the north side of the bay. Then double back and stroll the town—probably joined by roosters and barnyard beasts. Being here early will lessen concerns about navigating the narrow roads. When you drive back out—the way you entered—you may want to hike the first ten minutes of the Waikalai Road, which affords a view of the bay, or take the short jaunt down to Bellstone Pools.

Lipoa Point, Waikalai Road

Lipoa Point

MIDMORNING. DRIVE THE NORTH SHORE. Some of the best whale-watching bluffs are along the highway over the next several miles heading back toward Kapalua. You'll find the half-mile Ohai Loop Trail and other unmarked trails that skirt the cliffs and descend to seaside decks. Also keep an eye inland for segments of the alaloa, the King's Trail, that is identifiable because the ancient road builders didn't contour gullies, but instead went straight across, dipping and rising. You have an option of taking the short walk to Maui's sea geyser, the Nakalele Blowhole. Sometimes on this drive you will follow a whale family as it swims around the island.

Then continue on Highway 30, dropping through rough-sculpted Honokahau Bay. Farther down the road, stop in and catch the surf scene at Lipoa Point, where world-renowned waves roll in. From the overlook, you can also check out Honolua Bay to decide if this is a good morning to swim with the fishes in the marine preserve. Just as the road gets wider, you may want to swing in to check out D.T. Fleming Beach Park, a good place to let kids play.

Noon. Continue back on Highway 30 and then turn right on Office Road toward the Ritz Carlton and Kapalua. A tasty place to stop is the Honolua Store, where you can pick up treats to suit any yen. If you'd like to laze in luxury for a spell, check out the Ritz, one of Maui's best. Office Road connects with Lower Honoapi'ilani Road—turn left—and take your culinary prize to Ironwood Beach, to relax on the sand.

Continue south on Lower Honoapi'ilani. This is the Condo Coast that the highway bypasses. On the north end you'll pass Kapalua and Napili bays, which are snorkeling and strolling havens. Then continue south on the coast road, a drive-by-sight-see.

Afternoon. If you feel like an unfettered beach walk, pull into Kahekili Beach Park. Or, to gawk at the resort scene, try Dig Me Beach on the coast path at Ka'anapali. But save most of the afternoon for Lahaina. Visit the north end of town by veering right on Front Street, to see the Mala Pier and Jodo Mission. Then drive straight through the hoopla on Front to park at the south end of town at Shaw Street. Just follow your senses around Lahaina Harbor. If you wander around for a couple of hours, you'll see everything. The Thomas Edison vintage film at the Wo Hing Museum is … you gotta see it.

Breaching Humpback, Kahakuloa Head, Hanakoo Beach Park

Lahaina Harbor

SUNSET. Many will want to finish the shift in Lahaina, letting afternoon slide into evening, perhaps enjoying a cool beverage while watching the various vessels returning to harbor, or holding down a bench at Banyan Tree Square as the craft's fair winds down. Thoughts of moving to Maui might enter your mind.

Others can savor the waning hours with a drive south on Highway 30. Over the next few miles you'll pass several beach parks, beginning with Puamana where the local canoe club may be putting in for a late-day paddle. Each beach park offers a quiet spot under coco palms to view Lanai, and Haleakala to the south, which looks like an island from this coast. Inland are the green crags that gave Maui its nickname as the Valley Isle. The hot ticket for this experience is Olowalu Landing. If you want to look for the green flash of sunset from a higher elevation, continue on Highway 30 through the Lahaina Tunnel, and use the unimproved turnouts on the right, before reaching the logjam of sightseers at well-marked Papawai Point.

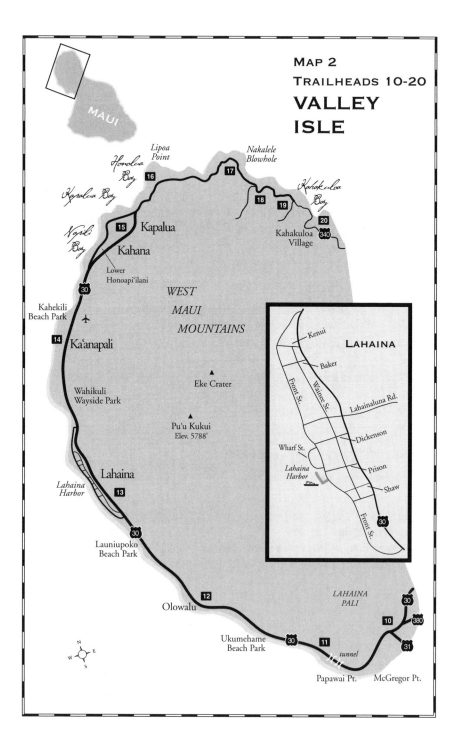

MAP 2
TRAILHEADS 10-20
VALLEY
ISLE

MAUI

Lipoa Point
Nakalele Blowhole

Honolua Bay
16
17
Kahakuloa Bay

Kapalua Bay
18
19
20
340

15 Kapalua
Kahakuloa Village

Napili Bay
Kahana

Lower Honoapi'ilani

WEST
MAUI
MOUNTAINS

30

Kahekili Beach Park

14 Ka'anapali

Kenui

LAHAINA

Baker

Eke Crater

Front St.
Wainee St.

Wahikuli Wayside Park

Lahainaluna Rd.

Pu'u Kukui
Elev. 5788'

Dickenson

Wharf St.

Lahaina

Lahaina Harbor

Prison

Lahaina Harbor
13

Shaw

30

Front St.

Launiupoko Beach Park

30

30

12
Olowalu

LAHAINA PALI

30

10

380

Ukumehame Beach Park
30
11

tunnel

31

N
W   E
S

Papawai Pt.   McGregor Pt.

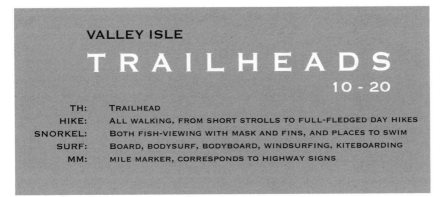

VALLEY ISLE

TRAILHEADS
10 - 20

TH: TRAILHEAD
HIKE: ALL WALKING, FROM SHORT STROLLS TO FULL-FLEDGED DAY HIKES
SNORKEL: BOTH FISH-VIEWING WITH MASK AND FINS, AND PLACES TO SWIM
SURF: BOARD, BODYSURF, BODYBOARD, WINDSURFING, KITEBOARDING
MM: MILE MARKER, CORRESPONDS TO HIGHWAY SIGNS

All hiking distances in parentheses are ROUND TRIP.
Elevation gains of 100 feet or more are noted.

10. LAHAINA PALI EAST   HIKE

WHAT'S BEST: This panoramic ridge trail was the easiest land route from Wailuku to Lahaina until about 1900. Traffic makes the trailhead approach tricky, meaning you'll encounter fewer fellow hikers.

PARKING: The approach to this trailhead is difficult. You need to being going south, toward Lahaina, on Hwy. 30 (the Hoʻonapiʻilani Hwy.) The trailhead road is on the right at mm5, just south of the traffic light that is the jct. of Hwy. 30 and Hwy. 380. It's just past a highway bridge and guardrail, near a huge power pole. Drive in .75-mi. on the dirt road (being careful not to dent the oil pan on high rocks) to a signed parking area.

HIKE: Lahaina Pali East (6.5 mi., 1,500 ft.)

*Talk Story:*The **Lahaina Pali Trail**—pali means cliffs—was constructed in 1825 over Kealaloloa Ridge as a way for missionary school children to get from Wailuku to the Mauna Olu Seminary in Lahaina. Think about that when you're slogging up its famed zigzags in the noonday sun. One of the teachers called it "the crookedist, the rockiest road ever traveled by mortals." Prior to this trail, most people going this direction traveled via canoe. In the early 1900s, a crude road was built nearer the coast, and the trail was abandoned. In 1993, the trail was restored and made part of the state Na Ala Hele hiking system. Huge electricy-generating windmills, comprising the Ukuhame Wind Farm, were added to Kealaloloa Ridge in 2006, placed along the rough road from McGregor Point Lighthouse to Puʻu Anu, at an elevation of almost 3,000 feet.

From the trailhead parking spot, a low-walled rock enclosure, the trail leaves the shade of kiawe trees and follows a rock-lined path. The shade will soon be a distant memory as you begin open switchbacks with big views unfolding at your back. The trail levels out after several miles (distances are marked on Na Ala Hele trails) and you'll contour a short distance on the rough road that comes up from McGregor Point. Then, following signs, take the trail leading from the road to your right to the turnaround and viewpoint at marker number 10. *Be Aware:* Bring plenty of water, sturdy shoes, and a hiking pole.

More Stuff: This trail connects with the following trailhead, creating the option of a car-shuttle hike. For a tamer stroll, drive north on Highway 30 to just past mm4 and head toward the King Kamehameha Golf Club. At the top of the hill you will find a clubhouse designed by Frank Lloyd Wright. Its domes echo the surrounding contours as well as the far off view of Haleakala. Also check out the Kahili Golf Course, whose grounds preserve heiau ruins.

11. LAHAINA PALI WEST   HIKE, SNORKEL

WHAT'S BEST: Get sweaty on one of the west side's best view hikes, and later cool off with a snorkel at a colorful cove that is frequented by tour boats. Then whale watch at sunset from several cliff lookouts.

PARKING: Take Hwy. 30 (the Honoapi'ilani Hwy.) west from Ma'alaea toward Lahaina. Pass through the tunnel after mm10, continue for .5-mi., and look for a signed, dirt turnout on the right at the bottom of the hill, amid trees. *Note:* As the highway rounds the cliffs before the tunnel, you will see several turnouts on your left. Due to traffic, these vantage points are best visited while heading the other way, toward Ma'alaea.

HIKE: Lahaina Pali West (5.75 mi., 1,600 ft.)

From the **Lahaina Pali West** trailhead parking lot, you hop up to a portion of the old highway that was constructed by prisoners in the early 1900s. This old highway, in turn, covered up parts of the ancient King's Highway, or alaloa—the long road. The Lahaina Pali Trail leaves the old road, to your left, after about 100 feet, beginning its steady climb up red dirt and boulders to a high point on Kealaloloa Ridge. During the climb you'll cross several gulches, all signed since this is a Na Ala Hele state hiking trail. On the way, watch for pioneer petroglyphs—rock etchings made by missionary school children and paniolos, or cowboys, who trod this path in the 1800s. Most are before and after the number 9 signpost.

You cross the canyonlike Manawainui Gulch almost 2 miles from the trailhead, and then walk an open grassy area. The high point comes near signpost number 10, serving up views toward Haleakala, Molokini, and Kahoolawe. But for a slightly more enticing view, continue just 10 minutes more, as the trail joins the McGregor Point road and contours Malalowaiaole Gulch—at signpost 11 you'll be able to see down toward the Lahaina Pali East trailhead, and also get a look at the ruins of a trailside shelter. *Be Aware:* Wear hiking shoes and bring water.

More Stuff: To access several whale-watching turnouts, and McGregor Point Light, head back toward Ma'alaea on Highway 30 from the trailhead parking. After leaving the tunnel, within the first .5-mile, look for two dirt turnouts that were part of the old highway. Inspiring viewpoints await. Farther along, after mm9, is the well-marked and popular turnout at Papawai Point. For more solitude with your view, continue a bit farther—past mm8 and just before mm7—and take a right on the dirt spur road that leads a short distance to the beacon light at McGregor Point. Safe, but steep, trails lead down to weirdly shaped formations.

SNORKEL: Coral Gardens is a small cove featuring acres of coral heads and waters that are calm on days when trade winds make other snorkeling spots choppy. To get there from the Lahaina Pali West trailhead, walk the back along the highway toward the tunnel a short distance to where the guardrail ends. Make your way down the rugged trail to a rock-and-sand beach. You can walk rocks toward the point or start swimming in that direction. Tour boats moor on both sides of the point, depending on wind and wave conditions. *Be Aware:* Due to currents and (rarely) sharks, this cove is for advanced snorkelers.

For easier access, go to **Papalaua Beach Wayside**, which is across the highway from this trailhead; walk down the beach to your left and swim out toward the rocks. Or, if more challenging entry is what you seek,

Coral Gardens bound, Lahaina Pali West

advanced snorkelers can try **Wash Rock**, which is below McGregor Point; walk down from the historical maker near the light and curl around to your right on the rocks.

12. OLOWALU & LAUNIUPOKO VALLEYS   HIKE, SNORKEL, SURF

WHAT'S BEST: Here are all the makings for a dream day: two classic tropical valleys, lots of snorkeling coral, rideable surf, and historical curiosities that span centuries.

PARKING: Take Hwy. 30 (the Honoapiʻilani Hwy.) toward Lahaina. *For Olowalu Valley-Petroglyphs:* At mm15, turn right into the lot for Olowalu Store. Drive around to the left and then turn right on a road near a small water tank. Parking is at a gate; you can also drive to the petroglyphs, which are .5-mile from the gate (though a sign says they are .25-mi.). *For Olowalu Landing:* Turn left from the highway directly across from the store at mm15. Go immediately left for .25-mi. to an unimproved parking area at a gate. *For Launiupoko Valley:* Continue on Hwy. 30 to the traffic light at mm18. Turn right (opposite the beach park) on Kai Hele Ku and continue uphill for about 2 mi. to road's end at a cul de sac.

HIKE: Olowalu to: Petroglyph hill (1.25 mi., 200 ft.), or Olowalu Valley (2.25 mi., 325 ft.); Olowalu Landing (.5-mi.); Launiupoko Valley (3.75 mi., 275 ft.)

The first .5-mile of the route to **Olowalu Valley** and **Petroglyph hill** leaves the huge monkey pod trees near the store and crosses fallow cane fields; the heiau-like rock platforms you see stacked in this area are piles workers made when clearing the fields. (Many people drive to the petroglyphs, subtacting 1 mile from the round-trip hiking distances.) On the north side of the hill's vertical face are the picture etchings made centuries ago. The exact origins of the pictures are the subject of Hawaiian legend and anthropological consternation. To the **top of Kilea cinder cone**, keep right on the road past the petroglyphs and curl right and up. Global warming tip: Sea shell fossils indicate that during geological yesteryear, when the earth had smaller polar ice caps, sea level reached within 15 feet of the top of this cone, making it a tiny island.

To **continue to Olowalu Valley**, cross the stream over the bridge that is just left of the petroglyphs, and stay right near taro fields. The road ends at a water tank almost .5-mile from the petroglyphs (again, you can drive this section if OCP gates are open). The area has been improved through the efforts of the Olowalu Cultural Preserve (see *Resource Links* page 235 to volunteer or get more info). There is no maintained trail all the way up the valley. But if you cross the irrigation ditch at the tank, and go left near picnic tables, you'll see a feeder trail that heads toward the stream bank. The forest is dense, but you can find adequate passage. *Talk Story:* The fascination with this trail is that it was the escape route in 1790 for Chief Kalanikupule when his troops were slaughtered across the island in the Iao Valley by the forces of Kamehameha the Great. *Be Aware:* Finding the same route back can be difficult if you wander off trail.

Ukumehame and Launiupoko Valleys

It takes time to fully soak in the beauty from the wharf at **Olowalu Landing**. The grounds (a short walk from the parking to the right) are adorned with coco palms, Norfolk pines, and several large native Hawaiian trees. In 1864 this was the site of one of Maui's earliest sugar mills and its most active pier. For the supreme vistas, head out the bench on the rock-and-dirt wharf. Sea turtles often pass, as do whales, just off the point. Inland is a museum quality view of Olowalu Valley, a jagged "V" above the treetops. *Talk Story:* This tranquil place was the setting of the Olowalu Massacre, in 1790, when American merchant Captain Simon Metcalf slaughtered about 100 villagers in a dispute over a stolen boat. Later, one of Metcalf's men, John Young, was kidnapped from another ship and forced to become a military advisor to King Kamehameha I. Years later, Young's granddaughter became beloved Queen Emma, wife of Kamehameha IV.

Olowalu Landing

Few tourists know about the **Launiupoko Valley** hike, which gives up spectacular seaward views of West Maui and takes you along the stream into the lush crease. From the cul de sac, head uphill from where large boulders are placed, and curl right to find a road that contours below a line of tall power poles and above the roof tops of a rural subdivision. This equestrian route has great views. After .5-mile, you'll reach signs for the Launiupoko Ahupua'a Archeaological Park (a village site whose remnants are obscured by brush). After another 10 minutes—keep left at a junction. You continue along a rock-lined dam and reach a reservoir. There you will find an appealing covered picnic table with a view.

Continue from the reservoir on grassy track that follows an irrigation ditch up the valley. The track becomes a trail, the valley closes in, and soon you will find yourself walking the tops of lava rocks that form the ditch. You lose the valley view for good when you enter trees, as century plants, guava trees, and wild coffee trees encroach on the path. Birds are abundant. About a mile from the reservoir, you cross the stream on a short, falling-down bridge supporting a water pipe. You have to enter the ditch in places over the next two hundred yards, until reaching its end, where the stream spews uncontained out of the dark shade of the jungle. Trailblazers can proceed with caution on a pig path that continues up the valley; falling rocks are a danger.

SNORKEL: For some of the best and most readily accessible snorkeling on Maui, try **Kaili'ili Beach**, commonly called, **Olowalu Beach**. Use roadside parking on either side of mm14. Coral shelves spread close to shore, as well as several hundred feet offshore, where tour boats anchor. *Be Aware:* Olowalu has a reputation for being a shark hangout; but only a few attacks (including one fatality) have been reported over a 15-year period. **Olowalu Landing** is also a good snorkeling area, far less frequented.

Look for the sandy ramp to the left of the long wharf, and in between a smaller boat landing. A coral bench is to your left within the reef, or, on calm days, swim out next to the wharf through a reef opening to explore deeper waters. You may spot a turtle. A small lawn under coco palms is the place to log towel time between swims.

Launiupoko Beach Park, at mm18, has a nice keiki pool, formed by a curve of rocks in the center of the park. Low tide can leave this pool high and dry. To the left is a sandy beach backed by lawn and tables. Offshore the park are good snorkeling reefs, but shallow waters and breaking waves can make this an iffy proposition. Launiupoko is a choice spot for a picnic, among palms and banyan trees, though traffic noise out-duels the surf as a soundtrack. For swimming with a sandy bottom, try **Awalua Beach**, which borders the highway south of the beach park, between mm16 and mm17.

SURF: During the summer, either side of **Olowalu Landing** is surfed, but a shallow reef break can be a problem. Just north of the wharf, a left-break surf spot also pops up during the summer. More reliable surfing in this area is to be had at **Launiupoko Beach Park** and **Awalua Beach**, directions to which are in the snorkeling descriptions. Launiupoko is a good beginners' break. In between these two is called **Kulanaokalai Beach**, but it's all the same run of sand. Small offshore reef breaks are reliable in the winter, and high surf will roll in during summer.

13. LAHAINA   HIKE, SNORKEL, SURF

WHAT'S BEST: Lahaina has always been where the action is—as the beachside enclave of kings and queens, as the bustling whaling town that was the capital of Hawaii, and, today, as night-life city and the point of departure of vessels of all sizes. Lahaina is one of Hawaii's best walk-around beach towns.

PARKING: Take Hwy. 30 (the Honoapi'ilani Hwy.) to Lahaina. On the south end of town, turn toward the ocean on Shaw St. *Choices:* Park in the lot at the corner of Shaw and Front streets, use on-street parking, or continue down Front St. two blocks to a lot at Prison St. Parking spots are at a premium from noon onward.

HIKE: Lahaina Town stroll (up to 3.25 mi.) and Lahaina Seawall (.5-mi.)

Talk Story: In 1802, his immense eminence, Kamehameha the Great, fresh from battles that made him the first ruler of all the southern islands, kicked back along the Lahaina shores with his entourage of several hundred family members and hangers-on, while his craftsmen fashioned some 1,000 war canoes, the peleleu fleet, in preparation for the invasion of Kauai, far to the north. A treaty was signed in lieu of an invasion.

By the early 1820s, Liholiho, or Kamehameha II, was king. Lahaina saw the arrival of both the whaling ships and missionaries—two disparate forces if there ever were.

The whalers—by the 1840s, some 400 ships called each year—believed "there is no God beyond Cape Horn." Alcohol fueled violence and rowdy behavior. In defense, Liholiho, along with his mother Queen Ka'ahumanu and Chief Hoapili, embraced the missionary influence. They built a stone prison to quell unruly whalers, and set into motion a series of social reforms that abolished the patriarchal system born of the previous decades of war. They developed an educational system that was more advanced than all but a few schools in America. After 34 years, in 1854, the kingdom's capital was moved to Honolulu, whaling subsided, and Lahaina became a sleepy cane town. Recent decades have seen its resurgence as a tourist destination.

From Shaw Street, begin the **Lahaina Town stroll** down Front Street. At the corner of the parking lot by the ball field, you'll find a plaque commemorating Moku'ula Island, the most sacred spot on Maui, where kings and queens had palaces and were interred. Common folk were prohibited. Then continue down Front Street, on the ocean side. The lawn area open to the beach is Hale Piula, and the foundation remnants are those for the never-completed palace of Kamehameha III—the king preferred sleeping in his grass hut nearby. Behind the hale is Lahaina Beach. Continuing on Front Street, after Kamehameha III school, you reach Canal Street.

Veer left at Canal Street, diagonally across the Banyan Tree Square. The sprawling tree was planted in 1873 by the sheriff on the town's fiftieth anniversary. Its canopy of limbs is now an aviary for chattering birds and an umbrella for scores of local artisans. Near the shore behind the tree are the old courthouse-visitors center, and the ruins of the first coral-block prison, which housed unruly whalers. First-class Hawaiian music and dance enliven the square on weekends.

The Lahaina Harbor is in front of the old courthouse, which is a visitors center with knowledgeable and free walking maps. For the **Lahaina Seawall**—a must-do side-trip—walk over to the prominent Lahaina Lighthouse, a 30-foot high beacon that dates from 1866 and was the first in Hawaii. Then walk down the paved road along the water, past an array of tour and fishing vessels, and take a right onto the seawall. You'll be walking on big flat boulders. The seawall, completed in 1938, is a spot to view surfers, the outer islands, and boating activity. But the real reason for being here is the romantic look you get back toward Lahaina: The opening shot for a South Seas adventure flick, with jagged green peaks as a backdrop to the palmy shore.

To **continue the town stroll**, return to the lighthouse and head over to the grassy area just north to see the remains of Kamehameha the Great's brick house, built in 1800, and the Hauola Stone, used by ancient Hawaiians as part of a birthing ceremony to portend healthy futures for their children. The ancient taro patch was also here, where the kingdom's first monarch labored to demonstrate the dignity of work. From here, cut back up to Front Street. There you'll find the Baldwin House Museum, the former home of Dwight D. Baldwin, one of the earliest missionaries, whose progeny became owners of vast tracks of land. Admissions is a couple of bucks.

Lahaina

Then, continue north on Front Street—and you're on your own. For several blocks, until things settle down again at Papalaua Street, you'll be in the heart of town, libation only steps away, galleries and shops plentiful, with brokers hawking adventure activities and tunes blaring from open windows. For the full effect, jog up Lahainaluna Street, the main drag that comes in from the highway. Follow your nose, but history buffs will want to stop in at the Wo Hing Museum. Built in 1912 as a gathering place for Maui's society of Chinese workers, the structure was restored as a museum in 1984. Behind the museum is the rustic cookhouse, in which is shown the Thomas Edison black-and-white footage of Hawaii. Shot in 1898 and 1906, these silent flicks impart volumes in a few memorable minutes. A minimal admission is charged.

More Stuff in town: Kids—and most everyone else—will want to see the Lahaina Prison, Hale Pa'ahao, or "stuck-in-irons house." It's two long blocks up Prison Street, which is between Shaw Street and Banyan Square. You'll see the high prison walls, built from the coral stones of the old fort at the banyan tree, on your left at the corner of Waine'e Street. During the 1850s, the prison housed sailors guilty of awa (kava) drinking, furious riding, and violating fishing taboos, along with your more run-of-the-mill adulterous fornication and assault. Making noise of any kind was prohibited.

Turn right on Waine'e Street and walk to the Waiola Church and Waine'e Graveyard. Buried here are Hawaiian royalty, including Queen Keopuolani, Kamehameha the Great's wife, and Governor Hoapili, as well as missionaries from the 1850s, such as William Richards. Commoners, sailors, elders, and children also rest here, persons of many races reflecting the multifaceted times when the world discovered Hawaii.

More Stuff close by: You'll also want to see the huge bronze buddha at the Jodo Mission; go a few blocks north on Front Sreet and turn left on Ala Moana. Then, if you're look-ing for an inexpensive, local-style plate lunch, try the Lahaina Cannery Mall, located at the far north end of town, off Front at Keawe Street. Yes, it is a mall, but locals hang out here and it's also the venue for excellent free hula performances, normally held weekends at noon and Tuesday and Thursday evenings at 7.

More Stuff up the mountain: For a look at a museum that housed Hawaii's first newspa-per, drive several miles toward the mountains on Lahainaluna Street, in the middle of town. You'll reach Lahainaluna High School, begun in 1831 and the oldest school west of the Great Divide. At the original schoolhouse—veer left at the top of the hill—is a historic landmark, Hale Pai, where Hawaii's first newspaper was printed in the 1830s. The view from campus makes you wonder how the kids get any studying done.

Talk Story: Some 1,400-foot up the hill from the museum is David Malo's grave, a short distance above the huge "L," which is maintained by students. David Malo, among Lahainaluna's first graduates, went on to be the kingdom's leading educator. But later in life he requested to be buried high on this hill, away from Western influence he felt would destroy the essence of Hawaiian culture.

Molokai south coast, Baldwin Beach, antherium, Big Beach

Jaws, Lahaina, Sliding Sands Trail Haleakala, Twin Falls

Wailea resort, Kahakuloa Head, Hookipa

Lahaina hula, Swinging Bridges, Ironwoods, Kamaole Beach Parks

View from Kahekili Beach Park

SNORKEL: Lahaina Beach, at the south end of town, is a .75-mile sand strip bordered by shade trees and a quiet neighborhood. A sheltering reef offshore makes for safe swimming and decent snorkeling. This was the beach of choice for Kamehameha I, a man who could do whatever he pleased. From the Shaw Street lot, access the beach behind Hale Piula to your right; or better yet, go to the more private end of the beach, by heading south to a Shoreline Access sign near 409 Front Street.

The action is at **Puʻunoa Beach**, also called **Baby Beach**, at the north end of town. From the highway, turn toward the ocean on Kenui to Front Street, and then go right. *Two access points: For the south end* of the .5-mile long beach, turn left on Kai Pali Place, and look for the Shoreline Access sign. This end of the beach features the popular baby, or keiki, beach. *For the north-end access,* and easier parking, continue on Front, turn left on Ala Moana, and park just past the Jodo Mission. A huge bronzed Buddha rests within the manicured mission grounds, a striking sight with the jungle ridge as its background. Before hitting the beach, you may also wish to walk north through the Puʻupiha Cemetery, to Mala Wharf, a monument to folly, since it was condemned just after completion in 1922 because offshore currents rendered it unusable. A reef just offshore Puʻunoa Beach provides a wave-free snorkeling zone, which can be shallow in spots at low tide. A ten-minute walk gets you to Baby Beach's south end.

Wahikuli Beach Park, alongside the highway just north of Lahaina, offers good snorkeling and numerous picnic huts set on the grass margin above the coast. The place can be busy on weekends. Use the second parking lot to the north. This spot has rocks at the shoreline, but you can walk both left and right to find sandy entrances to the water. Traffic can make getting into and out of these lots a hassle.

SURF: Puamana Beach Park, at mm19 just south of Lahaina, attracts low-key locals, both winter and summer. So does the **Lahaina Seawall**, both the north tip and off the elbow at its base. Access is via Lahaina Beach, behind Hale Piula, just north of Shaw Street. **Mala Wharf** also offers a long left-break, best during the summer.

14. KA'ANAPALI COAST   HIKE, SNORKEL, SURF

WHAT'S BEST: Take your pick between a glitzy, touristy resort path and a hike along an open beach backed by time shares. You'll find all manner of surf-and-sand sports.

PARKING: Take Hwy. 30 (the Honoapi'ilani Hwy.) north of Lahaina. *For Ka'anapali Beach Resorts:* Turn left before mm24, into Hanako'o Beach Park. Go to the right in the lot and park near the cemetery. *Note:* Alternate Ka'anapali parking spots are noted in snorkel and hike descriptions. *For Kahekili Beach:* Pass Ka'anapali exit and mm25 and turn left at a light on Kai Ala Place. Pass Westin parking and proceed to beach parking.

HIKE: Ka'anapali Beach Resorts walk (2.25 mi.); Kahekili Beach walk (2 mi.)

Ka'anapali is comprised of two long beaches, which are north and south of Black Rock, or Keka'a Point, which at the Sheraton. The resorts walk takes in south of Black Rock, and Hanako'o Park is at the south end of this segment. For the **Ka'anapali Beach Resorts** coastal path, cross over the little bridge at the north end of the beach parking lot (to the right as you face the water). You'll join the paved path that begins at Hyatt Regency. *Other Parking:* To park at the Hyatt (which will begin the hike at the essentially same place) continue north past the beach park and turn left at Ka'anapali Parkway. Then go left on Nohea Kai Drive, drive past Shoreline Accesses 209 and 210, and continue past the back side of the Hyatt to Shoreline Access 208. A paved path leads to the beach path. You could also park at 209 or 210, lots near the Maui Ocean Club, which will shorten the hike.

The gardens and man-made lagoon of the Hyatt highlight the first, quieter section of the walk. Joggers, pool boys, and people wearing name tags may share the flagstone walkway. You then pass the Maui Ocean Clubs, each with poolside gardens and chaise lounges supporting acres of glistening flesh. Here you may wonder why this path is called the Ka'anapali Historical Trail. Then comes Whaler's Village, a rather drab, open-air mall, which opens to the path, presenting an opportunity to Hawaiianize your wardrobe or eat battered shrimp. Not far after the mall, about 1.25 miles into the walk, is the deep run of sand that stretches in front of the old-timey Ka'anapali Resort and the fancy Sheraton. Black Rock will be visible ahead. The action-oriented 1970s surfer crowd dubbed this zone Dig Me Beach.

Kahekili Beach, north of Black Rock, is not quite the nature stroll, thanks to the addition of behometh time-share resorts in 2005—but you'll still find a run of open sand backed by kiawe trees. The walk begins at a pavilion, set among carefree palms and grassy banks. (Kahekili is also called Ahumanu Beach, or Old Airport Beach, or, at the south, Ka'anapali Beach.) You can walk left on the beach for about .5-mile to Black Rock, with the Royal Lahaina Resort looming on the bluff above. To the right, is open beach for about .75-mile, with ironwoods buffering the slopes and Molokai beckoning offshore.

More Stuff: Joggers and excercise walkers will want to know that the Wahikuli Interpretive Trail extends south for nearly a mile from Hanako'o Beach Park. The route hugs the coast through several beach parks ending near Lahaina.

SNORKEL: The south end of **Hanako'o Beach Park**, by the life-guard platform, is a calm area with sandy bottom, suited for novice snorkelers. This park is also called Cemetery Beach. Most snorkelers in the area head for **Black Rock**. *Other parking:* For the closest access to Black Rock, take Ka'anapali Parkway toward the Sheraton and use Shoreline Access 213 in the parking garage, just south of the ho-tel. If that lot's 20 spaces are taken,

Kaanapali Beach resorts walk

try the lot just south, for the Whaler's Village—you'll pay a few dollars per hour ('free' validated parking requires a purchase of $20 or more). Signs nothwithstanding, beach access is easy from Whaler's. Just north of access 213 (turn toward the Sheraton) is another pay lot. Okay, out of the car! Head for the sand just south of the point. Swim out along the steep walled Keka'a Point, where spirits of the dead were said to leave the island in ancient times, and where intrepid swan divers launch themselves these days. Fish are abundant, but visibility can be reduced by wave action. Bring your own shade, since Black Rock is a scorcher.

SURF: Boogie boarders and surfers like the area just south of **Hanakoʻo Beach Park**, sometimes called **Sand Box**. Winter rides are available, though summer is better, and this is not in the top ten Maui surfing beaches. When the surf is too hairy elsewhere, try the right-breaks here.

15. KAPALUA BAYS   HIKE, SNORKEL, SURF

WHAT'S BEST: Nature has scooped a series of sandy bays out of the rocky coast——providing surfers, snorkelers, strollers, wave-watchers, and sun-bathers with lots of choices to hang out amid the condos and resorts. Or, select a mountain hike from among the newly built trails offered by Kapalua Resort.

PARKING: Go north past Kaʻanapali on Hwy. 30, the Honoapiʻilani Hwy. Near mm29, turn left on Napilihau Rd. Then turn right on Lower Honoapiʻilani Rd. *Note:* Additional directions, going from south to north, are provided in the activity descriptions.

HIKE: Coastal hikes: Napili Beach to Kapalua Beach (1.25 mi.); Kapalua Beach to: Hawea Point Shoreline Conservation Area (1.25 mi.), or Oneloa Bay (2 mi.); D. T. Fleming Beach Park to Dragon's Teeth (.75-mi.).

Kapalua Mountain hikes: Village Walking Trails (up to 8 mi.); Maunalei Arboretum (3 mi..); Mahana Ridge (5.75 mi.)

Talk Story: Once the domain of Chief Piʻilani, who controlled six bays and the three islands—Molokai, Lanai, and Kahoolawe—that are visible from the shores, this 5-mile coastline today might well be called the Condo Coast. Creative site planners have blocked light from squeaking between the buildings in places, but these older places now seem folksy in view of some of Maui's larger resorts and timeshare "beach villas."

The coast walk from **Napili Beach to Kapalua Beach** is on a scenic path hidden in plain sight. The hard part is finding Napili Bay. *Driving directions:* Continue north on Lower Honoapiʻilani and, at about mm29.5, go left on Hui Drive; you should see a Shoreline Access sign, and signs for Hale Napili. The access path is where Hui Drive bends right. Park at will, amid weekend car jams. From the beach, walk to your right around the pretty crescent of sand, and hop up to the railed path with paved stones that goes in the direction of the point. Before the point, the path ends, and you'll need to step down to a route that is plainly visible on a lava shelf. This fisherman's trail hooks around the point, passing tide pools. Notice footprints carved into the lava. After rounding the point, step up to a lawn area of a resort, from which your route to Kapalua Beach will be visible. *Be Aware:* Don't try this walk during high surf.

In spite of its scenic charms, the hike from **Kapalua Beach to Hawea Point and Oneloa Bay** is taken by few people—though the route's populartiy may increase when a planned 4-mile Kapalua Coastal Trail to Honolua Bay is completed. *Driving direc-*

Kapalua Beach

tions: To get to Kapalua Beach, go north on Lower Honoapiʻilani Road and turn left after an uphill S-turn near mm30. A Shoreline Access sign points to a large parking lot (if arrving later, you will have to park on the shoulder before reaching the beach lot). Walk down the lot through a short tunnel to the beach and continue to your right along the sand, or on the grassy fringes of the huge new condos that sit above it.

Round the coastal bluff, turning slightly uphill to your right. You'll cross a road amid condos and then go left at a Public Shore sign, pointing toward the low-lying Hawea Point Shoreline Conservation Area—the most *au naturel* spot around these parts. Tide pools on its north side make for soaking tubs, when the conditions are right. To continue to Oneloa Bay (Ironwoods Beach), double back from the point, and head north on the lawn at the margin of nicely spaced condominiums. You'll see the bay ahead.

The **D. T. Fleming Beach Park to Dragon's Teeth** walk is a wave-watcher's special, leading from beach to the buttresses of Makaluapuna Point below the golf course at the Ritz Carlton Hotel. *Driving directions:* Take Highway 30 past both Napilihau Road and Office Road, which leads to Kapalua and the Ritz. At the bottom of the grade at mm31, turn left at a Shoreline Access sign, onto Lower Honokahua Road. A .25-mile drive takes you to the beach park. *Alternative:* You can also reach Dragon's Teeth by beginning from the lower end of Office Road, where it makes a left turn below the Ritz at a golf course. From the parking lot, cut accross the fairway at the edge of the burial site.

Dragon's Teeth

From D.T. Fleming Beach Park, go left along the sand (staying well back of the shore break) until it peters out, and then make your way up to the low bank that skirts the golf course, following the out-of-bounds markers beside the trees. The Honokahua Burial Site, dating from 850 AD, covers some 14 acres to your left. Respect for this site, and years of legal haggling, is what caused the Ritz to be set back so far from the coast. You then cut right through scraggly ironwoods, and pass the Dragon's Teeth, a line of sharpened tufts of whitish trachyte, four- or five-feet high. Beyond the teeth are lava flats and a grassy area, where on most days you can watch waves explode.

Other shoreline spots: Driving north from the beginning of Lower Honoapi'ilani Road, you will see a few of Shoreline Access points with fair-to-good recreational values. First up, going from south to north, is the minor gem of Honokowai Beach Park (see *Snorkel*). After that, as the road gets curvy, past Akahele Street that leads to airport, is Pohaku Park, or S-Turns, a scenic turnout in view of the Kahana Beach Resort. The best access, is just north here. Go left on Hui Road E at mm 28.7, to the end of the cul-de-sac. A tree-tunnel trail leads out to small Haukoe Point with tide pools; you can make your way north to a sweet sandy cove.

D. T. Fleming Beach

The **Kapalua Mountain hikes** are on the 22,000 acres owned by venerable Maui Land & Pineapple Co., which owns Kapalua Resort. As real estate has displaced pineapple in the company's portfolio, hiking trails—thankfully—have become part of the general plan. *Driving directions:* Take Highway 30 to near mm30 and turn left on Office Road, toward Kapalua and the Ritz Carlton. Make your second right (past the Golf Academy) toward the red-painted Kapalua Resort Center (See *Hikes* page 235 for phone numbers). A free trail guide with maps is availabe. You'll also get a free pass and shuttle bus ride. **Village Walking trails** encircle a nicely treed golf course that is just north of the center, on Plantation Estates Drive. The Master Loop Trail covers 3 miles with 400 feet of elevation. A half-dozen side trails add up to several miles.

For the **Honolua Ridge Trail**, with a side loop of **Maunalei Arboretum**, hop the free shuttle to another trailhead. The arboretum loop trails total about 1.5 miles, with 1,400 feet of elevation. The trails meander through the 1928 plantings made by D. T. Fleming. Hawaiian flora mingles with plants from around the world. The Honolua Ridge Trail, 2.5 miles, round trip, begins at the same place and climbs 1,700 feet past a sugi pine grove to the top of Pu'u Kaeo. From there, you'll have an option of hiking down the **Mahana Ridge Trail** nearly 5.75 to the Kapalua Resort Center. Or double back on the Honolua trail. For all Kapalua hikes, make sure you get the pick up time straight with the driver. *More Stuff:* Ever seen an ancient Hawaiian village being uncovered from a jungle valley? You can volunteer to help in the effort. Contact Malama Honokowai, a nonprofit group that is unearthing ruins: See page 234 in *Resource Links*.

SNORKEL: Go to the right at **Kapalua Beach** for easy entry and good snorkeling, as you stroke out toward the point. People also swim and snorkel below the bluffs on your left, as you come out of the pedestrian tunnel. Experienced snorkelers will want to check out the cove that is down to the left from the coastal trail to Hawea Point. **Napili Beach**, Kapalua's kissing cousin to the south, also has great swimming and decent snorkeling—to the right as you face the water. See hike descriptions for driving directions. *Be Aware:* Currents can be a strong offshore, near the tips of land.

Honokowai Beach Park is a bright spot at the south end of the Condo Coast. Go left from Highway 30 after mm25, and continue on Lower Honoapiʻilani Road for .5-mile. The park's protective reef makes for decent snorkeling and forms a very good keiki pool, with sandy entry. Bring the family and a cooler full of hulihuli chicken.

SURF: During the winter, surfers ride the tiers rolling into **Oneloa Beach**, a.k.a., **Ironwoods**. This is a big curve of white sand, not known for swimming, but it scores high marks among beach strollers. To get there directly, go north on Honoapiʻilani Road; pass mm30.5 and the Kapalua Resort, and take the left turn lane at the low sign for Ironwood Lane. You should see a sign for Shoreline Access (unless it's still missing). From the 20-space parking lot an improved path leads a short distance to the beach. You can also get here by turning left off Highway 30, towards Kapalua and the Ritz, on Office Road. Go downhill past the rows of ironwood trees, turn left, and then make a right on Ironwood Lane. Bodysurfing and bodyboarding is sometimes good at **D.T. Fleming Beach Park**, but the shore break and undertow can be dangerous when surf's up; lifeguards post hazard signs.

16. **HONOLUA MARINE PRESERVE**   HIKE, SNORKEL, SURF

WHAT'S BEST: At the beginning of Maui's wild north coast are a snorkeling sanctuary, a dramatic bluff walk, and world-class surfing waves—watch ʻem or ride ʻem.

PARKING: Take Hwy. 30 (the Honoapiʻilani Hwy.) north of Kapalua. The road narrows. *Mokuleia access:* Just before mm 32, look for a Marine Conservation District sign and paved turnout on your left at a chain-link fence. *Honolua access:* About .25-mi. past the Mokuleia access, on your left as the road curves right, is an overflow parking lot for Honolua Bay; from this overlook you can also observe conditions in the bay. Down the road from this lot (about .25-mi. past mm32) on a sweeping left bend, are marginal on-street parking spots for Honolua; more parking is on the left at a one-lane bridge just before mm33. *Lipoa Point access:* Continue to mm33.5 and look for a dirt road on your left, just past the guardrail at the top to the hill. *Be Aware:* Leave your car free of valuables at all these parking spots.

HIKE: Honolua and Mokuleia Marine Conservation District (up to .75-mi.); Lipoa Point (1.75 mi., 175 ft.); Windmill Beach (up to .5-mi.)

Railed concrete steps help on the short walk down to the small sand beach at **Mokuleia Bay**, which is known to surfers as Slaughterhouse Beach. To the right is Kalaepiha Point, the protuberance that separates this bay from its twin, Honolua, to the north. From the on-street parking for **Hononolua Bay**, a .25-mile trail—within a dense forest that includes banyans and dripping vines—takes you across a stream to the boulder shores. You'll find a concrete boat ramp, small patches of grass and sand, but no real beach. In 1976, re-created Polynesian sailing canoes took off from this bay and proved

Ironwoods

that the trip back to Tahiti would have been possible by the ancient voyagers.

With weird formations, crashing surf, and offshore views, **Lipoa Point** is a place you'll long remember if you sit for a while. From the highway, a rutted but passable dirt road curves down and right to where it's blocked by a gate and berm. Normally, surfer's cars will line the road. If you drive this part, subtract .5-mile from the round-trip walk. From the berm and gate, walk down the dirt road, keeping to your left. A pineapple field will be on your right, on a gradual descent. In the 1940s the field was a golf course, and this point is sometimes called Golf Links. You'll pass a grove of palms and then one of Norfolk pines, where a lava wall marks the remains of the old golf clubhouse. Bear left toward the point, through ironwood trees, and drop down through grassy patches and a rock-bordered path to the tip of the point. A smooth shelf is low enough to catch sea spray, but you can scramble up to perches on the craggy wall of trachyte that forms the point to get a point-blank view of Molokai. Below, little coves are pocked with caves, and you'll also see smooth tide pools that invite soaks.

Windmill Beach, officially called Punalau Beach, is north of Lipoa Point. Look for a gate and road to your left, near mm34.6. A path leads a short distance down an embankment through a stand of nicely spaced ironwoods to a long run of sand that is punctuated by sharp lava boulders. This is the last sandy beach going north, and its quiet shores are right for a picnic. *Be Aware:* Leave your car free of valuables.

SNORKEL: In spite of having no beach, **Honolua Bay** offers some of the island's best snorkeling. Enter at the boat ramp and swim out channels in the coral both left and right. Snorkeling tour boats often anchor farther out in the bay. Kalaepiha Point, to your left, hosts lots of fish but be mindful of choppy waters on days when surf is breaking. **Mokuleia Bay** is usually wavy and only suitable in the summer; flipper out to the point on your right. The northwest side of **Lipoa Point** has snorkeling pools awaiting for trailblazers willing to do the rock hopping it takes to find them. Also, at the outset of the hike as described above, look for a small coco palm beach down a ravine to your left, where snorkeling is good. *Be Aware:* Avoid Honolua after a heavy rain, when the stream muddies the waters.

SURF: Surfers like the right-break at **Slaughterhouse Beach**, that is, **Mokuleia**, just off the point on its north side. Bodysurfers also like Mokuleia, but rock hazards are present. The real action at this trailhead is at the north side of **Honolua Bay**— reachable via the Lipoa Point access—where fabulous right-breaks draw intermediate to advanced surfers. This is one of Hawaii's best breaks. The overlook is a magnet for surf photographers; a short, steep trail leads from turnout to an ideal viewing perch. **Windmill Beach** is less crowded. Scope out the offshore rocks before paddling out.

17.　NAKALELE BLOWHOLE　　　　　　　　　　　HIKE

WHAT'S BEST: A sea geyser erupts from a multicolored shelf on a rugged coast.

PARKING: Take Hwy. 30 (the Honoapi'ilani Hwy.) north of Kapalua. At mm38, look for a turnout on the left with a gate, from which a Coast Guard light is visible. *Alternate:* Some people take a slightly shorter, but much steeper, trail that is .5-mi. beyond this parking area. The blowhole is visible from the bluffs near beginning of this trailhead. *Be Aware:* Car break-ins have occurred at both trailheads.

HIKE:　Nakalele Blowhole (1.5 mi., 200 ft.)

The **Nakalele Blowhole** is a 3-foot circular opening in the roof of an underwater cave beneath a lava reef, where wave action compresses air with a hollow whooshing sound, followed by towering blasts of white water. Some bursts rise 50 feet or higher. From the parking area, head down the red cinder road through the eroded grassy area, bearing right of the Coast Guard light. Then go down the gray-rock gully to the right of the light, to a sandy spot at the bottom. The blowhole is about .25-mile away, to your right, on a trail leading though sea-scoured rocks that may remind you of a Nevada desert—gray, black, and red; pock-marked and smooth; swirled together at their seams, or lying about in cobbles and boulders. You'll cross a large sandy area, make passage through a tuft of these rocks, and come to the blowhole—set to your left, maybe 40 feet from the sea and 15 feet below on a broad, smooth reef. You can view from above or circle around inland to drop down to the lava shelf for an eye-level perspective. Unless you'd like a shower, get a fix on the spray's direction and magnitude before circling the hole. *Be Aware:* Stay well away from the actual opening. Anyone

Nakalele blowhole

slipping into that foamy maw is not coming out. Deaths have occurred.
More Stuff: On the way to the blowhole, Honokohau Bay is at the big bend north of
mm36. An intriguing wide stream flows into a rocky surfer's beach. There's no inland
access. Rough looking Bad Boys hanging around tend to dissuade tourists.

18. EKE CRATER & OHAI LOOP TRAILS   HIKE

WHAT'S BEST: Take a trekking journey from the grassy upsweeps of the north shore
to the fringes of the jungle at the wet heart of the island. Or forget that and opt for a
nature stroll along the coastal bluffs.

PARKING: Take Hwy. 30 (the Honoapi'ilani Hwy.) north of Kapalua and continue as
the road narrows along the north shore. *For the Eke Crater Trail:* About a mile after entering Kahakuloa Game Management boundary, turn right on dirt Poelua Rd., at mm41
and just before a speed limit sign. Drive in a short distance on a rutted road and park
at the small hunter check station. *Note:* Hunter's gate is open to vehicles on weekends
and holidays. *For the Ohai Loop Trail:* Begin at a signed trailhead on the ocean side of
the highway at mm41.7.

HIKE: Poelua Road-Eke Crater Trail (6 mi., 1,600 ft.); Ohai Loop Trail (1.5 mi.)

Talk Story: Eke Crater, also called Mount Eke, is in the wet center of West Maui, at an elevation of nearly 5,000 feet, getting some 30 feet of rainfall each year. You can't walk there—too far and too dangerous, with tangles of greenery, muddy rockslides, and lava tubes ready to slurp up a wayward hiker. But you can hike a few miles in toward the interior, where the jungle laps at your knees, and take a peek.

For **Poelua Road to Eke Crater Trail**, walk up the road to your left. You'll soon cross a metal gate, and curve to the right. Avoid two right-hand options as you arc around a red-cinder amphitheater, staying on the main road. The route climbs on a switchback amid koa trees, and then ascends straight up a ridgeline, with green Poelua Gulch down to the left. A little over a mile from the trailhead, you'll cross a grassy area—to the left across the field is a game-watering station—and reach a second gate. Then ascend a long straightaway through a tunnel of planted pine trees. The view up from here is of a knoll at the head of the gulch, where the trail will take you if you're willing.

After the steep walk to the top of the knoll, you'll be greeted by a garden of several kinds of ferns, and a forested bench that affords a view from the high rim. After this point, the plants that have been slapping shin-high start to reach crotchward. Continuing upward, you lose Poelua Gulch on the left, and start picking up views of a deep valley to your right, which contains Honokohau Stream. Through the greenery that chokes the trail, look up to head of the drainage to see a portion of inaccessible Honokohau Falls, which is one of the highest in the nation. Pick your own turnaround point. On the way back you'll enjoy the seaward views as you drop to the airy slopes that lead to the trailhead. *Be Aware:* Prepare for a full-fledged day hike, rain and shine.

The **Ohai Loop Trail** is a chance to get out of the car and go looking for whales (in the winter), soaring seabirds, and low-lying native plants, such as the trail's namesake ohai naupaka, and other species that thrive in salt air on the windswept bluffs. Less than .5-mile into the hike is a sea-viewing bench between two grassy hillock, the hike's scenic highlight. Sit down for awhile and watch the sea crash into Papanalahoa Point. A sign midway in the loop says, "end of trail." Whatever. You can easily continue on an inland loop, though backtracking is more scenic. *More Stuff:* The highway sweeps down to Hononana Bay. Near mm41, after a one-lane bridge, a path leads down to the boulder shores. If you rock-hop for about .5-mile to your right at the coast, you may find a seldom-seen blowhole. Watch for high surf.

19. WAIKALAI PLATEAU & BELLSTONE POOLS   HIKE, SNORKEL

WHAT'S BEST: Embark on a getaway hike, from the cliffs of the north shore to the grassy plateau and pine forests high above them, with close-ups of the peaks at Maui's interior. Or make your way down to swimming pools carved into a dramatic shoreline.

PARKING: Take Hwy. 30 north of Kapalua, as road narrows around the north shore. After mm42, Hwy. 30 becomes Hwy. 340 (the Kahekili Hwy.) coming around the other way, from Wailuku. *For Bellstone Pools snorkeling:* Pass mm42. About .75-mi. later, after a signed "dip" in the road, look for a dirt turnout on the ocean side. A "danger" sign marks the spot. *For the the Waikalai Plateau:* Continue past mm16 (the markers start descending from here), and about .5-mi. later, park on the left at a dirt turnout, across from the gate for Waikalai Game Management Road. *Note:* Hunter's gate is open to vehicles on weekends and holidays.

Bellstone Pools

HIKE: Bellstone Pools (.5-mi., 125 ft.); Waikalai Plateau (5.75 mi., 1,400 ft.)

For the **Bellstone Pools** (a.k.a. Olivine Pools), head down the red-dirt trail through dwarf ironwoods and make a little curl right at a second "danger" sign. The pools are visible on a shelf below, a straight-on descent. The tide pools are well worth exploring even if you won't swim—but watch for big waves. See *snorkel* for more on the pools.

For the **Waikalai Plateau** hike, start up from the gate and pass the hunter check station. You're headed into West Maui Forest Reserve to the lip of the Kahakuloa Natural Area, home to the endemic dwarf greenery that sprawls northward from the center of the West Maui Mountains. After ten minutes you'll hook around to a view of Kahakuloa Head, the shark-fin-shaped landmark that rises above the village. About a mile into the hike, after a switchback up and a straightaway beside koa trees, you'll reach a grassy field. A wildlife watering station provides a viewpoint to the coast, and inland you get a first look at Mount Eke, which lies far inland. From above the watering station, walk a narrow shoulder inland, and then dip down across a land bridge spanning a gorge. Atop the other side is a freshly scented pine forest. A little more than 2 miles in, the road leaves the ridgeline, alongside a cut bank that reaches the stream. You then embark on a serious uphill segment, which leads to a grassy tableland that is planted with pines. From here is a commanding view seaward, but press on as the route snakes gradually up and in. In a few minutes you'll see a plateau, the green hillock that is your destination, rising just above the tablelands.

Take the road to the top—spurs lead elsewhere—and you'll get a view of green, stepped ridge that climbs to flat-topped Mount Eke, a.k.a. Eke Crater. Pu'u Kukui, is also visible, to the right. Notice that the vegetation changes here, transitioning into the West Maui Natural Area Reserve, which is home to many plant species unique to Hawaii. At this end point, you may feel the hike is just beginning, such is the allure of the view. Go, if you must. *Be Aware:* Prepare for both hypothermia and heat stroke. Bring a hiking pole and plenty of water.

SNORKEL: The **Bellstone Pools** (a.k.a. Olivine Pools), are several natural tubs scooped into a sea shelf about 8 feet above wave-battered northeast coast of Maui. Greenish olivine is a semi-precious gemstone that is sluiced by wave action from the surrounding soils and comes to rest on the surface. To the left below the cliff, an intimate pool is tucked into a rocky point. The largest, sweetest, and easiest entry is the pool on the flat to the right, the most seaward. More fish reside here. When the waves cooperate, this is one of Maui's best experiences. *Be Aware:* High surf can make swimming dangerous. People have died here. Watch the waves for many minutes before getting in, and don't assume it's safe because people are in the water. *More Stuff:* The ancient Bellstone, or Pohaku Kani, lies at the roadside near the trailhead. Striking the stone on its mountain-side achieves a hollow, metallic sound.

20. KAHAKULOA VILLAGE   HIKE

WHAT'S BEST: Although wood-frame homes with electricity belie the image of "my little grass shack," this tiny village, with its dramatic location, is the island's best example of how Hawaiians lived in ancient times. And getting there is part of the thrill.

PARKING: Take Hwy. 30 north of Kapalua as road narrows along the north shore. Continue past mm42, when route becomes Hwy. 340—and road *really* narrows. Dip into the valley and park after steel bridge near mm14.5. *Note:* You can also get here by taking Hwy. 340 north of Wailuku; that option involves more narrow-road driving.

HIKE: Kahakuloa Village (up to 1.5 mi.); Kahakuloa Head lookout (.5-mi.)

After enduring the precipitous road into **Kahakuloa Village**, most drivers are anxious about getting out, so not many take the time to stop and appreciate the place—which is a blessing since there are few parking places. But the village is Maui's best example of how people lived in ancient times in an ahupua'a—a wedge of land that contained a seacoast with agricultural plain, bisected by a stream that originates in the mountainous woodlands. These were the geographic ingredients for generations of survival.

Backtrack to start your stroll. At the ourskirts of the village is the fetchingly sited Kahakuloa Protestant Church. Right on the road after that is the village's institution, Ululani's by the Bay Shave Ice, where you can talk story with Ululani. Then, from the parking by the bridge, take the dirt road that passes homes, whose stream-irrigated gardens display an array of Polynesian fruits. Ubiquitous wild chickens and poi dogs will sound a greeting. The road follows Kahakuloa Stream through large trees to the rocky beach—which is not on the list of Maui's most scenic. *Be Aware:* Although the road is public access, be polite and ask permission if you see a local person; tourism creates an impact on this quiet village. Then, backtrack and continue up the main road. On your right will be the driveway leading to the Francis Xavier Mission. Sitting on a rise above the village, the tiny church is open to all who want to come in and light a candle.

Kahakuloa Head is the 600-foot "Tall Lord" that presides in his "feather cape" over the northern end of the bay. For a close-up of this angular landmark often seen from afar, you need to drive through the village. After surviving the one-lane road along the cliff, the road bends right. You'll see the head on your left. Pull off on a dirt loop by a fence that provides parking for several cars. *Note:* If you're approaching the head from the south on Highway 340, look for this turnout on the right near mm14, after passing the Kaukini Gallery. You'll pass Puʻu Kahulianapa, a twin hillock that sits just inland from the head. The turnout is between the two.

From the pullout, walk through an opening in the fence and across the grassy swale between Kahakuloa Head and Puʻu Kahulianapa, which is to your right. Social trails lead seaward, down through an eroded area with large pocked-lava boulders. If you continue down to the ledges closest to the ocean, and go left, you'll get a look at Mokeʻehia Island Seabird Sanctuary. Frigate birds, shearwaters, and tropic birds may grace you with a fly by. You'll also see Haleakala and the east shore. Trade winds are often in your face from this perch, but on quiet days during the whale migrations in the winter, you'll be in a natural echo chamber that amplifies the exhales of the big mammals as they laze by. *Be Aware:* When walking below the head, be mindful of falling rocks.

Kahakuloa Protestant Church.

Windward Coast

Champion Dan Moore rides a 68-footer at Jaws

WINDWARD COAST

The reef-protected beaches and mountain ridges on this working side of Maui are often bypassed by visitors—but not by surfers and windsurfers. Several strolls invite wave-watchers and history buffs, and adventurers will find roads to hidden heiaus, lofty mountain ridges, and sea cliffs where gargantuan waves arrive.

DRIVING TOUR
PICKING THE RIGHT DAY

Select Saturday for this driving tour to see locals at play at the Maui Swap Meet, and avoid the traffic in town during the workaday week. On days when clouds hang in the West Maui Mountains, avoid the high stuff and retreat to the sunnier coast. Featuring some indoor activities, this is a good tour when the weather is not the greatest.

THE ROADS

You'll at least be on regulation-sized roadways during this drive, although traffic bogs down mornings and evenings in Kahului, like sand going through this hour glass-shaped island. Traffic also clogs headed into Paia late in the afternoons, as commuters head Upcountry. Also respect Mother Nature, by avoiding Highway 340 north of Waiheʻe during or after heavy rains, as flashflooding occurs. For those wishing to circumnavigate West Maui from this direction, one-lane road segments begin about mm8 and continue for some 9 miles—but the only white-knuckle segment is the short stretch through Kahakuloa.

THE COURSE

Follow along on the Windward Coast map, page 84. Refer to trailhead descriptions beginning on page 85 for more details.

BEGIN EARLY MORNING. MAUI SWAP MEET, KAHULUI. People-watch, souvenir shop, pick up exotic flowers, and expand your art collection at this Saturday morning scene. Good deals abound. Items range from strictly tourist stuff to some guy selling what's left of his apartment before moving back to Des Moines. A good time to arrive is about 8:00 a.m., after the early birds. Think about picking up some homemade bread, organic veggies and fruits for a fresh picnic lunch.

MID-MORNING. TAKE KAʻAHUMANU AVENUE, WHICH IS HIGHWAY 32, TO IAO VALLEY STATE PARK. Every day is a weekend at Iao, and you're bound to see a tour bus or two in the parking lot. The Needle is Maui's signature landmark, and it deserves its reputation. Stop at Kepaniwai Heritage Gardens and Hawaii Nature Center on the rebound. After that, if you feel like getting high on an out-of-the way trail, try Kapilau Ridge.

Kepaniwai Heritage Gardens, Iao Valley, Bailey House Museum

HEAD UP THE COAST ON HIGHWAY 330, WHICH BECOMES HIGHWAY 340. This route takes you up Market Street in Wailuku, where you can pop out of the car to take some of the old-town stroll. Then continue north on the highway. You can use pullouts or the short trails to check out the coast at Hulu Island Seabird Sanctuary. Hikers can also take side trips for the stream walk at Swinging Bridges, or the uplands of Waiheʻe Ridge. But the best bet for a daylong tour is the short walk to the Kukuipuka Heiau, a big-mana viewpoint for the Kahului coastline, which you'll explore during the rest of the day. It's at the same parking for Waiheʻe Ridge.

NOON. HEAD BACK DOWN HIGHWAY 340. In a few minutes you can take a side-trip in Waiheʻe to see the town's hidden, pleasant beach park. Then roll the wheels south, making sure to keep left on Highway 340, which is Waiehu Beach Road. This will give you a chance to pull in to see the Halekiʻi-Pihana Heiaus State Historical Monument, hiding in plain sight.

HUG THE COAST AS THE ROUTE BE-
COMES KAHULUI BEACH ROAD, AND
KEEP LEFT AT A MERGE WITH HIGH-
WAY 32. Keep left, turn left on Hobron, and turn right on Amala to get to Kanaha Beach Park. Here you can enjoy your picnic and be entertained by kite-boarders and windsurfers. This place is a never-ending action movie. Across the street is the Kanaha Pond Wildlife Sanctuary.

AFTERNOON. DOUBLE BACK AND GET ON THE HANA HIGHWAY, HIGHWAY 36. You'll want take to a few minutes to do a drive-by at the locals' beaches mentioned in the Spreckelsville trailhead—and, hey, nobody's going to sue you if you decide to flop back for the rest of the afternoon at one of them. Or, continue driving, through Paia to check out some country scenery, either by taking the fairly long walk to Pauwela Point, or a shorter one to Halehaku Heiau and Kahuna Point. The Halehaku option is a respite among tropical trees, before you backtrack to Paia.

SUNSET. PULL IN AT THE HOʻOKIPA LOOKOUT. The world has few better places to finish out the day than from this overlook of the surfer and windsurfer scene. You can follow up with a meal and stroll of Paia after dark. Don't worry about a dress code. Or, if you need to get back to another part of the island, cruise down the road to Baldwin Beach Park for sunset. Coco palms fringe a long sand trip, giving way to a view of the Iao Valley and, far to the north, Kahakuloa Head. It's easy to pop a whole chip of images here—big sky, ultra-aquamarine water, perfect light. Island-style rules, as locals gather to savor another day in paradise.

Iao Theater, Baldwin Beach

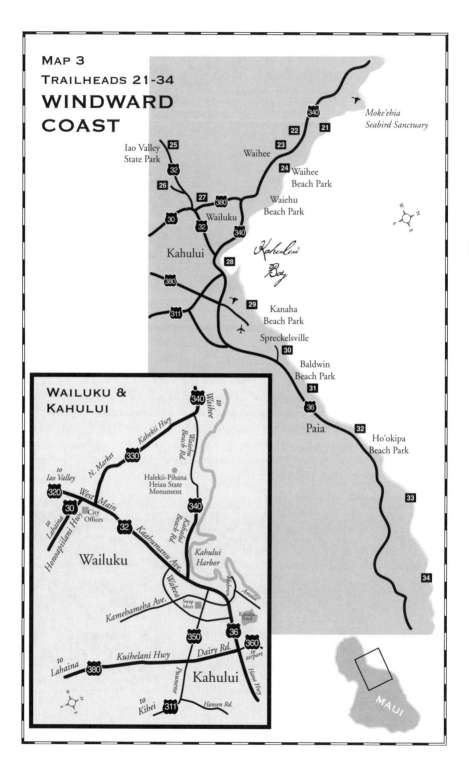

MAP 3

TRAILHEADS 21-34

WINDWARD
COAST

Moke'ehia
Seabird Sanctuary

340
22   21

Iao Valley   25
State Park

Waihee   23

32   24 Waihee
              Beach Park

26

27   380

30   Wailuku   Waiehu
                     Beach Park
32

340

Kahului   28   *Kahului
                     Bay*

380

311   29   Kanaha
                 Beach Park

Spreckelsville

30

Baldwin
Beach Park

31

36

Paia   32

Ho'okipa
Beach Park

33

34

WAILUKU &
KAHULUI

340   to
         Waihee

Kahekii Hwy

N. Market   330   Waiehu
                       Beach Rd.

to
Iao Valley   Halekii-Pihana
                Heiau State
320   West Main   Monument

30   City   340
        Offices

to   32   Kahului
Lahaina   Beach Rd.

Honoapiilani Hwy

Wailuku   Kahului
                 Harbor

Waiehu

Kamehameha Ave.   Swap   Amala
                     Meet

                     Kanaha
                     Pond

350   36   360   to
                         airport

to   Kuihelani Hwy   Dairy Rd.   Hana Hwy
Lahaina
380

Kahului

to
Kihei   311   Hansen Rd.

MAUI

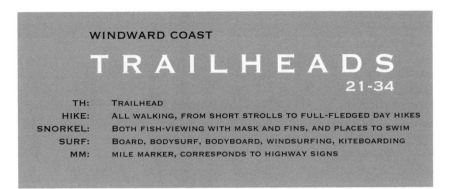

TRAILHEADS
21-34

TH:	TRAILHEAD
HIKE:	ALL WALKING, FROM SHORT STROLLS TO FULL-FLEDGED DAY HIKES
SNORKEL:	BOTH FISH-VIEWING WITH MASK AND FINS, AND PLACES TO SWIM
SURF:	BOARD, BODYSURF, BODYBOARD, WINDSURFING, KITEBOARDING
MM:	MILE MARKER, CORRESPONDS TO HIGHWAY SIGNS

All hiking distances in parentheses are ROUND TRIP.
Elevation gains of 100 feet or more are noted.

21. SEABIRD BLUFFS   HIKE

WHAT'S BEST: Wander grassy bluffs above a wild coast and tiny islands that are a sanctuary for seabirds.

PARKING: Take Hwy. 340 (the Kahekili Hwy.) north of Wailuku and Waiheʻe. Look for a white-railed fence beginning at mm5.5, and park at a large turnout at mm5.9. This trailhead is apparent public access on private property. Use your own judgment. Landowners are not legally responsible for your safety. Homemade signs along the fence line say 'malama aina,' meaning, 'love the land.'

HIKE: Seabird Bluffs to Hulu Island view (.75 mi., 150 ft.)

Talk Story: Extending several miles north of Waiheʻe is a roadless coast with cliffs and bluffs that embrace the trade wind's waves. The bluffs were the Western world's first glimpse of Maui, by Captain James Cook in 1778. Offshore the southern end of this coast is Hulu Island, a nationally designated bird sanctuary. Its sister sanctuary, Mokeʻehia Island, is to the north, just offshore of the 500-foot Hakuheʻe Point.

For the **Seabird Bluffs to Hulu Island** hike, pass left of the gate and walk down the wide gravel road amid ironwood trees. Where the road hooks left, continue straight for a couple hundred feet on a weedy path, until you break into the open on a grassy, red-dirt embankment. From there, make your way farther down, veering left. Hulu Island will come into view, about 200 feet below in an often churning seas. Several other small islands extend northward, including the farthest north, and largest, Mokeʻehia Island, some 4 miles distant. In the winter, trade winds supercharge the flights of seabirds, the giant frigatebird among them. *Be Aware:* Maui is a geologic work in progress. Some bluff edges are precipitous and unstable. Stay back.

Waihee Ridge

22. WAIHEʻE RIDGE   HIKE

WHAT'S BEST: Start high and get higher on Maui's best tropical ridge hike to a view of the mountains at the center of the island. Or take shorter strolls: Nearby is a jewel of a heiau with a view, and not far away are two waterfalls with swimming holes.

PARKING: Take Hwy. 340 (the Kahekili Hwy.) north of Wailuku and Waiheʻe. *For Waiheʻe Ridge and Kukuiipuka Heaiau:* Turn left at mm6.75, across the highway from Mendes Ranch. Drive .75-mi. up a paved road and curve left to a signed trailhead; the heiau trailhead is a few hundred feet across the pasture toward the ocean. *For Makamakaole Falls:* Continue northward on the highway to a bridge on the inside turn at mm7.75, and park at a turnout on the left. A sign notes "do not walk tractor on road." Walk about 100 yards back on the road (watch for traffic) to a turnout that is on an outside turn at the top of a rise (you could park here also).

HIKE: Waiheʻe Ridge (4.75 mi., 1,500 ft.); Kukuipuka Heiau (.25-mi., 100 ft.); Makamakaole Falls (.75-mi., 200 ft.)

From a cow gate, trudge up the steep concrete ramp that begins the **Waiheʻe Ridge Trail**. Part of the state's Na Ala Hele trail system, the route is well constructed and marked. At the top of the ramp, go left through a gate and ascend through a bird-rich tree tunnel that includes Norfolk pines and strawberry guava. After .5-mile, you'll come to overlooks of Waiheʻe Valley—one has a viewing bench that is a worthy end-point for hikers with less time, or on days when the clouds are hanging on the interior ridges.

From this first overlook the trail climbs with the aid of staircase sections, to a knob and spiny ridge that affords both the big look back toward the windward coast and the ridges that rise inland. The trail then veers away from the valley, across a depression of native scrub, before exacting another climb that is made easier by stair sections. Trail's end is an open hillock at 2,500 feet. A picnic table marks to enjoy the vista and to wave at the occasional tour helicopter. Inland, about a mile away and not much higher, is Mount Lanilili. Puʻu Kukui, West Maui's highest, is behind that peak, and flat-topped Eke Crater is north and inland. *Be Aware:* Prepare for rain and slippery conditions on this hike. The trail beyond the fencing is hazardous and not maintained.

Kukuipuka Heiau is a place that radiates beauty in all directions. The trailhead steps begin at the the hill that rises above the meadow. You soon reach an open promontory, and the heiau, whose low, white-limestone walls—about 75-feet square—invite visitors to stop and enjoy. Native flowers and trees accent sweeping coastal views toward the Kahului Bay coast as it sweeps toward Paia, with Haleakala rising above. The heiau has been restored by Leiʻohu Ryder and other community members; see *Resource Links.*

Makamakaole Falls are two 'secret' adventures enjoyed mainly by locals on weekends and small hiking tour groups. From the outside turnout, go straight down the steep shoulder to a telephone pole, and continue down little zigzags from the pole (other trails veer left into the gorge). You'll reach the first pool at the top of a 20-foot cascade, where people leap for a chilling dip. Walk-climb down to the right of the pool and then cross left over its outflow. After a hop up to some rocks, the trail continues downstream over mossy bedrock and ferns and reaches to the top of the second, 40-foot falls, beside a large banyan. The route down to the second pool is more difficult: you need to back down a 15-foot rocky face with root handholds to the left of the banyan. *Be Aware:* Landowners are not responsible for your safety.

Makamakaole Falls trail

First swinging bridge, Waihe'e Ridge Trail

23. SWINGING BRIDGES

WHAT'S BEST: Take an adventure hike over plank suspension bridges that lead upriver in a tropical canyon—to where waterfalls drop from on high. The bad news: Landowners have prohibited access. Call for the latest information; see page 235.

PARKING: Take Hwy. 340 (the Kahekili Hwy.) north from Wailuku. Pass the school in Waiheʻe and turn left at mm4.8 on Waiheʻe Valley Rd., before the bridge at mm5. Drive in .4-mi., turn right on a dirt road, and continue a short distance to the check-in station for Waiheʻe Valley Plantation. *Notes:* Admission formerly was around $6. Permission to enter is also required from Wailuku Water Co.

HIKE: Swinging Bridges (3.5 mi., 250 ft.)

This inviting trail follows the river up Waiheʻe Valley, which is nearly 3,000 feet deep. Waiheʻe means "slippery waters," made so by algae, so be extra careful with your footing on wet rocks. For the **Swinging Bridges** hike, walk the dirt road from the concession stand at the trailhead, passing a decrepit cable gate. The road starts up through dense subtropical forest, with the river and taro patches down to your right. After about .25-mile, the road begins a contour alongside an irrigation ditch, which periodically disappears into dripping tunnels. Just after .5-mile, you'll drop to the first bridge, a plank-and-cable strand some 125 feet long and 10 feet above the water. Just after the first bridge is the second, set in a profusion of jungle greenery. The second span is maybe 175 feet long, with a slightly uphill grade nearly 20 feet above the river. Both bridges were originally built to ease the way for agricultural workers.

Okay, you made it. From the second bridge, the trail follows the water amid a garden of bamboo, ti, and ginger and then crosses the river on rocks. After that, you weave up the other bank in a hau and banyan thicket, drop down, and cross the stream again. Continue up through rocks and ferns. The trail forks—either way works, but the left fork follows a an interesting concrete ditch. After a short distance you'll reach a decrepit dam and spillway, with an 8-foot waterfall and swimming pool. Upstream is a view of the 3,000-foot-high amphitheater carved by the Waiheʻe River, often draped with a waterfall. *Be Aware:* Flash floods in this valley present a significant hazard. Stay out during rains. If you get stuck on the wrong side of a torrent, wait it out.

24. WAIHEʻE BEACHES

WHAT'S BEST: This long, scenic beach offers a quiet relief from resort strips. Nearby heiaus are a historical surprise, hidden above the neighborhoods.

PARKING: *For Waiheʻe Beach Park:* Take Hwy. 340 (the Kahekili Hwy.) north of Wailuku. In Waiheʻe, just after the ball field and before mm4, turn right on Halewaiu Rd. At the bottom of the hill, veer right toward Shoreline Access sign, and then turn left just before the golf course into the beach park. *For Haleki'i-Pihana Heiaus:* Take Highway 340, or Waiehu Beach Rd., south from its junction with Highway 330; you can also approach from Kahului Harbor on Hwy. 340. From Waiehu Beach Rd., turn inland on Kuhio Place (across from Ka'ae Place) and then turn left on Hea Place.

HIKE: Waihe'e Beach Park (up to 4 mi.); Haleki'i-Pihana Heiaus (up to .5-mi.)

At **Waihe'e Beach Park,** the 600-foot-high walls of the northeast shores have tapered down to sea level. This long curve of tree-fringed sand and coral reef is seldom visited by tourists (indeed, permanent campers and nearby affordable housing give this park a local feel.). Tall ironwoods surround a spacious lawn, creating a choice beachside picnic spot. From Waihe'e Beach Park, you can walk about a mile north, or left, on the sand, but rocks make the going tough before reaching Waihe'e Point—site of Kealakaihonua Heiau, located just south of where the Waihe'e River joins the Pacific. *More Stuff:* Hundreds of coastal acres are part of the Maui Coastal Land Trust; to explore natural and cultural sites, or to volunteer with the trust, call 808-244-5263.

Going to the right, is a pretty walk for about a mile to Waiehu Beach Park, which abuts the other side of the golf course. The sand dwindles along the fairways, and you may have to skirt margins of the golf course. You then hit the sandy, open beach at Waiehu Beach Park (see *Surf* below for driving directions to this beach).

The huge **Haleki'i-Pihana Heiaus** are a State Historical Monument, with some ruins dating from the late 1500s. The monument is on 10 weedy acres atop the hill, with views of the Iao Valley and Kahului coast—as well as the warehouses and modest suburbs that engulf the site, providing visual irony. The Pihana Heiau remains are farthest from the parking lot. The Haleki'i Heiau ruins spread from the lot's interpretive signs. *Talk Story:* Kamehameha the Great made human sacrifices here in 1790 to prepare for his conquest of Maui in the Iao Valley. Both these heiaus were partially dismantled when kapus against sacrifice and other decrees were made in the 1800s.

SNORKEL: A coral reef offshore **Waihe'e Beach Park** limits shore break and provides for colorful swimming, the best on this coast when conditions are right. Local spear fishermen love this place. The park is an excellent picnic choice. *Be Aware:* Waves breaking on the reef mean rip currents may exists. Waters will be shallow at low tide.

SURF: In recent years, both kiteboarders and windsurfers have discovered little **Waiehu Beach Park.** Take a seat on the open lawn and check out the colorful scene—but be sure to give them plenty of space. Short-board sufers will also be around. *Driving directions:* The park is located at the end of Lower Waiehu Beach Road. Take Highway 330 north from Wailuku, turn right at the junction with Highway 340 (Waiehu Beach Road), and then turn toward the ocean .25-mile south of this junction on Lower Waiehu Beach Road. *Alternate:* Highway 340 north from Kahului and then turn right on Lower Waiehu Beach Road, before you reach the junction with Highway 330.

25.   IAO VALLEY   HIKE

WHAT'S BEST: The Iao Needle is Maui's signature spire. And surrounding tropical ridges, cascades, gardens, and ocean panoramas woo hikers and strollers alike.

PARKING: *For all hikes,* take Hwy. 320 (Iao Valley Rd.) from Wailuku. Iao Valley Rd. is where Hwy. 32 meets Hwy. 30, near city hall. *For Tropical Gardens of Maui:* Look on the right before mm1. *For Kepaniwai Heritage Gardens-Hawaii Nature Center,* look for the gardens at a bend in the road near mm1.5. Turn left into a lot that is a little farther up the road; the nature center sits above the gardens. *For Iao Valley State Park hikes,* continue 2 mi. to a large paved lot. *Notes:* Don't leave valuables in car. A fee is charged to park.

HIKE: *Before the state park:* Tropical Gardens of Maui (about .25); Kepaniwai Heritage Gardens (about .25-mi.) and Hawaii Nature Center (up to 2 mi.);

Iao Valley State Park to: Botanical Gardens and Iao Needle Overlook (.75-mi.), or Iao Tablelands vista (1.5 mi., 250 ft.), or Iao Stream (1.25 mi.)

Featuring a bridge over wide Iao Stream and a pond-side gazebo, privately owned **Tropical Gardens of Maui** is well worth a look on your trip to the park (admission is about $5). Concrete paths swerve through several acres of plantings that are at once manicured and profuse—a result of 25 years of hands-on care. A plant export nursery near at the entrance allows you to send some of the greenery home.

The **Kepaniwai Heritage Gardens** sit at the gateway to Iao Valley, where steep green ridges rise alongside rushing Iao Stream. The county park features banyans, coco palms, taro, and a variety of Polynesian flora, growing amidst a stone-foundation grass hut and other exhibits that recreate village life on Maui. A Japanese garden and Chinese pagoda also grace the park, along with the architectural styles of Portugal, the Philippines, and New England—all meant to pay tribute to the many people who have called Hawaii home. If you're headed to the state park, these gardens are the best spot to stop for a picnic on the way back. *Talk Story:* On a less harmonious note, Kepaniwai means "damming of the waters," in reference to the mounds of fallen warriors that virtually stopped the flow of Iao Stream during the great battle of 1790.

Some 35 acres of streamside rain forest surround the nonprofit **Hawaii Nature Center**, a place for the family to enjoy both the botanical and historical bounty of the island. The center's gift shop is well worth a browse, and the attached museum will wow the kids. It features a large sun room, burbling stream, and touchy-feely exhibits that will elicit giggles and impart knowledge. You can opt for a two-hour guided hike (distances vary to suit the group) into the rain forest. *Note:* Admission to the museum is $6 for adults, less for kids. Hiking tours are about $30 per person.

Most tourists, some in buses, visit **Iao Valley State Park** to pay homage to the Iao Needle, the poster-boy for Maui travel brochures. Nonetheless, you'll find plenty of room to roam. For the hike to **Botanical Gardens and Iao Needle**, take the paved path past the restrooms, and go left down the stairs before the bridge. You can wander around among the signed plants, both indigenous and Polynesian-introduced, and ponds. At the far end of the gardens, face upstream to observe the confluence. Kinihapai Stream, which flows under the bridge from the Needle, joins Iao Stream, which comes from the valley to the left. Then retrace your steps out of the garden, cross the footbridge—a Kodak moment—and take the paved path to the right. After hopping up a few dozen stairs, you will come to the small covered viewing area for the 2,250-fot Iao Needle. *Note:* Iao rhymes with "meow."

The boundary for the 6-acre state park is the railing at the Needle Overlook. To continue to the **Iao Tablelands vista**—the choice hike for the valley and one of the best on Maui—you need to step over the railing at the overlook and continue up the well-used trail. *Note:* Signs at the rail ask that you "stay on designated walkways" and warn that cars left after park closure (7 p.m.) will be towed. The trail is hiked frequently. Use your own judgment.

The Iao Tablelands is the area between and above the two streams, which join below at the botanical garden. The trail at first is cut into the side of a narrow ridge, with an embankment rising to your left and a steep valley on the right. As you climb, during the first .25-mile, you'll rise above the Needle and be able to observe that the backside of the spire is anchored up high to a ridge, eliminating the needle effect. After another .25-mile, the trail climbs so that there is no rise to your left. Amid strawberry guava saplings, double-back a few hundred feet down the trail that runs along the ridge, parallel and slightly above the main trail.

Iao Valley Botanical Gardens

You'll come to a little clearing with astounding views: Inland is the the Iao Valley and seaward is the Kahului Coast. Both streams are visible. On the north is the Wall of Tears, a 3,000-foot fissured cliff that at times will have a half-dozen silvery falls; at times, water vapor falls down the cliff faces. And then turn around. The craggy green Kapilau Ridge is equally captivating. *Be Aware:* Stay back from trail edges, where greenery disguises dangerous drop-offs. *More Stuff:* From the vista point, the trail continues into the tablelands for more than a mile, and gradually up. Although flora encroaches at times—ferns, koa, ti, bananas, guava—the route is easy to walk. You won't achieve a view comparable to the vista point, and forget about taking the ancient route to the Olowalu Valley: It's overgrown and washed out. Make sure to memorize your trail junctions, as coming back can be confusing.

For the **Iao Stream** walk, cross the bridge at the stream on the improved path. At the stairs leading to the Needle, go to your left on a path and stairs down to the forested banks of Iao Stream. A social trail leads upstream. The improved trail makes a loop downstream, passing near the confluence across from the botanical garden. *Talk Story:* The Iao Valley has become known for the gruesome battle. But for centuries is was also the place on Maui where the Makahiki was celebrated in the fall—when the god Lono returned to bring peace and renewal, and to bless the land's bounty.

26. KAPILAU RIDGE   HIKE

WHAT'S BEST: A little-used trail takes you up to a sweeping view of the isthmus' two coasts and a goat's-eye look at Iao Valley. Or, a nearby old-style garden and visitors center offers families a more leisurely option.

PARKING: *For Kapilau Ridge:* Take Hwy. 320 (Iao Valley Rd.) from Wailuku. After about .5-mi., veer left toward Wailuku Heights on W. Alu Rd. Continue about .25-mi., to where guardrail ends and the road makes a big left. The trail is on the right at telephone pole #5. Park at a shoulder on the left *before* reaching the turn. *For Maui Tropical Plantation:* Take Hwy. 30 (S. High St.-Honoapi'ilani Hwy.) about 2 mi. south from Wailuku; it's off the highway just south of Waiko Rd.

HIKE: Kapilau Ridge to: Wailuku Cross (1.5 mi., 850 ft.), or Pu'u Lio (4.5 mi., 2,100 ft.); Maui Tropical Plantation (up to .5-mi.)

Talk Story: Around 1960, parochial school students from Wailuku erected a large cross on the Kapilau Ridge, which is the one to the left as you look toward the Iao Valley. Repairs and improvements have been made on yearly pilgrimages. You can see the white cross from Highway 30 south of Wailuku, and from Highway 340 going north.

For **both Kapilau Ridge hikes**, step up the grassy embankment to the right of telephone pole #5 and begin the steep climb through trees made less dense by a recent fire. Roots help with footing. The trail flattens before you reach the wooden **Wailuku Cross**, contouring along through koa, ironwoods, and even paperbark trees. For the aerial views from **Pu'u Lio**, continue past the cross. The trail makes several steep rises, followed by flatter segments on knolls. Not far above the cross, century plants may block the trail in one spot, but good passage follows for the rest of the hike. The first big pitch from the cross reaches a clump of ironwoods. From there you'll ascend two eroded, red-dirt ramps. The more forested Puʻu Lio is above these; a small grassy area, which is often at cloud level, lets you look through leaves and century plants, down at the Iao Needle, and the Kinihapai Stream side of the valley.

Maui Tropical Plantation's 60 acres sprawl from the base of the West Maui Mountains, planted with an orchard of tropical fruit trees and flowering shrubs, and surrounding a large pond that is home to feedable fish and quacking ducks. The grounds feature a large gift store, no-nonsense restaurant, and a monkey cage. Kids will love it. You can see it all on a 40-minute tram ride (about $11 for adults, $4 for children), or by taking a stroll of the central grounds. It all adds up to an old-timey, relaxing visit.

27. WAILUKU TOWN   HIKE

WHAT'S BEST: Do some quirky souvenir shopping while you get a sense of small-town Maui, circa 1950. Or roam other buildings that date from a century earlier.

PARKING: Go north toward Wailuku on Hwy. 30, which becomes S. High St. At a traffic signal, S. High St. meets Hwy. 32, which is also Main St. *For the Historical Buildings:* Park at public lot across the street from the library, just before reaching Main. *For the Old Town Stroll:* Turn right on Main St. and then turn left on N. Market St. Park on-street, or in a public lot that is on the left before reaching Vineyard St.

HIKE: Historical Buildings Tour (up to .5-mi.); Old Town Stroll (.25-mi.)

Talk Story: At the opening to the Iao Valley, Wailuku's site was the chosen spot for the kings, or aliʻi, of ancient times. This is also where Kamehameha I's forces won the final battle that united the islands as a kingdom, where the missionary movement and educational reforms were centered, and, finally, the capital for sugar industry's growth during the late 1800s and well into the 1900s. All of these historical threads are braided together within a few blocks on the Historical Buildings Tour, featuring some 10 buildings listed on the National Register of Historic Places.

The **Historical Buildings Tour** begins at the Old County Building, under the huge monkeypod trees at the parking lot, dates from 1925. Next door, the Circuit Court-house, was built 18 years earlier. Both are National Historic Places. So are the Wailuku Public Library across High Street, and the Territorial Building, which sits with a lawn buffer just above it. At the corner of High and Main streets are the Kaʻahumanu Church, built in 1876 to honor Hawaii's favorite queen, and a small cemetery in Honoliʻi Park, where Hawaiian aliʻi and missionary families lay side by side.

Walking to your left, toward Iao Valley, on Main Street, you'll see the Alexander House, built in 1836. And just up the street is the stone-and-stucco Bailey House Museum, one of the better small museums in Hawaii. Built on lands donated to the missionaries by Hawaiian royalty, the plantation-style structure was home to the Wailuku Female

Seminary from 1832 to 1932. Today, you'll find native Hawaiian artifacts and paintings by Edward Bailey, who also made much of the furniture. Displays tell the story of Maui's golden era, when educational and cultural reforms took place in the 1800s. Outside is an exotic garden with inviting benches and a view of Haleakala, and the entrance to the gift store, which is run by the Maui Historical Society. *Note:* The museum is open Monday through Saturday, 10 to 4. Admission is around $5.

Although the county seat since 1905, the high tide of commerce has been receding from Wailuku since the 1960s, as evidenced in the 'charming,' art deco-meets-Old West buildings along the **Old Town Stroll**. Antique stores, bonafide junk stores, Hawaiian crafts, used records, galleries, second-hand clothes, old books, and espresso cafes, are strung along one block, all set around the crown jewel of funk deco, the Iao Theater. Old Wailuku is not trying to be cool, although some brochure writers have dubbed Market Street, "Antiques Row." On side streets, are neighborhoods with sugar shacks covered with sprays of flowers and tropical greenery. Way at the end of Vineyard, at the corner of Ilina Street—you'll probably want to drive—is another cemetery. The headstones are a history of Maui, and the view of the Iao Valley from here is one to make most of us take time to reflect. Alright, back to the beach.

28. KAHULUI HARBOR   HIKE, SURF

WHAT'S BEST: Catch the gargantuan open market and swap meet on Saturdays. Then see if there's a canoe race or big surf at the harbor.

PARKING: Take Hwy. 311 (the Mokulele Hwy.) north to Kahului. Mokulele becomes Hwy. 350 and Pu'uhene Ave. Follow several blocks to just before Kamehameha Ave. *Alternate route:* Take Hwy. 30 to Wailuku and turn right on Hwy. 32, which is W. Main St. Follow as Main St. becomes Ka'ahumanu Ave., and turn right on Hwy. 350, Pu'uhene Ave. *Note:* Event organizers anticipate moving the swap meet to south of Keopulani Park near Maui Community College, which is between Ka'ahumanu Ave. (Hwy. 32) and Kahului Beach Rd. (Hwy. 340) on Wahinepio Ave. Call 808-877-3100 for an update.

HIKE: Maui Swap Meet (about .5-mi.); Kahului Breakwater and Keopualani Park (up to 2 mi.)

Locals gather before 7 a.m. on Saturday for the **Maui Swap Meet**, in search of good deals on fresh flowers, sunglasses, T-shirts, books, jewelry, ethnic snacks, native crafts, castaway junk, baked goods, trinkets, and a mind-boggling assortment of locally grown fruits, herbs, and vegetables. You may arrive just to roam the several-acre scene, but few will depart empty handed. The event winds down around noon.

To get from the swap meet to the **Kahului Breakwater** and **Keopualani Park**, head up Pu'uhene Avenue to Ka'ahumanu Avenue, or Highway 32. Turn left, and then veer right on Highway 340, which is Kahului Beach Road. At the far end of the harbor, turn right into a paved lot at the foot of the wide breakwater that forms the west side of the harbor. Park near the gate and walk about to view the big ships, incoming surf, fishermen, and surfers. Keopualani Park, home to the Maui Art Center, spacious play areas, and Maui Nui Botanical Garden, is directly accross Kahului Beach Road. The state-run gardens are slowly growing into one of the better exhibits of Polynesian and native plants. To drive there, turn right leaving the breakwater and make your first left on Kanaloa Avenue. Hours are Monday through Saturday, 8 to 4. *More Stuff:* The Hawaiian Canoe Club puts in at the grassy shores of Hoaloha Park for paddles out Kahului Harbor. To get there, continue on Puʻuhene Avenue, turn left on Highway 32 (Kaʻahumanu Avenue), and turn right on (unsigned) 2nd Avenue toward Shoreline Access. If you're driving east on Kaʻahumanu Avenue, turn left past Lono Avenue, just before the light at Puʻuhene. The small park offers a view of Pier 2, where the cruise ships, the Superferry, and container vessels dock.

SURF: The breakwater at **Kahului Harbor Park** presents a choice for surfers: a left-break inside the harbor, or a larger, right-break outside on the ocean side. The outside break is often better reached from the **Paukukalo** neighborhood. Take Highway 340 north as Kahului Beach Road veers right and becomes Waiehu Beach Road. Several Shoreline Access points are on dead-end roads: Kainalu, Linekona, Kaikoʻo, and Kailana. The Paukukalo neighborhood is very local.

29. KANAHA BEACH PARK   HIKE, SNORKEL, SURF

WHAT'S BEST: Beach walk while trade winds froth the waves inside a long coral reef, supercharging the sails of windsurfers and kiteboarders. You can find both action and or a private beach. Or take an even calmer stroll at the nearby historic wildlife pond.

PARKING: *For Kanaha Beach:* Go east from Kahului on Hwy. 32, Kaʻahumanu Ave., and continue straight at the jct. with Hwy. 36 (the Hana Hwy.) which goes to the right. Turn left on Hobron Ave. (32A), and then turn right on Amala Pl. Continue for 1.75 mi., as Amala becomes Alahao St. The beach park covers more than a mile along the street; the primary entrance is the second paved road on your left. *Alternate:* Go to the airport, loop around the terminal, and turn right toward the rental car returns on Kaʻa St. Kaʻa joins Alahao St.; turn right for beach park. *For Kanaha Pond:* From its jct. with Hwy. 32, take Hwy. 36. Veer left toward the airport on Hwy. 36A. Then veer left off 36A toward the airport on Keolani Pl. and make the first left on Palapala Dr.

HIKE: Kanaha Beach stroll (up to1.25 mi.); Kanaha Beach to Spreckelsville Beach (2 mi.); Kanaha Pond Wildlife Sanctuary (up to 1.75 mi., permit required)

Try the **Kanaha Beach stroll** in the afternoon, when the kiteboarders are airborne and dozens of colorful windsurfer sails accent the breaking waves. Many visitors overlook this scenic park because it is off main roads and near the airport. About .5-mile after making the right on Amala, on the left before a bridge, is the pipe gate for the Kaʻa

Maui Swap Meet, Hoaloha Park

Point section of the beach park that is the kiteboarders' hangout; a second access is about .4-mile beyond the first. These athletes from around the world stand on a short board with toe clips, while harnassed into a kite—which has just enough lift to swing them into the air, but not enough to yank them into the wild blue yonder. Farther down Alahao Street, at the farthest lot for Kanaha Beach Park, is the take-off spot for the windsurfers. Stroll down the beach to your left and continue past the rounded point to reach the kiteboard beach. On the way you'll weave through the expansive picnic and camping area, shaded by ironwoods and tall broadleaf trees.

Kanaha Beach Park

Start the **Kahana Beach to Spreckelsville Beach** hike from the farthest last parking lot at the beach park. This is one of Maui's pleasant surprises. Head to your right along the coarse sand, at the edge of a backshore of ironwoods, palms, and kukui trees. You'll pass a little black-rock jetty and reach a nice run of sand, from which Kanaha Park will no longer be visible. Cross a second black rock point, leading to another, smaller beach. Nice beach homes are set back from the beach, and you'll have to walk the tops of the bulkheads of their yards to round the point. One last section, with Spreckelsville Beach now visible, is easiest wading—and not that easy at high tide.

The **Kanaha Pond Wildlife Sanctuary** walk covers 150 fenced acres. Paths encircle four ponds, creating a walking track with options. Wandering these tree-shaded land patches between still waters will be a memorable experience for bird watchers. *Note:* You'll need a permit from state wildlife (available from September through March, when birds are not nesting). Hikes are possble Monday through Saturday, 8 to 4; call 808-984-8100. The free permits can be processed on the day of your request. *Talk Story:* The pond was built to raise fish and waterfowl, more than 200 years ago by

King Kapiʻiohoʻokalani. Today this National Natural Landmark provides habitat for native Hawaiian species, such as the coot, stilt, and duck—all endangered. Migrating waterfowl and shorebirds also touch down here in the winter.

SNORKEL: The long Spartan Reef offshore **Kanaha Beach Park** provides for colorful snorkeling on calm days, but windsurf action makes swimming iffy. A roped-off pool near the lifeguard station is a safe place to take a dip; or, show up before 11, the start time for the wind worshipers. Your best bet for a beach day is to take the walk toward Speckelsville, described above. Bits of seaweed and wave-borne sand detract from water clarity, but you won't find a more private and pretty beach scene on Maui.

SURF: **Kanaha Beach Park** is a windsurfing and kiteboarding Mecca, both for those who take part and those who want to kick back and watch the spectacle (see *Hike* above for directions). These guys and wahines are among the world's best.

30. SPRECKELSVILLE   HIKE, SNORKEL, SURF

WHAT'S BEST: Three beaches present different ways to get away from it all, without having to go far to do it.

PARKING: *For all beaches:* Take Hwy. 36 toward Hana past its jct. with Hwy. 37 and mm3. *For Spreckelsville Beach:* As Hwy. 36 bends to the right (before the senior center), turn left at mm4.4 on unsigned Spreckelsville Beach Rd., a.k.a. Stable Rd. *For Sugar Cove, Baby Baldwin:* Continue as Hwy. 36 bends right, pass the senior center, and turn left at mm5 on Nonohe Pl. Further directions in hiking descriptions.

HIKE: Sprecksville Beach (up to 2.5 mi.); Sugar Cove (up to 1.25 mi.); Baby Baldwin Beach (1.25 mi.)

Talk Story: Claus Spreckels came to Maui already a millionaire in 1877. He left 20 years later a multi-millionaire known as the "Sugar King" of Hawaii, after he bought up thousands of acres and built mega-irrigation ditches that captured stream flows on the north slope of Haleakala. Known also by some as a robber baron, Spreckels' former compound, Spreckelsville, was where the Maui Country Club is today.

You'll see several potholed spur roads to **Spreckelsville Beach** after you pass coco palms. Dunes and beach succulents appear on your right. The access roads are within .5-mile from the highway turnoff, before reaching homes at road's end. Park off the pavement at the farthest, and walk through the pinkish sand dunes to the beach. To your right you can walk about 1.25 miles, passing rounded Papaula Point, to Sugar Cove. Small black-rock points intrude into the sand along the way. *More Stuff:* To your left, alongside the road, is the bike path that goes to Kanaha Beach Park. You can also beach walk to Kanaha.

Baby Beach, Kanaha

To **Sugar Cove**, drive .2-mile to the bottom of Nonohe Place and turn left on Pa'ani Place for another .2-mile. Park at road's end, near a sign for Shoreline Access 302. A short sand trail leads along a lava seawall to a .25-mile cove set below unobtrusive, high-end condos. You can walk left to Spreckelsville Beach—the reverse of the hike described above—but this beach is more a place to catch a few winks or count grains of sand. To **Baby Baldwin Beach**, stay to the right on Nonohe at the bottom, and then immediately turn left toward Shoreline Access, on Kealakai Place—instead of going to the golf course. The unimproved parking is at Wawau Point, where a mosaic of red banks, black rocks, and white sand make for an interesting stroll. The beach hike seamlessly connects with Baldwin Beach Park.

SNORKEL: A finger from Wawau Point's reef curls just offshore for several hundred feet at **Baby Baldwin Beach**, making a sandy-bottomed oval that can accommodate large numbers of swimmers. The beach is a well-known dipping pool for families, safe even during trade winds—although be mindful of the current flowing to your right as water returns out the open end of nature's pool. Sand dunes and ironwoods buffet the shore. Not many fish are in the pool, but this is a five-star swimming spot. You'll also find a very good **baby beach at Speckelsville**. Go the access road that is .5-mile in from the highway, just before the private road begins. A long oval is carved out of the shelf, open to the sea on its left side, which also opens to the big look at Iao Valley. Soak and stare. *Be Aware:* Wave action will bring current, usually right-to-left. It's normally safe. Local families will show up on weekends, but not many tourists will find this sweet place.

SURF: Windsurfers catch the breeze off **Wawau Point**, near Baby Baldwin, but offshore rocks make this less popular than other spots not far away, both up and down the coast. The offshore tiers at **Sugar Cove** occasionally attract local shortboard surfers and kite-boarders.

31. BALDWIN BEACH PARK   HIKE, SNORKEL, SURF

WHAT'S BEST: Baldwin is one of Maui's sweet spots, where coco palms fringe golden sand and turquoise waters—the perfect place to enjoy life on a waning afternoon.

PARKING: Take Hwy. 36 (the Hana Hwy.) past the Maui Country Club to mm6. Turn left into signed beach park lot. Hours are from 7 to 7.

HIKE: Baldwin Beach to: Baby Baldwin (.75-mi.), or Paia via State of Mind Beach (1.5 mi.)

Talk Story: The beach park is the former home for families who worked the sugar cane for Harry A. Baldwin—whose grandfather Dwight Baldwin was one of Maui's original missionaries in Lahaina in the early 1800s. Harry furthered the efforts of his father,

Baldwin Beach Park

Henry P., and the family by the 1930s was one of the Big Five, who controlled more than 90 percent of the state's sugar production—and virtually ran Hawaii's government. Local mills have shut down, but some of the workers and their descendents still gather at the park. If you're lucky, you'll arrive on a day when blade-wielding Tongans are climbing the park's willowy coco palms to trim. A 2007 flash flood brought a wave of silt that closed the park pavilion, and repairs were slow in commencing.

Late afternoons are a good time for **Baldwin Beach**, as locals gather to frolic in the surf and unwind. **Baby Baldwin Beach** is a sand-and-surf walk. In the background

State of Mind Beach

is the jade tunnel of the Iao Valley, and to the right in the distance you'll see the shark fin of Kahakuloa Head. Going to your right from the pavilion, toward **Paia**, you'll cover a stretch of sand and then hop up to a dirt fisherman's path, protected by riprap. After rounding a point, you'll reach isolated **State of Mind Beach** (a.k.a. Montana Beach). The path continues just above its narrow run of sand, a couple hundred yards long. After a copse of ironwoods—where at shore a large, washed-up concrete block is spray-painted with "state of mind"—come the sands of Lower Paia Beach Park, which is on the outer edge of the town.

SNORKEL: **Baldwin Beach** is not known as a snorkeling beach, but you will find spots to take a dip. The best is to the right a hundred yards from the pavilion. A curve of rocks creates a fairly protected pool. Ample sands and shade trees lure locals and a smattering of kicked-back tourists. Ask lifeguards about surf conditons.

SURF: The shore break to the left of **Baldwin Beach** parking draws bodysurfers and bodyboarders in the winter. But be careful, as head plants can be scary at times. The lifeguards normally post hazard signs, but you shouldn't rely on them. Board surfers head for the reef break, to the right of the pavilion in the direction of Paia.

32. PAIA-HOʻOKIPA   HIKE, SNORKEL, SURF

> **WHAT'S BEST:** Shop for surf shoes, espresso, or island art in this back-to-the-earth beach town. Then just down the road is the world capital of windsurfing.

Paia, Hookipa

Paia

PARKING: *For both hikes,* from Kahului take Hwy. 36 (the Hana Hwy.) past mm6. *For the Paia stroll:* As you approach the first buildings, at the first crosswalk and reduced speed sign, look for public parking sign on your right. On-street parking is also available. *For Hoʻokipa Beach walk:* Drive beyond Paia. At about mm8.5, pass the first entrances to the beach park and turn left past a sign for Hoʻokipa Lookout. Park at the upper lot.

HIKE: Paia stroll (.75-mi.); Hoʻokipa Beach walk (1 mi.)

For the **Paia stroll,** wander up the Hana Highway to its T-intersection with Baldwin Avenue. All the action is a block or two on either side. If you need a beach break, begin by doubling back a short distance to the Lower Paia Beach Park, at the youth center. The scene amps up on weekends with surfers and sunbathers.

Paia reinvented itself in the 1980s, when the studly new sport of windsurfing married the fetching waves of nearby Hoʻokipa Beach. The fading Old West wood-frames, plantation cottages, and sugar shacks got new coats of pastel paints, as the sandy-footed set created a demand for a host of low-key tourist shops—boutiques, hemp-reggae wear, surfer-Joe outfitters, espresso internet cafés, seafood grills, and some of Maui's best art galleries. The with-it epicenter for Paia is Mana Foods—up Baldwin Avenue on the left—where tribe members of organic enclaves and other low-key locals seek whole-grain goodies and stimulated conversation. If dining out in Paia, don't bother to shave or blow dry, since this is a dress-down place, even for island-style.

Surfers catch the point break below the **Hoʻokipa Beach Lookout**, riding in toward the shore as spectators view from a pipe railing. At the far end of the railing, a social trail curves down a grass embankment to the smooth lava shelf. You can get a board's eye view on the action. *Be Aware:* Big surf can be a hazard at this lower area. Then, for a closer look at the beach scene, take the road down to the pavilion. Late in the day, the long parking lot along the beach is filled with surfers enjoying their day at Hookah, er, Hoʻokipa. The lower part of the beach extends for about .25-mile, with a reef close in on the east end below the lookout. Windsurfers from around the globe gather off the point extends on the west end of the beach. Grassy bluffs are designed for photograhpers and gawkers.

SNORKEL: Paia and Hoʻokipa, with reefs close in and wave action, arenʼt good for swimming, particularly in the winter. To take the plunge, try **Mamaʼs Cove**. Driving toward Hoʻokipa from Paia, turn near mm8, into the Mamaʼs Fish House; a dozen shoreline access parking places should be on the right, marked by blue cones. *Alternate parking:* Turn toward the ocean on Kaiholo Place at mm8 (close by on the Paia side of Mamaʼs) and park at Poho Place; then walk up Kaiholo on a grassy drive toward cottages, up steps, and then right on another street to a shoreline access path. Either way, youʼll pop out to this sandy cove, on the beach fronting Mamaʼs. The cove has a reef close in that creates a keiki pond, normally safe for swimming—but donʼt expect lots of fish. *Be Aware:* Low tide brings poor swimming conditions.

SURF: Body boarders ride the tiers of fast-breaking near-shore tubes at **Lower Paia Beach Park**, which is on the left as you come into Paia. Lots of friends and onlookers hang out on the few hundred yards of fine sand. **Hoʻokipa** has been home to the world championships of windsurfing; they normally gather at the west end of the beach, where the Spartan Reef begins. Much of the sportʼs equipment, including Simmer, is designed in Paia. Some of Mauiʼs best board surfing waves are off the lookout, several tiers of wedges that break to the right. In the little settlement of **Kuau**, about .5-mile from Paia, are two Shoreline Access spots that host a lower-key surf scene. The best is at mm7.4, down dirt cul-de-sac that is just past Kuau Beach Place.

33. JAWS   HIKE, SURF

WHATʼS BEST: Behemoth, perfect waves form off the bluffs above the pineapple fields. When Jaws goes off, big-wave surfers come fast. On other days, take a sea-view hike.

PARKING: Take Hwy. 36, the Hana Hwy., past mm11 and the turnoff to Haiku. *For Pauwela Point:* After another .7-mi., park on right near the Haiku Community Center, which is between Pauwela Rd. and Pili Aloha. *Note:* On dry days, you may be able to drive the first mile of the hike. *For Jaws:* After mm13 and E. Kuiaha Rd. park at an ocean-side turnout at a gate; itʼs just before the memorial park cemetery—across the highway from a fruit stand and where a sign notes that E. Kuiaha Rd. is coming up. *Alternate:* 4WD vehicles can drive to Jaws. Continue to mm13.5 and turn on Hahana Rd., which turns to dirt after .25-mi. When the surfʼs up, too many cars make this road tough.

HIKE: Jaws (2.5 mi., 275 ft.); Pauwela Point (up to 3 mi., 200 ft.)

Talk Story: Maybe two or three times each winter, waves 25- to 70-feet high form off Peahi Point, attracting intrepid surfers from all over the world—including the king of big-wave surfing, Laird Hamilton (star of American Express ads). Check the forecast or, better yet, head to the decrepit county boat ramp at Maliko Bay: On an inside

Jaws

bend at mm10, turn inland and then turn right again before the old bridge, driving under the highway. Jet skis transport surfers from here, and when Jaws is going off, the lot fills with trucks and jet-ski trailers. (The spoil-sport County of Maui is thinking about closing Maliko and making the guys come from Kahului.)

To walk to **Jaws**, head down the road to the left from the gate, but then make sure to jog right directly toward the ocean across the pineapple fields, and not stray down the gulch to the left. After crossing the field, go left along a treeline with another gulch on your right. About 15 minutes into the hike, go right at a berm into the gulch on a road. You'll drop down and then curve left and up. At the top, go right for a short distance. Then go left, on a long straigthaway sloping down, now with a gulch on your left. This road curves right at bluff's edge and comes to a 100-foot dirt circle that is the lookout for Jaws. *Notes:* The road from Hahana reaches Jaws from a different direction. Access to this hike may be limited; landowners are not responsilbe for your safety.

More Stuff: To get down for a sea-level look, go right from the lookout down a spur road through ironwoods to where the road ends amid a tree filtered view. To the left is an easy-but-steep trail down 100 feet; a rope aids the way in places. You reach the bouldered beach and stream where the white foam of Jaws' waves reach shore.

For **Pauwela Point**, walk across the highway from Pili Aloha (look for a 'no dumping' sign). An unpaved and unsigned Lighthouse Road skirts the east end of the broad wedge of pineapple fields that slopes downward. As you walk down, the field will be on your left, while on your right, bananas and tropical trees will give way to a steep gully that eventually falls to tiny Kuiaha Bay. Keep heading seaward toward a white light beacon, which is on the point. Acres of grassy bluffs surround the light beacon. You can loop to your left along the edge for a view toward Paia, West Maui, and Molokai, and then peel off right, following decrepit concrete stanchions along a path with the view toward the Hana Coast. The path eventually comes around to the road you walked in.

SURF: Jaws breaks a couple hundred feet offshore, farther out as wave size increases. Most guys tow in to take the right-break on the perfectly formed monsters, since the left-break presents a rock hazard. Jet skis are needed to get enough speed to ride these big boys, which appear to be moving in slow motion from land. The jet ski partners also whiz in to pick up surfers after a wipe out. Head to Maliko Bay to watch them coming back in and to listen to war stories told with an adrenaline rush. The lookout is a good spot for photographers, but the spur road to the right also presents perches for shutterbugs. On days when Jaws breaks, this place is jumpin'.

34. HALEHAKU HEIAU   HIKE

WHAT'S BEST: Contemplate the sea overlooking this secluded bay, or take a short walk that leads centuries into the past, to the ruins of a village.

PARKING: Take Hwy. 36 (the Hana Hwy.) past the Haiku turnoff. Just after mm16, turn left on Haumana Rd. Continue on a country lane for .4-mi., veer right on Kulike Rd., and follow 1 mi. to its end, where it becomes unpaved. Park near guardrail.

HIKE: Kahuna Point (.25-mi.); Halehaku Heiau (1 mi.; 200 ft.)

Halehaku Heiau is a place you may not think much of as you go on your merry Maui way, and then two weeks later you won't be able to get it out of your mind. **For both hikes**, take the trail that leads from the left of the guardrail, and walk straight out the visible perch that sits about 200 feet above the west side of Halehaku Bay. **Kahuna Point** affords both details and a panorama of the wild bay and the steep, lush walls that frame its opening to the sea. You're bound to see whales offshore in the winter, and down below don't be surprised if sea turtles swim by.

To get to **Halehaku Heiau**, double back 50 feet from Kahuna Point and take the trail that traverses inland. You'll veer down through koa, kukui, and hau trees, which provide hand supports when this trail then drops straight down. Cross the stream at the bottom, and make your way across the grassy bench that sits just above a boulder beach. After a few hundred feet, hook right and walk in to see the big heiau and wall remains, built under a canopy of trees.

Talk Story: In 1790, King Kamehameha, having ventured from Hana during his invasion of Maui, won a decisive battle near here, bolstering his flagging confidence on his way to the final victory at Iao Valley. Trees grow through places in this landmark, but its terraces and enclosures are fundamentally intact. Built of beach rock, its duel platforms each measure roughly 125 feet square. Some remains in this area date from the 1500s. *Be Aware:* As with all such sites, be careful not to disturb anything.

Hana Highway

North from Keanae Peninsula

HANA HIGHWAY

More than 50 one-lane bridges allow passage on a squiggly blacktop that hugs the cliffs and valleys of a rain forest—and in typical Hawaiian fashion, each has a name, such as, "open laughter," "heavenly mist," "land of deep love," and "lightning flash." Waterfalls are strung like confetti. The coast is wild with waves doing battle with sculpted lava. Then you reach Hana and its hidden beaches, pastoral slopes, historical strolls, and freshwater pools. After Hana, the twisting highway takes a curtain call, offering more waterfalls and forest, as the journey continues to the Kipahalu section of Haleakala National Park, at the Pools of Oheo.

DRIVING TOUR
PICKING THE RIGHT DAY

Every day is a weekend on the Hana Highway, although you'll see less local traffic on the real weekend. The main concern is to avoid this tour during and right after tropical storms, when mud slides and flash floods present a hazard. Of course, a safe time after storms is when the road's greenery sparkles and waterfalls are most plentiful. Overcast weather will not spoil a day here, since this is not a fun-in-the-sun adventure, and the rain-forest greens deepen under cloud cover.

The wisest advice is to depart early, if you would like a more private experience. Rental cars seem to form a train beginning from about 8 a.m. to 10 a.m. If you are taking the half-trip—see below—you could also opt to depart after the rush.

THE ROAD

Provided the weather is fair, the Hana Highway is not in the running for Maui's most dangerous drive. Cars tend to plug along in a mellow samba line. The one-lane bridges have clearly marked yield lines. Although some publications say that cars headed toward Kahului yield to cars headed toward Hana, this etiquette is rarely practiced. The car that gets to the bridge or one-lane road segment first goes through, along with the cars in the same posse. If you arrive behind that stream, pull over and yield to the oncoming traffic from the other side of the bridge.

Exceptions to the yield rule are surfers hell-bent on catching the next wave down the road, and pick-ups and other commuters who drive the highway with a certain reckless abandon. *Give the locals a break. If cars are on your tail, pull over.* Everyone will be happier. Also remember to fill up on gas before leaving Paia. You also want to cart any garbage you produce back with you, since the Hana landfill is nearly full.

THE COURSE

Follow along on the Hana Highway map, page 118. Refer to trailhead descriptions beginning on page 119 for more details.

Note: Visitors who have an extra day on Maui can consider breaking this tour into two trips: The first would end at Nahiku, where the highway leaves the rain forest, and the second would begin there, and continue around to the pasturelands of Hana and the Pools of Oheo. If you want to do two trips, then take advantage of the side trips and hikes. Otherwise, take the side trips sparingly. The times outlined in the course below are for the longer tour.

BEGIN EARLY MORNING. TAKE HIGHWAY 36 PAST MM16 TO WHERE IT BECOMES HIGHWAY 360. Consider grabbing a steaming caffeinated beverage and baked goods to-go in Paia, just before sunrise. Just before the road narrows, you'll pass Twin Falls, which is one of the better, and longer, inland hikes on the coast. After that, the road starts living up to its reputation.

Over the next 10 or more miles, you weave in and out, on the fringe of the Ko'olau Forest Reserve, where the Waikamoi Ridge Nature Trail and Garden of Eden, as well as several state hunter's roads, lead into a rain forest that gets denser the farther you go. Waterfalls appear at inside bends, beginning around mm6.

MID-MORNING. After mm12 you come to the Kaumahina State Wayside, an excellent rest stop that received a complete makeover in 2005. A short path leads to a view that previews the Keanae Peninsula that lies just down the road. Beyond the wayside, down in the next valley, is rugged Honomanu Bay, the only place the highway reaches the water until you get to Hana. After climbing out of this valley, you reach the Keanae

St. Augustine Shrine, Wailua

Keanae Arboretum, Hana Highway cascade

Arboretum. If you were to take just one short walk along this stretch of the highway, this is it. Just after the arboretum are the side trips to Keanae and Wailua, both of which impart a sense of Old Hawaii.

NOON. After Keanae, the Hana Highway really does the hokey-pokey, offering cascades and steep hillsides dripping with flora in a constant turn of the wheel. Inland is the Hanawi Natural Area Reserve, one of the wettest places on earth. A side trip to mysterious Nahiku awaits at mm25. After rounding the bend in Nahiku, fruit stands and occasional homesteads appear, as the highway changes character. The overhanging jungle lifts, giving way to bucolic slopes, pocketed by tropical woodlands.

Just before Hana, at mm31, is one side-trip that is tough to pass, to Kahanu National Tropical Botanical Gardens and Pi'ilanihale Heiau—where you can appreciate the Hawaiian culture at its zenith. And just down the road from these attractions is the Blue Pool, unsurpassed in scenic beauty by any of the island's other pools. Beyond the turnoff to the gardens is the road to Waianapanapa State Park. You could easily spend the day here, and the park's picnic grounds are the best around. If you're looking for a long coastal walk next to exploding waves, this is the place.

Travaasa Hana

AFTERNOON. If you're on a day trip, and plan on doing some walking around at the Pools of Oheo, you might have to give Hana short shrift. But make time for the Hana Cultural Center and a stroll around wharf area—and for that matter, the .25-mile hike to Kauiki Head and the Queen Ka'ahumanu Birthplace is a bell ringer. For an overview of Hana, hump up to Fagan's Cross on Pu'u o Kahaula. Come to think of it, Red Sand Beach isn't that far, and it is a sight you'll never forget; although the trail can be hazardous, this beach is unique.

Keanae

Koki Beach

As you head out of Hana—and Highway 360 becomes Highway 31—you'll have time to hook seaward and see Koki Beach Park and Hamoa Beach. Haneoʻo Road loops back out to the highway. Unless you bypassed all the stuff early in the day, you may have to skip Venus Pool. About five miles later—passing waterfalls through deep forest on some fairly hairy one-lane segments—you reach Kipahulu Visitors Center at the lower part of Haleakala National Park.

At Kipahulu are the Pools of Oheo Gulch, formerly known as the Seven Sacred Pools, scooped out by Pipiwai Stream before it enters the ocean. Fantastic as they are, the pools are not the epitome of the Hana Highway tour. In fact, they may play second fiddle in this neighborhood to the trail that leads inland to the Falls at Makahiku and Waimoku Falls—up a jungle crevice and bamboo forest, over a hard-rock stream on bridges. If pressed for time, do the falls walk to the bridges—for a big scenic payoff. Darn it, we wish we were there now instead of writing this book.

SUNSET. Unless you left yesterday, your waning hours will be spent behind the wheel going home. But that's good news, no matter which route you select. One choice is to continue around on Highway 31, past Kaupo. The road is actually an easier drive than the Hana Highway—with the exception of a mile-long segment about three miles from Kipahulu, near mm39 at Lelekoa Bay. It's narrow, but you can find marginal turnouts and the traffic, what there is of it, is almost all headed the same direction (clockwise). If you go back this direction, you can dip in to see Charles Lindbergh's grave, before that narrow stretch. Look at the Haleakala driving tour for more on this route. You'll see sunset on the backside of the big volcano, as well as have a sunset ocean view. *Note:* This route may still be closed due to a rockslide.

An equally good choice is to retrace your route on the Hana Highway. You may need to do this just to believe all the sights you beheld earlier in the day. Certainly, you can drive the Hana Highway a dozen times and see fresh sights. The place is overflowing with them.

Koʻolau Forest Reserve

Hana Highway, Kipahulu Campground, Waianapanapa State Park, Kipahulu Fruit Stand

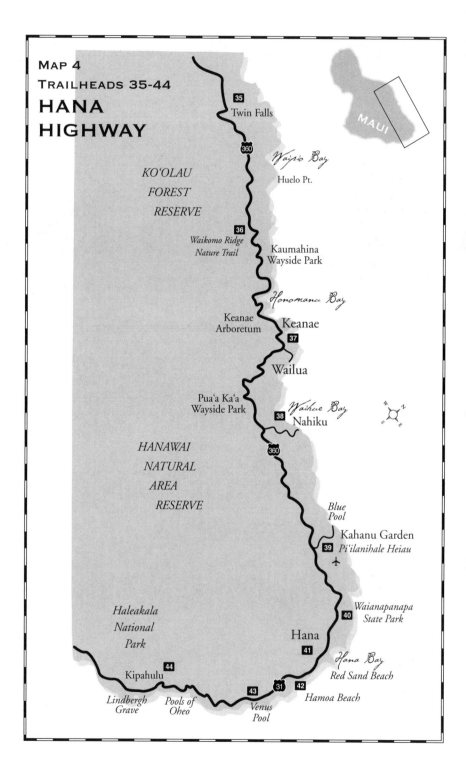

MAP 4
TRAILHEADS 35-44
HANA
HIGHWAY

MAUI

35
Twin Falls

360

Waipio Bay

KO'OLAU
FOREST
RESERVE

Huelo Pt.

36
Waikomo Ridge
Nature Trail

Kaumahina
Wayside Park

Honomanu Bay

Keanae
Arboretum

Keanae
37

Wailua

Pua'a Ka'a
Wayside Park

Waihue Bay

38
Nahiku

360

HANAWAI
NATURAL
AREA
RESERVE

Blue
Pool

Kahanu Garden
39 *Pi'ilanihale Heiau*
✈

Haleakala
National
Park

Waianapanapa
40 *State Park*

Hana
41

Hana Bay

44
Kipahulu

Red Sand Beach

Lindbergh
Grave

Pools of
Oheo

43   31   42

Venus
Pool

Hamoa Beach

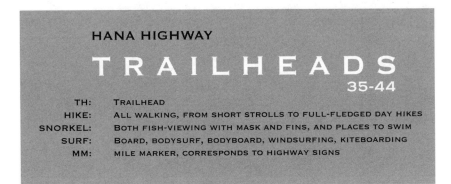

TH:	TRAILHEAD
HIKE:	ALL WALKING, FROM SHORT STROLLS TO FULL-FLEDGED DAY HIKES
SNORKEL:	BOTH FISH-VIEWING WITH MASK AND FINS, AND PLACES TO SWIM
SURF:	BOARD, BODYSURF, BODYBOARD, WINDSURFING, KITEBOARDING
MM:	MILE MARKER, CORRESPONDS TO HIGHWAY SIGNS

All hiking distances in parentheses are ROUND TRIP.
Elevation gains of 100 feet or more are noted.
Please pull over for locals when driving the Hana Highway.

35. TWIN FALLS   HIKE, SNORKEL

WHAT'S BEST: A half-dozen waterfalls tumble into swimming pools amid tropical flora. Amazing, but don't try to fit this adventure in with the long drive to Hana.

PARKING: Take Hwy. 36 (the Hana Hwy.) beyond mm16, where route becomes Hwy. 360 and mile markers restart from zero. *For Twin Falls Botanical Preserve:* At mm2, pull out to the right on the shoulder of a wide bridge at the Twin Falls Fruit Stand.

HIKE: Twin Falls Botanical Preserve (2.25 mi., 250 ft.)

Talk Story: The preserve is where two streams with waterfalls, pools, and very long names join together, fall some 20 feet over a lava ledge, and depart as one: Hoʻolawa Stream, which then descends over two more falls-with-pools before reaching Hoʻolawa Bay. Trails are on lands of the Twin Falls Botanical Preserve—*please* make a donation. Their organic produce is a deal in both price and quality.

People meander on the various trails through the **Twin Falls Botanical Preserve.** Here's a semi-loop option to see it all efficiently: Immediately after the gate at the fruit stand, leave the road and go left on a trail that soon reaches the stream, where you go right, upstream (a left forking trail here leads to the top of Lower Twin Falls). Then immediately take a left-bearing trail that drops to a beautiful, 100-foot oval pool with a 25-foot cascade falling through basalt columns under a huge banyan tree; most tourists miss this one. Then backtrack to the trail and continue upstream, above this cascade. Within minutes, the trail drops to and crosses the streambed, reaching a wide, 10-foot falls. Roots line the walls of a cavern and a rope swing invites swimmers to take a ride and plunge. From here, climb up the trail, which will take you to the main preserve road, where you go left. (On the way out, stay on this road and

enjoy its floral delights—papayas, hibiscus, ti, guava, bananas—that rival the falls as this hike's main attraction.)

The road crosses the stream at a spillway and, a few minutes later, reaches a three-fork junction at painted rocks—your gateway to both 'Left Twin Falls' and 'Right Twin Falls.' For both, go left at the painted rocks and, a few hundred feet later, go right. To **Left Twin Falls**, take an immediate left and walk for several minutes over a rooty trail. A rope aids the easy 30-foot descent to the pool and ferny amphitheater. You can swim behind the sheet of water or take a tame rope swing ride.

Twin Falls

To the **Right Twin Falls**, the most popular, backtrack on the rooty trail and go left, as if you had not visited the Left Twin Falls. The road dips through paperpark trees and reaches an irrigation channel. Cross a plank 'bridge' and go left along the rock wall of the ditch, then across roots and rocks, and you'll reach the Right Twin Falls—cascading 35 feet from a curved cliff into a pool, all of it under a leafy ceiling. To reach the top to of the falls (and the jumping rocks) take a steep route that is to the right at the edge of the pool. Only the first part requires hands. Go left at the top. *Hot tip:* Stay on the trail from the top of Right Twin Falls, through lovely paperbark and pandanus trees. In a couple minutes you'll reach the jewel of the preserve: 'Upper Right Twin Falls,' a sunny, 12-foot waterfall into a private swimming oval!

SNORKEL: Bring your swimsuit and camera. After school and on weekends, zany highschool kids and locals leap from overhanging rocks and branches, with the premier show at Right Twin Falls. Left Twin Falls will better suit tourists. The most attractive for visitors may be the basalt-column falls, that is to the left off the main road, immediately after the entrance gate. *Be Aware:* Submerged rocks and shallow waters are a hazard. Get advice and test the waters. Don't dive.

More Stuff: You can access the bottom Lower Twin Falls from the old highway: Backtrack on Hwy. 360 about .1-mi. and turn right on unpaved Ulalena Loop. Continue .4-mi. to an old concrete bridge at the stream, and park. Walk upstream (you have to cross) a short distance to the 15-foot cascade. Also, trekkers will want to note Lupi Road which climbs several miles into the pleasant treed birdlands and flowering shrubs of the Ko'olau Forest Reserve. Look to the right and up, as you face the fruit stand.

Another attraction nearby: Built in 1853, on a grass clearing in a jungle setting, Kaulanapueo Church is poetically situated. The church's thick walls are plaster-covered basaltic boulders that rise to a steeple. Palms and Norfolk pines accent several acres of lawn. Sitting next to the building is a small cemetery whose tombstones link history today. *Driving to the church:* Continue to mm3.6, as the Hana Highway narrows. Turn left toward Huelo at a bus stop with a public phone. After .25-mi., turn left on a short, rough uphill driveway.

36. KO'OLAU FOREST RESERVE   HIKE

WHAT'S BEST: Pick a tame or wild adventure from among these walks into the rain forests and waterfalls just off the Hana Highway.

PARKING: Take Hwy. 36 toward Hana past mm16; route becomes Hwy. 360 and mile markers start at zero. Continue to mm6. *For Bamboo Forest Falls:* Park at a turnout near an opening in a bamboo hedge at mm6.6. Leave car free of valuables. *For Waikamoi Ridge Trail:* Park at a signed turnout at mm9.5. *For the Garden of Eden:* Use a turnout at mm10.5 and proceed up a signed entranceway. *Note:* Some Ko'olau Forest Reserve lands

Ko'olau Forest Reserve

are leased by East Maui Irrigation Company. To enter, you may need a waiver from the irrigation company. Waivers normally are granted only to members taking hikes with the Sierra Club or Mauna Ala Hiking Club. See page 235 for contact information.

HIKE: Bamboo Forest Falls (.75-mi., 150 ft.); Waikamoi Ridge Nature Trail (1.25 mi., 200 ft.); Garden of Eden (up to 1 mi., 125 ft.)

Talk Story: The Ko'olau Forest Reserve runs for about 10 miles along the highway, extending inland to an elevation of about 4,000 feet. Roads connect an elaborate system of tunnels and irrigation ditches, many dating from the late 1800s, a remarkable engineering feat led by Henry P. Baldwin. Son of missionary Dwight Baldwin, Henry gained fame in 1876—one month after losing his arm in a sugar mill accident—when he belayed 120 feet down a gorge after his work crews balked at the precipice. The massive water conveyance project was completed in the nick of time to prevent a takeover by the rivals of Baldwin, and his partner and boyhood friend, Samuel T. Alexander.

For the quick jaunt to the **Bamboo Forest Falls**, duck through the rabbit hole in the bamboo and head down to your right. Cross a small stream, continue on either fork of the trail on the other side. Then cross the main stream on rocks (when flow rate allows) and go left on an upstream trail. You'll reach a first falls and pool, after only 10 minutes into the hike. To see the second falls, continue for about 5 minutes upstream on the trail through a bamboo tunnel. *More Stuff:* After the bamboo forest, at mm6.75, a gate is on your right marking Papaʻaea Road, which passes a large reservoir at the outset and leads over several streams to an immense hillside of ferns.

Featured in many brochures, the **Waikamoi Ridge Nature Trail** attracts a fair number of visitors stopping midmornings on the way to Hana. The hike climbs through native and planted trees, many identified, with view benches along the way. You'll find picnic areas at the trailhead and at the top. To start, go to the left as you face inland, and keep left to the first lookout. From there the trail makes a long switchback among pandanus at eye level. Then comes a second lookout, above the dense flora of a bend in the highway. The trail levels through a lovely paperbark and bamboo tree tunnel, at the end of which is a picnic hut. To your right is the Kolea Road, a route that descends through bamboo to trailhead parking to make this a loop hike.

The 26-acre **Garden of Eden**, begun in 1988, has family walking trails, one of which features a look at Keopuka Rock, which appeared in the opening sequence of *Jurassic Park*. At several picnic tables you can commune with coco palms, mangoes, ti, bananas, and a host of flowering botanicals. A few of the plants were contributed by the late Beatle George Harrison, friend of owner (and musician) Alan Bradbury. On the way out, visit the small flock of exotic birds who pose for snapshots. *Note:* Admission is about $10 per person. For free you can visit the beautifully sited Garden Gallery.

More Stuff: To the right at the Garden of Eden turnout is Wahinepeʻe Road, leading through 'Little Jurassic Park' to Wahinepeʻe Falls, as pretty as any in Hawaii (3.5 miles

Garden of Eden

Wahinepee Falls

round-trip, 300 foot climb). Head up the road, which skirts the garden. Stay left at a fork, and then left again, going up a double road. At a main, contour road, go left again. You'll swerve through a lush gully of ferns. Keep right, following a stream up to the 100-foot double free-fall and cascade, which flows under an artful 1925 concrete bridge. Not many visitors see this baby. For an easier .25-mile walk to Puohokama Falls, a 30-footer into a pool, begin at an inside turnout near the bridge at mm11 past the garden. *Note:* Heed signs and use these trails at your own risk.

37. KEANAE

HIKE, SNORKEL, SURF

WHAT'S BEST: Wild seascapes, village taro fields, historic churches, pools, falls and a tropical arboretum: Old Hawaii lives on.

PARKING: Activities take place over a 6-mile section of Hwy. 360 (the Hana Hwy.) taking in both sides of the Keanae Peninsula—from near mm12 to mm18.

HIKE: Kaumahina Wayside Nature Trail (.25-mi); Honomanu Bay (up to .5-mi.); Keanae Arboretum (1.25 mi.); Keanae village and pools (up to 2 mi.); Wailua Valley State Wayside (less than .25-mi.)

At mm12.2, pull off at an outside bend into the **Kaumahina State Wayside,** which was given a facelift in 2005. Head up the railing of the park's nature trail to a view straight down to the bay and toward the low lava peninsula that is Keanae. An unofficial trail at the top loop through forests and back to the parking. Wild **Honomanu Bay**—the only place the highway reaches sea level between Paia and Hana—features a large jungly stream, trees dripping with vines, and a smooth-rock beach, all enclosed by high cliffs drilled with sea caves at water level. *Driving:* At mm14.1 (after the bridges at the bottom) veer left and drive steeply down .25-mile to a streamside flat area. At the boulder-and-black-sand beach, walk right to the sea caves beneath the cliff. (An additional, walk-in access is on the way down the highway, at mm13.5. An old road is now closed to cars.)

The **Keanae Arboretum** is the best family leg-stretcher on the coast, featuring a wide path alongside Piʻinaʻau Stream, in the shade of huge trees brought here from both sides of the equator. A paved trail slopes to a grove of tropical trees from around the world, extremely large considering the arboretum dates only from 1971. A giant bamboo is inspiring. The paved path becomes dirt as you continue upstream and enter the native Hawaiian and Polynesian species—including taro, papaya, bananas, and ti. From here the path becomes a trail that crosses a tributary stream and then deteriorates while heading into the rain forest along a second tributary. *Driving:* Look for the signed turnout and gate on your right near mm16.6—and heads-up because the mm16 sign may still be missing. Additional parking is on the left, just past the gate.

Keanae Arboretum

The Keanae Peninsula came into being after one of Haleakala's more recent eruptions, when lava flowed out the Koʻolau Gap and fanned out into the Pacific. For the **Keanae village and pools** hikes, turn left just down the hill from the arboretum, before reaching mm17. Continue on the sleepy road for almost .75-mile, and park at the big turnout on the left across from the church and ball field. Start out by walking to the point toward lava stacks, nature's

statuary that fight a losing battle against oncoming waves.

Village life centers around a little church with a big name—ihiʻihioiehovaona Kaua—sitting dreamily below green ramparts and on the edge of taro fields. The edifice dates from 1860, but it was substantially rebuilt in the 1900s. From the church you can waltz over to munch a petite loaf of Aunty Sandy's righteous banana bread at the Keanae Landing Fruit Stand.

ihiʻihioiehovaona Kaua

The **pool** is a large lagoon formed where Keanae Stream, hemmed in by the cliff above the peninsula, meets a gravel bar at the beach. From the ballfield parking, walk with the ocean on your left, and keep left as the road forks passing by houses. (Ask permission if you see someone; the public is normally permitted.) You'll reach a turnaroud and gate. Continue on the grassy road. Veer left before reaching the ironwoods and palms, and descend several feet to lagoon level. Under most conditions, you'll be able cross the stream or just walk onto the gravel bar that separates the lagoon from the ocean. At the far end of the long pool, is a cascade of Keanae Stream. *More Stuff:* On the way south from Keanae, for the supreme view of the village, look for a turnout near mm17, at a guardrail, where a tidal wave siren hangs above telephone pole #41.

Keanae Peninsula

More Stuff: The scenic Wailua churches and taro fields get far fewer visitors than Keanae. Veer left from the highway near mm18.25, on Wailua Road. Just down the blacktop on your left are St. Gabriel's Church and, in the gardens behind it, St. Augustine Shrine—both cared for by some big-hearted local folks. Across the road, taro fields carpet the rich valley floor, encircled by green cliffs rising a thousand feet. Down the road (look inland toward Waikani Falls) you can park near a 'local traffic only' sign and walk to a rocky beach at Wailua Bay, where two streams coverge.

Leaving Wailua, look for the **Wailua Valley State Wayside** on the right as you come up the grade, just before mm19—and before the turnout on the left where most people stop. The parking is through a cut bank. The overlook is up a mere 40 steps to an on-high view of Wailua. *More Stuff:* A road leads from the parking into the Keanae Valley. Trees occlude an inland view initially, but after a short downhill grade, the road swerves right into rich birldlands. Then, not far past the wayside (at the bridge near mm19.5) is Upper Waikani Falls, a standout beauty among the Hana Highway's darlings.

SNORKEL: You can get a swim in at the lake-sized **Keanae Pool**. Higher upstream are several popular swimming pools, locally known as **Sapphire Pools**. *Driving:* Continue a short distance toward Hana from Keanae and park after the second bridge (where Piʻinaʻau Road goes inland). Scramble down from the bridge and you'll find clean, pure tubs. *Be Aware:* Flash floods make this a bad choice during or after rains.

SURF: Surfers who want to get away from it all ride the tiers of offshore wedges at **Honomanu Bay**. Winter swells of 4- to 8-feet break within the mouth of the bay.

38. NAHIKU   HIKE

WHAT'S BEST: Subtropical sunbeams strike rich soils moistened by 300-plus inches of rain per year. See the green results at the dramatic, remote coast at Nahiku.

PARKING: Take Hwy. 360 (the Hana Hwy.) past Keanae. Highlights for this trailhead take place over a 4-mile section from near mm21 to mm25.

HIKE: Nahiku (up to .75-mi.)

Talk Story: The Hana Highway climbs inland from Keanae and zigzags through a botanical crescendo over a 4-mile run that crosses some 10 streams. Botanists counting species will hit triple figures in no time. Prominent among them are huge banyans and rubber trees. Some 25,000 rubber trees were planted near the coast, launching the Nahiku Rubber Company in 1905, which failed in spite of fabulous production due to geographic isolation. In more recent times, the Nahiku environ gained fame as a retreat for former Beatle, the late George Harrison.

To explore **Nahiku**, veer left from the highway after the bridge at mm25. Getting there is half the fun, as the narrow, but well-paved road descends 1,000 feet over 2.5 miles before coming to an end at ocean-scoured Opuhanu Point. About .5-mile from the top is a cavelike lava tube, which is near Big Spring, the largest on Maui. As the road levels, .25-mile from the ocean, you'll see a 4WD road to the right that invites further exploration, among tin-roofed sugar shacks and the occasional honor-system fruit stand. The Catholic church near the school dates from the early 1867s, a time when Catholics were persecuted on the island. You'll cross a stream and bridge, snap a picture, and come to road's end at big-bouldered Honolulunui Bay. The point's lava tongues extend into the powerful seascape, accented with heliotropes, palms, and pandanus. Walk to the right along the shore to see a waterfall entering the sea at a decrepit bridgeworks. *Be Aware:* Big waves are a danger at the shoreline.

More Stuff: Look for Wailuaiki Road near mm21.25, just after an uphill grade and sharp right turn; the gate and sign sit above the road making it difficult to see. A fabulous waterfall and deep gorge lie less than .5-mile in on Wailuaiki Road (permission to enter may be required by State Department of Fish and Wildlife). Farther along is Pua'aka'a State Wayside, a 5-acre developed park at mm22.5. It can be dreary in rains, but absolutely idyllic when sun shines on the lush greenery, 20-foot waterfall, and pool; an excellent picnic stop. Just before the bridge and turnoff to Nahiku at mm25 is Makapipi Road. It leads toward the Hanawi Natural Area Reserve; showered yearly by more than 30 feet of rain, the reserve is nature's storehouse of endangered plants. Finally, just after the road to Nahiku, at mm25.3, is the Kuhiwa Bamboo Forest, a chance for quick immerison into greenery, but going gets rough early for hikers.

39. PI'ILANIHALE HEIAU-KAHANU GARDENS   HIKE, SNORKEL

WHAT'S BEST: A huge temple dates from the 1500s and now resides within a National Tropical Botanical Garden. A nearby blue pool rests beneath a waterfall next to crashing surf—but its popularity has made access iffy at best.

PARKING: Take Hwy. 360 (the Hana Hwy.) almost to Hana. At mm31, turn left on Ulaino Rd. *For Kahanu Gardens and Pi'ilanihale:* Continue 1.5 mi. on the partially paved road to the entrance on the right just after a stream crossing. *For Blue Pool:* In dry conditions, you will be able to drive nearly to the beach. Park at one of the signed, private lots ($2 or $3) that are 1.25 mi. from Kahanu Gardens. *Be Aware:* Locals, tiring of crowds, have discouraged visitors by claiming that this coastal access is closed.

HIKE: Pi'ilanihale Heiau-Kahanu Garden loop (1.25 mi.); Blue Pool (.75-mi.)

Kahanu Gardens is a 123-acre living exhibit of Hawaiian culture, and also one of only five National Tropical Botanical Gardens set up by an act of Congress to preserve and study endangered plants. From the entrance station you drive almost .5-mile across a

Nahiku

sprawling lawn, through a grove of 200 breadfruit trees, as well as other species. On your left is one of Hawaii's last pandanus forest ecosystems. You can backtrack to roam this grove later on. *Note:* Admission is about $10; hours are weekdays, 10 to 2.

From the parking area, cross left through a little tunnel greenery and come upon kamani trees and a "canoe" garden, so named because it replicates the growing cycles for some 27 plants the voyaging Polynesians brought with them across uncharted seas

Kahanu Gardens

nearly 2,000 years ago. But you may not notice this garden at first because, across the grass field, **Pi'ilanihale Heiau** looms out of the jungle foliage. This 'House of Pi'ilani' is named for a beloved king of the 1500s, a time that in many ways was the zenith of Hawaiian life. The platform stone structure—roughly 300 feet by 300 feet, with walls terraced about 50 feet high—will remind some of the ancient civilizations in the Americas. It was refurbished in the late 1990s. The path continues toward the heiau, dipping in and out, and then up a short distance to an interpretive hut. *Be Aware:* Visitors are not allowed to use trails that circle the structure.

From the interpretive hut, the path loops away from the heiau, along low lava cliffs at the ocean's edge, before reaching a cabin, Hale Ho'okipa. The cabin was part of the area's former life as Kaeleku Plantation in the 1800s. Old Hawaiian and home-steader gravesites are nearby. Several families, and the Hana Ranch, donated property to form the gardens in the 1970s. Complete your loop by circling right to the lava ledges behind the hale, and continuing through the Wishard Coconut Grove, back to the parking area.

SNORKEL: To see the **Blue Pool**, walk down the road from the parking lot, a perfumed and shaded journey that ends about 100 yards in from the surf at a green lagoon of Heleleikeoha Stream. Follow the stream to the boulder beach, cross, and go left for less than .25-mile. You'll see whitewater sheeting down about 100 feet of ferny cliff—known as Blue Angel Falls—and into Blue Pool. From the lip of the 30-foot oval, the ocean's waves are a short throw away. *Be Aware:* Don't cross the stream during high water. Nudity is not allowed. Some locals discourage visitors.

WHAT'S BEST: The ancient King's Trail hugs a sea-sculpted lava shelf, which features fountains of whitewater and historical sites. Enjoy the tropical flora, caves, and Black Sand Beach at one of Hawaii's top state parks.

PARKING: Take Hwy. 360 nearly to Hana. At mm32, turn left at sign to Waianapanapa and follow the road .4-mi. to the state park. Go left and park at the picnic area.

HIKE: Waianapanapa Caves (about .25-mi.); North coast: Kipapa O Kihapiʻilani Trail (2.75 mi., 150 ft.); South coast: Ohala Heiau (1.5 mi.)

Talk Story: Coco palms, pandanus, heliotrope, hala, and a wealth of other flora soften the sharp lava that paves the coast at the 122-acre Waianapanapa State Park. Burial sites and ruins hint at the history. The picnic grounds are picturesque, and the park's 12 coastal cabins, though not exactly cheap, offer the best rustic lodging on Maui. The campground is also very good.

The **Waianapanapa Caves** trail dips down from the parking area and loops through a lush streambed, where caves are carved at the base of mossy rock knobs. *Talk Story:* Legend proclaims these dripping caverns were the tryst site for a Princess Popoalaea and her lover, until her husband found out and killed her here. In the spring, the waters turn red with the memory of her blood—or from tiny shrimp hatching, take your pick.

Kipahulu Camptround Trail

Black Sand Beach

For the **Kipapa O Kihapiʻilani Trail**, which crosses the Kapukaulua Burial Site, take the trail from the railing at the picnic area, which drops to the Black Sand Beach, a.k.a., Pailoa Bay. Trod the sand-slash-pebbles and climb up to the low point at the far end of the beach. Part of the King's Trail, circa 1550, the rocky path weaves through a lovely grove of pointed-leaf pandanus and passes two small, black-boulder coves—Pokohulu and Keawaiki. The path heads across the sharp lava to the north side of Pukaulua Point, where the burial mounds and heiau remains are located, about 20 minutes into the walk. After that you will pass a large lava tube (down left) and then reach an orange, blank sign that marks the remains of a heiau. *Be Aware:* Take care not to disturb any of these sacred ruins. Wear sturdy shoes, as many trail sections are on unstable rocks. Prepare for harsh sun.

To see the **Ohala Heiau** remains and breaking waves do battle with tufts of lava, walk right along the railing at the picnic area from the signed trailhead. You'll pass the park's buildings as the trail hugs a frothing coast and passes a natural arch. Within .25-mile you'll pass the cabins, set back from the trail; a road to the right just after them leads back to the park, making for a .75-mile loop option. Next comes a blowhole and a lava bridge and, a distance farther, are the the walls of the Ohala Heiau. *More Stuff:* Stay on the trail, hugging the coast over lava, to continue to Hana, several miles away.

SNORKEL: **Black Sand Beach** is the best snorkeling spot along a coast with few choices. On the right day, it's something to write home about. If surf is small, under 2 feet, you can swim out to the right toward the natural arch, and also to the left toward Pokohulu Cove. *Be Aware:* Rip currents may exist in the bay, especially when surf is up. For a chilling freshwater dip, head for the pool at **Waianapanapa Caves**.

41. HANA

HIKE, SNORKEL, SURF

WHAT'S BEST: After the precipitous curves through the rain forest to get here, Hana's sloping pasturelands and open bay will come as a surprise and a relief. Pick from several short walks—a cultural stroll, powerful seascapes, or a panorama.

PARKING: Follow Hwy. 360 (the Hana Hwy.) to mm33.7. *To Fagan's Cross:* Keep right on Hwy. 360, pass Keawa Pl., and park at mm34.5 in a lot across from Travaasa Hana (formerly Hotel Hana Maui). *For all other hikes and activities:* Veer left on Uakea Rd., continue 1.5 mi., and park at the bay, which is just past Hana Cultural Center.

HIKE: Fagan's Cross (1.75 mi., 400 ft.); Hana Bay stroll (.75-mi.); Kauiki Head-Queen Ka'ahumanu Birthplace (.25-mi.); Red Sand Beach (1 mi., 200 ft.)

Don't come looking for action in Hana. Low-key aloha rules here, with quiet cottages set above the harbor, and a few Hawaiiana shops and cultural sites spread about. **Fagan's Cross** is atop Pu'u o Kahaula, visible from the parking lot. Follow the paved path as it takes a gentle rise through the pastures of Hana Ranch. As you near the base of the pu'u—also known as Lyon's Hill— the trail curves around to the right and does its serious climbing. The view from the top is a geography primer for Hana and its coastline. *Talk Story:* The cross is a memorial to Paul Fagan, who introduced cattle in the 1940s to found the ranch, and later started the Hotel Hana Maui. Across from the trailhead parking, the hotel is quietly one of Hawaii's best. Check out the open pool near the sea cottages. *More Stuff:* In the pasture not far from the trailhead, the Hana Maui Trail takes off to the left, a

Travaasa Hana

Hana Wharf

4-mile, round-trip excercise jaunt through the ranch. It comes out near the highway before Haneoʻo Road; see TH42.

Begin **Hana Bay stroll** by backtracking the road to the Hana Cultural Center and Museum. The small center is an educational work of love, with artifacts, crafts, quilts, photographs, and exhibits that reflect both ancient times and contemporary. Outside is a re-creation of a village, including a Hawaiian Ethno-Botanical Garden that grows all the essential plants from ancient times and changes seasonally. Also on the grounds is the Old Historic Courthouse and Jail, dating from 1871.

Hana Beach Park rims the bay, where visitors are released from shuttle buses to sit under coco palms and ironwoods and enjoy the cuisine of Tutu's Snack Shop, or perhaps Bill's Lunch Wagon. At the far end of the bay is Hana Wharf, a T-shaped intrusion several hundred feet onto the water. *Note:* Damaged by a storm in 2004, the wharf may not be officially open to the public, but people walk out daily.

The **Queen Kaʻahumanu Birthplace** is at a sheltered rock near the tip of Kauiki Head, which is the furry 400-foot rise that frames the south end of Hana Bay. Begin at the wharf and take a red-cinder trail that skirts the shoreline among ironwoods. Stay near the shore. At the beginning, one eroded spot requires handholds and will dissuade some hikers, as will mini-slides of red cinder that tend to cover the trail. But it's a short ordeal, and the payoff is big. *Talk Story:* In the 1700s, the Kauiki Head was a stronghold for warriors during the ongoing battles between Maui and the Big Island— typically these Hana slopes were controlled by the Big Island's forces, since open sea was easier to cross than the terrain of East Maui. Near the tip is a plaque commemorating Queen Kaʻahumanu, who was born in 1768 and went on to become Kamehameha the Great's favorite wife, as well as a beloved and enlightened ruler. A tiny island with a light beacon, Pu'uki'i Island, lies a long jump from the tip—too long when the big seas are galloping in. This ten-minute hike gets you a million miles away.

Red Sand Beach, officially called Kaihalulu, is on the other side of the head from the bay. To get to the trailhead, continue a few blocks on Uakea Road, past Hauoli Street, and park on-street near the Hana Community Center. The striking cove is scooped out of a towering red cinder cliff, protected by the jagged teeth of a black-rock reef that is just offshore. Traverse the county park lawn just beyond the cultural center, and drop down through ironwoods—a cemetery will be on your left, and the sea cottages of the Hotel Hana Maui on the right. Stay right at the end of the lawn and drop down to the right of a knarled ironwood tree, reaching a coastal trail. A slide in 2008 took out a section of the trail, and you need to hop down to the beach for a segment. You then climb a little to a ledge above the water and reach a point. Around this corner is the eye-popping view of the beach. The trail is cut into the cliff (watch your step) as you descend to the red sand. *Be Aware:* Although the trail is used frequently by the public, it is on property of Hana Ranch; use your own judgment. Avoid this trail during heavy weather. Once on the sand, don't sit under the crumbly cliff at the far end.

More Stuff: To see some of the dozen churches and other sites in town, stop by the Hasegawa General Store, which is on your left at the edge of town as you continue south. A free Hana Visitors Guide with map is available. The venerable general store is also one of Hana's main attractions, run by the same family since 1910, as well as being the best place to buy snacks, trinkets, and supplies.

Red Sand Beach

SNORKEL: The best snorkeling at **Hana Bay** is between the base of the wharf and the light beacon on Puʻukiʻi Island. Currents sweep out the bay during higher surf, so stay close to shore and avoid swimming when the surf's up. Due to natural silt, the bay is not known for clear near-shore waters. Your best chance is during the winter, **Red Sand Beach** is a spectacular swimming hole, inside the black-rock breakwater. Lots of fish reside. *Be Aware:* Waves indicate rip currents may be present. Also, in spite of the bare bottoms you may see, nudity is not permitted on Hawaiian beaches.

SURF: Mostly during the summer, you'll find the wave riders off the **Hana Wharf**, a nice deep-water break. This is also a good place to be a spectator.

Hamoa Beach

42. HAMOA BEACHES   HIKE, SNORKEL, SURF

WHAT'S BEST: A short side trip from the Hana Highway passes two beaches, including the south shore's most luxurious swath and one with an offshore bird sanctuary.

PARKING: Take Hwy. 360 through Hana. After mm33, the road becomes Hwy. 31. You begin at mm51, with numbers *descending* as you travel away from Hana. Turn left on Haneoʻo Road, .7-mi. past mm51. Haneoʻo loops back to the highway at mm49.2.

HIKE: Koki Beach Park (up to .5-mi.); Hamoa Beach (.25-mi.)

Koki Beach Park, a tranquil place with an exciting view, will be on your left, .4-mile from the highway at call box 18. From the shoulder parking, an ample strand of sand leads left toward a red cinder cliff. Look for a natural arch near the point. To the right, you can cross a small stream and walk a grassy area shaded by palms, ironwoods, and an occasional Norfolk pine. Offshore the tip of land is small Alau Island Seabird Sanctuary, with a few coco palms pointing askew from its crest like wayward hairs.

Koki Beach

Hamoa Beach is around the point on Haneoʻo Road, a little more than a mile from the highway. Look for a bus stop and low lava wall on the left. Concrete steps and ramp lead down to a good-sized white sand crescent—the beach used by guests of the Travaasa Hana (formerly Hotel Hana Maui). A lawn and garden, part the hotel's private beach facilities, border the sand. From the shore is a spot-on look at the Big Island, rising from the far horizon. From Hamoa Beach, Haneoʻo Road travels .5-mile through the quiet homes of Hamoa and loops back to Highway 31.

SNORKEL: Enter **Hamoa Beach** to the left as you face the water, and swim out the lava tongues and submerged rocks. *Be Aware:* Shore break and rip currents may present hazards. Avoid swimming at Koki Beach except on the calmest of days.

SURF: The conditions are often good for bodysurfing and bodyboarding at both **Koki Beach** and **Hamoa Beach**. The same is true for Lehoula Beach, mentioned above in *More Stuff*, although there's no approved public access.

43. VENUS POOL   HIKE, SNORKEL

WHAT'S BEST: Freshwater pools await at ocean's edge, a short walk in from the highway.

PARKING: Take Hwy. 360 through Hana. After mm33, the road becomes Hwy. 31 coming from the other direction. You begin here at mm51, with numbers *descending* as you travel away from Hana. Cross a bridge at mm48, and park off the road on the shoulder to the right at telephone pole #88 (don't block driveways).

HIKE: Venus Pool (.5-mi.)

To reach the **Venus Pool**, walk back across the bridge and hop through a gatelike opening in the fence. A path leads down the sloping pasture, with Waiohonu Stream on your right. A few minutes into the walk you'll come upon a dome-shaped rock kiln, where the path curves right toward the stream. Fringed with greenery, the pool reveals itself only when you come upon it from about 15feet above. *Be Aware:* Although this trail is used by the public, a Hana Ranch sign at the trailhead warns of tresspassing.

The waves from a rocky nook in the coast mingle with the leading edge of Venus Pool, while upstream of the 75-foot oval, freshwater enters from bedrock ledges that are carved out in places, forming smaller pools. Pool conditions will vary depending on both the surf and runoff. The pastures above the pool extend seaward toward the black-rock point, providing room to roam with a Big Island view.

More Stuff: Some 73 acres at Muolea Point in 2005 were conveyed to the county, thanks to contributors and the Trust For Public Land. The park features a nice sand beach, heiau ruins, and the site of King David Kalakaua's summer residence. *Driving:* About .75-mile past mm47, look for an access just after a one-lane bridge. Public access may not yet be established, so heed posted signs.

SNORKEL: On sunny days, **Venus Pool** is ideal for swimming around.

44. POOLS OF OHEO   HIKE, SNORKEL

WHAT'S BEST: The Hana pilgrimage leads to a series of terraced pools that a stream has scoured from bedrock. Inland, the stream tumbles from two of Maui's highest waterfalls, alongside a trail that penetrates a bamboo jungle. Farther down the road, a shorter hike leads to a more secluded falls.

PARKING: Take Hwy. 360 through Hana. After mm33, the road becomes Hwy. 31 at mm51—with numbers *descending*. After mm43 you'll pass Haleakala National Park boundary, and then a bridge over Oheo Gulch. Just after mm42, turn left into the parking for the Kipahulu Visitors Center. *Notes:* An entry fee of about $10 per car is charged; the fee is good for a week, and also applies to the summit area of Haleakala National Park. Additional directions follow for Lindbergh and Alelele Falls hikes.

HIKE: *National Park:* Pools of Oheo loop (.75-mi, 150 ft.); Pipiwai Trail to: Falls at Makahiku (1.25-mi., 300 ft.), or Waimoku Falls (4.25 mi., 850 ft.); *Other hikes:* Kipahulu Point Park-Lindbergh Grave (.25-mi.); Alelele Falls (1 mi.)

Talk Story: Just when you thought it was safe to get back in the car … the pasturelands of Hana give way to a rolling rural area, lush with gardens and blue-water vistas, which in turn transition to a narrow, twisting road that is punched through steep rain forest

and across eight streams over five miles. Then comes the visitors center for the Kipahulu section of Haleakala National Park. This portion of the park is located on the ahupua'a of Kipahulu, a village of antiquity that was one of the largest on Maui. *Be Aware:* The Pools of Oheo can be a zoo during peak hours on sunny days. Get there early.

For the **Pools of Oheo loop**, walk to the visitors center and take the signed Kuloa Point Trail. You'll meander in the shade of a huge banyan before reaching the stream and its pools (formerly dubbed the Seven Sacred Pools). When nearest the ocean, jog right a short distance to see the ruins of Kipahulu Kauhale heiau and its four-star view bench. Then take the path upstream to the highway bridge before looping back to the visitors center. *Be Aware:* All the pools present a danger due to flash floods. Normally,

Pools of Oheo, Pipiwai Trail

a gate will close access during flood conditions. *More Stuff:* A half-dozen or so pools are up Oheo Stream from the highway bridge—yes, there are more than seven.

The **Pipiwai Trail** is one of Hawaii's best waterfall hikes. Begin by taking the trail to the left of the visitors center, or backtrack on the highway toward the bridge, to where the trail crosses. On the leg to the **Falls at Makahiku** you cross a pastureland and then climb the forests above the stream, lying steeply below to your right. You'll come to a falls overlook sign, where the 200-foot watery ribbon is visible. Fine, but be sure to take the spur to the right just afterwards that leads to the top of the falls and a view down the gulch. *Be Aware:* Stay back from drop-offs, especially during rains.

To continue to 400-foot **Waimoku Falls**, ascend the trail past a gate and under the boughs of a huge banyan. The trail levels as you get a first glimpse of the higher falls from a stand of guavas. Stream overlooks will be to your right. About a mile from the trailhead, the stream narrows as it crashes through a rocky gorge, falling in cataracts and pools that are spanned by two footbridges—one of the hike's highlights. During much of the hike's final run, you'll be on long sections of boardwalk and stairs, through towering bamboo forests straight out of Borneo. The trail ends with two crossings at a stream confluence, just before the skyscraper amphitheater of Waimoku Falls. Walk up the rise opposite the falls for a point-blank view.

More Stuff: For a mile-long coastal stroll away from the crowds at the pools, go right as you face the visitors center, driving toward the campground. A grassy shoreline trail loops around small Kukui Bay to Puhilele Point and the ruins of the heiau.

Kipahulu Point Park and **Charles Lindbergh Grave** are a mile beyond the visitors center, past St. Paul's Catholic Church and mm41. Then turn left on a lane lined with century plants (at Maui Stables' sign). Then go left again to Palapala Ho'omanu Church. The church is also called Kipahulu Church, dating from around 1860. At the small cemetery next to the church is the gravesite of the most famous American of his time. Lindbergh was laid to rest here in 1974. Down the lawn from the church is the small county park with shaded tables and a big view back across the wide channel to the Big Island. *More Stuff:* When you leave this area, turning right on Highway 31, look on the left for the big smoke stack and other ruins of Kipahulu Sugar Mill, which shut down in 1922. If you turn left on the Highway 31, about .25-mile away, is Laulima Farms, an organic smoothie and espresso shack whose surrounding gardens grow virtually everything they serve. You may not want to leave. Lastly, for guided cultural hikes (2 to 4 hours and a bargain), contact the Kipahulu Ohana; see page 235.

The **Alelele Falls** trail is several miles from the Kipahulu visitors center, heading toward Kaupo on Highway 31. It's about a 15-minute walk, under kukui trees and over some rocks, to the 100-foot falls—one of Maui's more hidden treasures. *Driving:* Highway 31 drops into the hairy, narrow section between mm40 and mm38 at Lelekea Bay. Park near the middle, one-lane bridge (inscribed 'Alelele') and take the trail upstream. *Be Aware:* Rockslides in 2007 closed the road near mm39.5 for two years. Stay clear of this area during rainy conditions, when flash floods are a hazard. Also, don't linger on the roadway sections near cliffs: falling rocks have caused at least one death. *More Stuff:* Alelele Falls and Lelekea Bay are part of a finger of Haleakala National Park that extends down from the volcano. At the next bridge (Kalepa) a rough trail heads inland and makes an undulating contour for almost 4 miles, and comes out to the road near Lelekea Stream. Experienced hikers only—and on sunny days.

More Stuff: Going back toward Hana from the Pools of Oheo—between mm44 and mm45—are the double bridges of Wailua Falls. The turnout at the first bridge is normally frequented by crafts vendors. Additionally, on the uphill grade after the first bridge is the marker for the so-called trail to Helio's Grave. The route is a precipitous butt-slide 300 feet down an overgrown embankment to Wailua Cove. A 20-foot cross memorializing Helio is jon high ground. Helio and his brother, Peterto, led a Roman Catholic movement on Maui in the 1840s.

SNORKEL: You'd look silly with a mask and fins in the **Pools of Oheo** but not swimming around. Between the highway and the ocean are five pools, with waters up to 40-feet deep. The middle two are most popular. *Be Aware:* Flash flood hazard exists here, so dip only when skies are blue. Some days these pools are brown, even when it's not raining. For a secluded dip, try a small black-sand beach on **Lelekea Bay**, near the Alelele bridge.

Waimoku Falls

Haleakala

Sliding Sands Trail, Haleakala National Park

HALEAKALA

You don't need to leave Maui to cure tropical malaise, just drive up 5,000 feet to the rolling hills and pine forests of Kula. Or, put on the outerwear and head up 10,000 feet to leave the planet altogether on a journey into the Haleakala crater. As a third choice, go to the unexplored Kaupo coast for a trip to Arizona with an ocean.

DRIVING TOUR
PICKING THE RIGHT DAYS

Seeing sunrise from the summit of Haleakala is a quest for many Maui visitors, and if you're one of them, bring every stitch of warm clothing you have, plus the beach towels. Perhaps this quest has derived from the myth surrounding the volcano's name "House of the Sun." In ancient times, the demigod Maui snared the sun with his fishhook, thereby insuring a longer planting season and well-being for the people. The sunrise expedition, aside from being cold, also must begin in darkness, meaning you can't reliably check out visibility on the summit from down below, and it's too early to call the rangers for a forecast. When clear, the Haleakala summit is an eye-popper. Consider leaving just after sunrise, which will put you ahead of the tour buses and allows you to enjoy the scenery on the way up in daylight.

Regardless of what your watch says, when the weather appears clear at the top is the time to head for Haleakala. Bear in mind that Kula clouds often hang at about 5,000 feet, making the peak appear socked in when it's not—you wind up with an airplane's view of these clouds. And, aside from full-on storm conditions, clouds get tossed around up there, so be patient. Cloudy days have clear moments.

Kula is a scenic drive any day, but it doubles as a fallback alternative when weather forces a retreat from the summit. The Kaupo coast is Maui's least visited region, and therefore is a good choice if seeking quietude on a busy weekend. In the shadow of Haleakala, it's also the most arid, and the most likely place to find sun, even when rains are lashing West Maui and the Hana coast. During droughts, and mostly in the summer, the Kaupo coast will be dry grasses, save the coastal Kiawe trees and the upper reaches of the Kahikinui Forest Reserve. But during normal winters and springs, a green carpet of low-lying vegetation fills in around the lava formations.

THE ROADS

The Haleakala Highway has the most elevation gain per horizontal mile covered of any paved road on earth. But it's built on the mountain's relatively gentle north slopes, and using long switchbacks without vertigo-inducing hairpins. Provided your brakes hold out on the way down, and you avoid the stream of downhill bicyclists as you go up, the road is a snap. Kula is made for convertibles. Along several miles well below the summit, the Kula and Haleakala highways run on parallel contours—with old Lower Kula Road between them—providing loop options for touring the Upcountry.

The southern Kaupo coast—where Highway 37 circles around to become Highway 31—is also an easy one to navigate. New steel and concrete bridges appear to have been built in advance of commute traffic, and the county crews are extending the pavement toward Kaupo. But currently, the smooth pavement ends before the road reaches sea level at Nuʻu Bay, and becomes pothole-patched and dirt-graded after that, but no problem for passenger cars. Lack of shoulders present hazards in some areas. Just follow the yellow-paint line. Traffic is wonderfully sparse, increasing only in late afternoons when the Hana commute comes through on the clockwise circumnavigation. The only dicey, narrow section is past Kaupo, near mm39 when the road narrows to one lane at Lelekea Bay on its 8-mile finale to Kipahulu. Even with this challenge, you might consider visiting the Pools of Oheo from this direction, rather than coming around from Hana. Go in the morning, and double back to visit the Kaupo coast in the afternoon. (The road from Kaupo to Kipahulu was scheduled to reopen in 2009 after many months of closure due to rockslides.)

THE COURSE

Follow along on the Haleakala map, page 152. Refer to trailhead descriptions that follow on pages 153 for more details.

Note: Three tours for this trailhead section: Haleakala, Kaupo coast, and Kula. The Kula tour can be combined with either of the others, or done independently, but to do all three would be more like work than a vacation.

From Puu Maneoneo, Kaupo Coast

HALEAKALA TOUR. BEGIN EARLY MORNING. THE HALEAKALA HIGHWAY STARTS AS NUMBER 37, CHANGES TO 377, AND FINALLY BECOMES 378 AS IT MAKES ITS SWITCHBACKING ASCENT INTO THE HALEAKALA NATIONAL PARK. The highway segment, after Pukalani, is through rolling horse country, sensuous hills dotted with eucalyptus as well as native Hawaiian trees. The tight turns of Highway 378 at first cut through the flower farms and gardens, and then the road tops out on the broad shoulders above the tree line. Keep your eyes peeled, because you

Haleakala, Kaupo Coast

Haleakala Visitors Center

pass through different biological zones in minutes.

You enter Haleakala National Park at mm10, where an entrance fee is charged. Consider saving Hosmer Grove—to the left after the park entrance—for the return leg of the tour, but a visit to Park Headquarters is a recommended stop for an introduction to the visit. Then, push the wheels toward the top. The Kalahaku Lookout, after mm18, can only be accessed on the downward trip.

Must stops are the Red Hill observation area at the summit, and the White Hill walk at the Haleakala Visitors Center, just before the road's end. At the summit, observe the sinking phenomena described by author Jack London when he rode a horse up here: Since you see more of the horizon as you climb, the summit of Haleakala can be perceived as a downward journey. After taking in the summit, energetic travelers will want to immerse themselves in the red cinder of the crater, by taking the Sliding Sands Trail.

On the way down, check out at the Leleiwi and Kalahaku overlooks. Highly recommended is Halemau'u Trail to the Ko'olau Gap overlook—a place that exceeds imagination. You'll be able see most everything on this tour, since Haleakala is the right size for a full-day visit. And you'll feel like you've been gone for a week after descending to the sandy beaches and coco palms.

KAUPO COAST TOUR, BEGIN EARLY MORNING. TAKE HIGHWAY 37 PAST KULA AND CONTINUE AS IT BECOMES HIGHWAY 31. Traditionally, people see this area on the last leg of a long day, coming around from Hana. Consequently, it's passed over as an "eerie moonscape" you pass by on the way back to the resort for the evening's Mai Tai. For many visitors, however, the Kaupo coast will be Maui's most pleasant surprise—gulches becoming canyons along a rugged wilderness coast rich with archeological sites, and all of it under the towering relief of Haleakala.

After rounding the bend at Kula, you may wish to take a first rest stop at Sun Yat Sen Park at mm18. But save a refreshing wine-tasting and historical tour at Tedeschi Winery, just down the highway, for the homeward leg. Don't miss it—the sublime, parklike grounds were a favorite stop for Hawaii's last king, David Kalakaua, as well as author Robert Louis Stevenson.

A couple miles past Tedeschi, which is on the grounds of Ulupalakua Ranch, the road narrows, and you start to pick up views down to the lava flow on the Kinau Peninsula at La Perouse Bay. Cinder cones rise from the desert flora of the slopes. The road begins

Tedeschi Winery grounds, Nene, Huialoha Church

a long descent, passing the Lualailua Hills and reaching near sea level at Manawainui Gulch. From the turnout at Manawainui, you can walk a short distance to see the natural arch and fishing shrine ruins on a remote portion of the King's Trail.

The highway stays near sea level for the next several miles. Stop at will. Along this coast, you truly can explore. You will mostly likely want to see the petroglyphs at Nu'u Bay, as well as the view of Haleakala you get from the boulder beach there. After Nu'u, the highway climbs to Pu'u Maneoneo, where you can hop out of the car for a perspective on where you've just been. This is one of Maui's eye-popping scenes.

For the next several miles, the partially paved road winds through ranchlands, passing St. Joseph's Church, and reaching the sanctum sanctorum of this coast, the Kaupo Store. That this country-funk place is the center of commerce for the entire coast speaks wonderful volumes. Sit a spell. From here, adventurers wanting the area's best hike can try the Kaupo Trail, that scales Haleakala and reaches the park through the Kaupo Gap. Beyond the store, the remaining 8-mile trip to the Pools of Oheo is one of Maui's most scenic. But even if you don't go that far, be sure to check out Huialoha Church, which is about a mile from the Kaupo Store.

KULA TOUR. ADD ON TO THE HALEAKALA OR KAUPO TOURS, OR DO SEPARATELY. The Kula, or Upcountry, portion of Maui runs along a contour at several thousand feet in elevation on the west slope of Haleakala. Cool temperatures, moderate rainfall, and trade-wind clouds prevail here, an ideal environ for gardens, forests, and arboretums. Put Bruddah Iz Kamakawiwo'ole's version of John Denver's *Country Road* on the CD player and roll.

Haleakala downhill biking

I'iwi, Hosmer Grove, Sliding Sands Trail

TAKE HIGHWAY 37 TO HIGHWAY 377. A horse's life may seem appealing as you see them grazing up here on the rounded hillsides, with enough shade and windbreak offered by eucalyptus and native tree groves. Near mm5 is Kula Lodge, a venerable eatery with an art gallery downstairs and Upcountry Harvest gift store nearby. But seekers of all-things-Maui should head next door for the Kula Marketplace, set just below its on-highway parking lot. You'll find local art, jewelry, books, a wealth of souvenir ideas, and a totally tempting array of island baked goods, fruit and veggies, sandwiches, and local delectables. Guys, buy a newspaper, you'll have a long wait.

Farther down the road, on either side of the junction with Highway 378, are protea flower farms, and then the entrance to the old-timey Kula Gardens, Maui's oldest garden. It's ambitious plantings are backed by a great view. Kids will love it.

If you're doing a full day in the Upcountry, you'll want to take a spin up Waipoli Road to the Kula Forest Reserve; the road will be on your left before Highway 377 joins Highway 37. At least drive up about .5-mile to check the scene at Ali'i Kula Lavender (turn right from Waipoli at a dragonfly sign just before the cattle guard).

From there, Waipoli Road wiggles upward to about 6,000 feet, over hillsides favored by model airplane buffs and parasailors, before becoming unpaved and entering the sublime trails of the Polipoli Springs State Park. It's the relatively secret side of Haleakala.

FROM THE JUNCTION OF HIGHWAYS 377 AND 37. Take Highway 37 around the mountain for some 7 miles to Tedeschi Winery that is within Ulupalakua Ranch. On the way you'll pass through the historic Chinese settlement of Keokea, just past which you can veer left up the hill to see the movie-like setting of the Kula Sanatorium. Also on the way, near mm18 is Sun Yat Sen Park, where views of Makena open up. And down the road from the park is Uluapalakua Ranch and the Tedeschi Winery—offering tasting

Tedeschi "shipmast" tree and a history tour of its arboretum.

BACKTRACK TO JUNCTION OF HIGHWAYS 377 AND 37. JUST PAST THIS JUNCTION, TURN RIGHT ON LOWER KULA ROAD. You don't want to miss this slice of old Maui, left intact since bypassed by the newer highways. At the turn is Rice Park, with rolling lawn and a commanding overlook toward West Maui. Down

the road is Calasa Service, built in 1932, where gassing the car will be an experience. Down the street from the service station are the Morihara Store and Café 808, which may not have an identifying sign—both are places for local-style libation. Farther along from these establishments is the centerpiece of Kula, the Church of the Holy Ghost, an octagonal edifice built in 1894.

Protea

Makawao Forest Reserve

Note: Beyond the church, Lower Kula Road pops back out to the highway. You can take another section of the road—a right turn shortly after coming out to the highway—to see the Mormon Pulehu Church, built in 1851. This segment of Lower Kula becomes rougly paved and joins Highway 37 again a few miles ahead.

CONTINUE ON HIGHWAY 37, TURN RIGHT ON HIGHWAY 377, AND TURN LEFT ON KEALALOA HANAMU ROAD. This maneuver takes you through dairy-lands—also the descent route for Haleakala bicycle tours—and joins up with Olinda Road. *Note:* You could also continue on Highway 37 to Highway 365 and reach Olinda Road a little farther down the mountain in Makawao. Either way, you can turn right on Olinda for a spin to the upper Upcountry, ending at the Waihou Springs Forest Reserve. On the way up you pass flower and succulent farms, near mm11, and the Maui Bird Conservation Center.

On the way down Olinda are big views toward the Kahului coast. Makawao, the Upcountry's cowboy town is well worth a walk through; turn left at the stop sign on Highway 365—across from which Olinda Road becomes Baldwin Avenue. You can then return to the lowlands via rural Baldwin Avenue, which is Highway 390, down to Paia. On the way are the venerable Baldwin Estate (now Hui Noeau Visual Arts Center) and the Father Damien memorial at the Holy Rosary Church.

Let me see some ID

MAP 5

TRAILHEADS 45-52

HALEAKALA

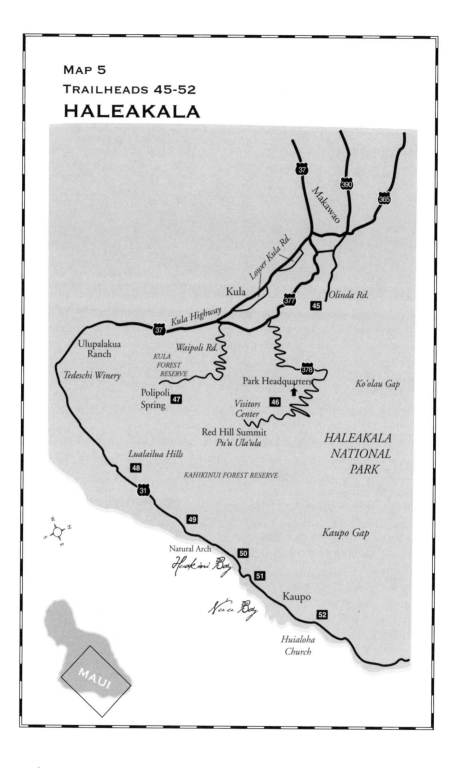

HALEAKALA

TRAILHEADS
45-52

TH: TRAILHEAD
HIKE: ALL WALKING, FROM SHORT STROLLS TO FULL-FLEDGED DAY HIKES
SNORKEL: BOTH FISH-VIEWING WITH MASK AND FINS, AND PLACES TO SWIM
SURF: BOARD, BODYSURF, BODYBOARD, WINDSURFING, KITEBOARDING
MM: MILE MARKER, CORRESPONDS TO HIGHWAY SIGNS

All hiking distances in parentheses are ROUND TRIP.
Elevation gains of 100 feet or more are noted.

45. OLINDA UPCOUNTRY-MAKAWAO   HIKE

WHAT'S BEST: Take a walk around Maui's cowboy country town, or choose an excercise hike on two trails into higher-elevation forest reserves where few tourists venture.

PARKING: Take Hwy. 36 to Paia and turn right on Hwy. 390, Baldwin Ave. Follow about 5 mi. to Makawao. *For the Makawao stroll:* Park on-street, near the T-intersection of Baldwin and Makawao avenues. You can also get to Makawao from the Hwy. 37 (the Haleakala Hwy.): turn left at Pukalani on Makawao Ave. *Waihou Springs Forest Reserve:* Continue straight at jct. with Makawao Ave., as Hwy. 390 becomes Olinda Rd. At mm11.9, park at a sign for Tree Growth Research Area. *For Makawao Forest Reserve:* Turn left on Makawao Ave., go .25-mi. and turn right on Pi'iholo Rd. (Hwy. 394). After 1.4 mi.. veer left on Waiahiwi Rd. Then continue .4-mi., turn right on Kahakapao Rd. and drive about 1 mi. to signed, on-street trailhead parking.

HIKE: Makawao stroll (up to .5-mi.); Waihou Springs Forest Reserve (up to 2.25 mi., 450 ft.); Makawao Forest Reserve (6.5 mi., 475 ft.)

Makawao (rhymes with 'wow') is Maui's dark-horse contender for best walk-around town, where love-the-earth locals and the low-key Hollywood types mingle at galleries, eateries, boutiques, and upscale gift stores. The place has an Old West look that reflects its paniolo (cowboy) culture. Follow your instincts, or get the lowdown at Gecko Trading Company, which hosts the art of Deybra, and Aloha Cowboy, where Willie Nelson buys his boots. Chow down at Makawao Steakhouse, a family institution, groove to Upcountry tunes at Casanova Restaurant, or eat green at Down to Earth.

Olinda Road winds skyward from Makawao. **Waihou Springs Forest Reserve**, part of the state's Na Ala Hele trails system, was test-planted with pines and other species in the 1920s. Head down the needle-cushioned road through the orderly pine grove. After

about .25-mile, turn right toward the overlook, and then, to reach Waihou Springs, go right again, amid spindly ash trees (you will backtrack to this junction). You reach an overlook with a bench among sugi pine, where the springs trail drops steeply on switchbacks. The springs seep from a 200-foot mossy wall that is bored with cavelike irrigation tunnels—a mysterious Hobbit-land. In summer, and drought conditions, it may be dry. Backtrack to the trail junction and go right. The trail continues on an undulating circle, through a variety of trees that include cypress and koa, as well as some good-sized pines. Then you reconnect with the main path back to trailhead parking. *More Stuff:* Olinda Road ends about .25-mile past mm12. From just above the road's gate is the lower part of Waikomo Ridge Trail, which descends from Hosmer Grove. Permission to hike may be required from The Nature Conservancy; see page 235.

Enter the **Makawao Forest Reserve** for a bird-lover, tree-hugger exercise jaunt on the peaceful and pretty Kapahakapao Loop Trail. You start down a wide paved road. After .5-mile (before the reservoir) go right on a dirt road at a trail sign, and then, .5-mile later, go right again on the West Loop Trail. The trail ascends beside a drainage and loops left, ever upward. A new drainage will appear on your left, which the trail crosses, through lovely ti and tree ferns. You'll reach a junction for the East Loop Trail; go left. You're now on the downward leg, which swerves through baby ferns and tall Norfolk Pines, before returning to the start of the West Loop Trail.

More Stuff: Head down Baldwin Avenue from Makaweo (to below Hali'imaile Road at mm3.75) to take a 15-minute walk around Hui Noeau Visual Arts Center, set on groomed acreage of the former Ethel and Harry Baldwin Estate. Pastoral serenity and towering trees are a backdrop to the 1917 Mediterranean buildings, the work of famed architect C. W. Dickey. On site now are a gift shop, photography studio, jewelry and ceramics workshops, and art gallery.

Makawao Forest Reserve

WHAT'S BEST: A journey to a volcanic planet two-miles in the sky in the middle of the Pacific. Choose from hikes that will suit every energy level: forests, craters, and overlooks with aerial views of Maui and beyond.

PARKING: Go inland on Hwy. 37, the Haleakala Hwy. After Pukalani-Makawao jcts., turn left on Hwy. 377. Follow for 6 mi. and turn left on Hwy. 378. The national park boundary is near mm10. Additional directions follow below, beginning at the boundary. Admission is about $10 per car, per week. Bring warm clothes, food, and water.

HIKE: LISTED FROM BOTTOM TO TOP: Hosmer Grove Nature Trail (.5-mi.); Halemau'u Trail to: Ko'olau Gap-crater overlook (2.25 mi., 250 ft.), or Holua Cabin (8.25 mi., 1,200 ft.); Leleiwi Overlook (less than .25-mi.); White Hill (.5-mi, 150 ft.); Sliding Sands Trail to: cinder cones overlook (2 mi., 400 ft.), or Ka Lu'u o ka O'o (5.25 mi., 1,400 ft.), or Kapalaoa Cabin (11.5 mi., 2,500 ft.), or Bottomless Pit (11.25 mi., 2,600 ft.); Red Hill Summit (less than .25-mi.); Skyline Trail (up to 13 mi., 3,200 ft.)

Talk Story: Climbing to 10,000 feet over a few horizontal miles, the Haleakala Highway is the steepest roadway in the world. Yet its sweeping curves are a mellow drive, by Maui standards, unless your brakes fail coming down. The crater (19 square miles and 3,000-feet deep) is not technically a crater, but an eroded valley, whose moonscape is dotted with about a dozen red cinder cones. These mini-craters, called pu'us, are vents from separate eruptions. Haleakala is an active volcano—it will erupt again, say the experts. Clouds bring wintry conditions to the summit. Weather changes rapidly. Frequently, clouds hangs near Kula, near 4,000 feet, making the top appear socked in from below when it's actually rising into the sun—Haleakala, "House of the Sun."

The **Hosmer Grove Nature Loop** through native shrubs will be of most interest to botanists and ornithologists. The trailhead begins at the campground, a .5-mile drive on a left turn just after entering the park. The first part of the loop goes through cedar, spruce, and other conifers planted in the early 1900s by forester Ralph Hosmer. The second part is through native shrubs, where our feathered friends live. *More Stuff:* The Waikomo Ridge Trail is near a restroom a few hundred feet from the end of the road into the campground. The catch: Call The Nature Conservancy for permission to enter; see page 235. No catch: The Supply Trail, which climbs 500 feet over 2.5 miles to join the Haleamu'u Trail, a wonderland of low-lying native plants and a good choice when fog lingers higher up. It begins on the right, before Hosmer Grove. For other hiking information, stop at the Park Headquarters, just up the road near mm11.25.

The **Halemau'u Trail** parking lot is at an elevation of 8,000 feet, just after mm14. The hike to the **Ko'olau Gap** and **crater overlook** reaps a big return for the investment of energy. After descending through low shrubs you reach a precipice. On your right is the west side of the Haleakala Crater, a jumble of black lava here, speckled with

Holua Cabin, Silversword, Sliding Sands Trail

greenery. You walk the spine of the precipice toward the gap, where a lava fall created the Keanae Peninsula off the Hana Highway, down to your left.

To reach the **Holua Cabin**, the trail takes a herky-jerky descent of nearly 1,000 feet down a weirdly formed escarpment. On the bottom, your feet briefly are comforted by a grass patch, before the trail again ascends up a lava bench. Atop the bench, on a small lawn below the towering Leleiwi Pali, is the cabin. Often waddling around this rustic oasis are the endangered nene, or Hawaiian goose, the state bird. Please don't feed them. A trail leads south from the cabin, eventually connecting with trails coming down from the top of the crater (see *More Stuff* below). *Be Aware:* Caves formed by lava tubes in the area can be dangerous; venturing inside of them is inadvisable.

The kiosk **Leleiwi Overlook** offers a view from the high cliffs above Holua Cabin, as well as the entire crater. Look for a signed turnoff after mm17. Late in the day at the overlook is a good time to observe the surreal ho'okuaka effect, or what the Germans call "Bröckenspector": With clouds in the crater and the sun at your back, your shadow sometimes will appear in the mist, illuminated by a halo of color. This effect, or another variation of a sky-high view, can be seen at the Kalahaku Overlook, which is up the road on the left, but can only be accessed when coming down from the summit. Below the overlook, clouds often gather and vanish like wisps of smoke.

The stone **Haleakala Visitors Center**, featuring a fabulous view from its perch on the edge of the crater, is almost to the top, at mm20. This is the place to chat with rangers, or wait for clouds to clear. A trail from outside its door winds to the top of

From Kalahaku Overlook

White Hill, a.k.a. Pa Ka'oao. The exquisite view is a prime destination for short-walk specialists. Off the trail are remains of ancient Hawaiian celestial observation huts.

The **Sliding Sands Trail**—the premier trail at Haleakala—departs from the right as you enter the visitors center parking lot. Descending with long traverses over red sand,

From Sliding Sands Trail

this trail has many options and a way of drawing hikers deeper than they intended, so begin prepared for a long hike. Austere beauty envelops hikers from the get-go. The **cinder cones overlook** will come up on your left, an unmarked spur. The **Ka Lu'u o ka O'o** crater will be directly below. To get there, continue down and make a left at the first junction—at a confusing outcropping among some silverswords, the jewel of the Haleakala plant world. When you reach the crater, be sure to take the thrilling trail around its rim.

To the **Bottomless Pit**, a.k.a. Kawilinau, continue on the Sliding Sands for nearly 2 miles past the above junction. The last part will be a steep descent. Then take a left at a trail junction, beginning a moderate fall over about 1.5 miles, keeping two cinder cones to your right. The pit—with a bottom clearly visible—is on the north side of the cinder cones. To reach the **Kapalaoa Cabin**, keep on trekking past the Bottom-

less Pit-Halemau'u Trail junction, for 2 more miles. The cabin lies near the edge of the Kaupo Gap, and the 7,000-foot escarpments that fall to the south coast. *Be Aware:* Coming back up the Sliding Sands at this elevation can be a grind. Don't bite off more than you can chew. *More Stuff:* One of the park's best long hikes is a car-shuttle from Sliding Sands, past Holua Cabin, to the Halemau'u trailhead. The hike is 11.5 miles with 2,800 feet of elevation gain. Hikers without a second car to shuttle commonly hitchhike back to the top. Head toward the Bottomless Pit (Kawilinau) and go left at a signed junction.

To **Red Hill Summit** (elevation 10,023) drive to road's end, which is at mm21. A covered, octagonal hut with picture windows provides shelter, informative displays, as well as staggering views. Red Hill's real name is Puʻuʻulaula—try it, it's easy. For another panorama, don't forget to take the rim trail, which encircles the parking lot.

The fabulous **Skyline Trail** is outside the park boundary and not shown on the visitors maps. *Driving:* Go left .3-mile from the visitors center, opposite the spur road to Red Hill. Conintue .75-mile and go left to trailhead parking—the no tresspassing sign refers to the road to Science City, which veers right. Sometimes a gate is locked at this junction, adding 1.5 miles to round-trip hikes. (Science City is a defense department and University of Hawaii research center; God knows what goes on there.) The trail gives up big ocean views from an open, red cinder ridgeline. It continues way down to Polipoli State Park, but you can achieve a grand panorama after only .25-mile.

47. KULA FOREST RESERVE-POLIPOLI SPRINGS PARK   HIKE

WHAT'S BEST: Ascend the green side of Haleakala, where some trails achieve lofty heights with ocean views, while other paths wander misty conifer-and-broadleaf forests that have been battered by nature. Or choose a more relaxing visit in cool Kula: flourishing botanical gardens, a lively lavender garden, or a historic winery.

PARKING: Take Hwy. 37 (the Haleakala Hwy.) up the mountain and keep right as Hwy. 37 becomes the Kula Hwy. *For all Kula Forest Reserve hikes and the two gardens:* Just after Rice Park and before mm14, turn left on Hwy. 377. *For Kula forest and lavendar garden:* After .25-mi., turn right on Waipoli Rd. Aliʻi Lavendar Garden will be on your right after .5-mi., after crossing a cattle guard. The Kula Forest Reserve is *up* for 5.75 mi. on Waipoli Rd; see hike descriptions for further directions. *For Kula Botanical Gardens:* Pass Waipoli Rd. and .25-mi. later, turn right off Hwy. 377 up a signed driveway. *Tedeschi Winery* is about 7 miles away on Hwy. 37 (Don't turn left on Hwy. 377). The road changes to Highway 31 near mm20, and a mile after that is the winery.

HIKE: *In the Kula Forest Reserve and Polipoli Park:* Waipoli Road to: Boundary Trail loop (6.5 mi., 900 ft.), or Haleakala Ridge view (7 mi., 150 ft.); Skyline Trail to: Mamane Trail loop (5.75 mi., 950 ft.), or Haleakala Park summit (up to 13 mi., 3,200 ft.); Polipoli Springs-Redwood Trail loop (3.75 mi., 900 ft.,); *Nearby short hikes:* Aliʻi Kula Lavender garden (.25-mi.); Kula Botanical Garden (.25-mi.); Ulupalakua Ranch-Tedeschi Winery (.25-mi.);

Talk Story: Mother Nature smacked the Kula Forest Reserve in 2006 and 2007 with wildfires, torrential rains, and hurricane-force winds. The parklands were closed for many months. More than 100,000 seedlings have been planted and roads were improved. From the end of pavement, Waipoli Road maintains a contour through the 12,000 acre Polipoli Springs State Park, which is part of the reserve. It's nippy up here, from 6,000 feet on up. Bring warm clothing.

The **Waipoli Road hikes** are for those who decide not to drive past the end of the pavement—though the unpaved portion is normally okay for passenger vehicles. Begin walking from the parking area (where the paragliders take off). After .5-mi., you'll round a bend and enter the forest and pass the junction with the Boundary Trail. The road undulates, but basically maintains a contour.

For the **Boundary Trail loop**, go right, after about 2.25 miles from the parking area, at the right-hand junction with the Waiohuli Trail. You will drop 900 feet and join the Boundary Trail. Turn right and enjoy views toward the Kihei coast as you return on a more gradual climb. For the **Haleakala Ridge view**, just stay on the road. At 3.25 miles from the parking area, you pass the junction with the spur road that drops to Polipoli Springs. From that junction it's another .5-mile farther up to a big open turnout, where you can look up the Haleakala Ridge and down to the vast sheets of lava on the southern coast. The Skyline Trail begins its ascent to the summit here, and hardy hikers can continue.

For the **Skyline Trail-Mamane Trail loop**, *drive in* about 2.25 miles from the end of the pavement, and park at signed junction for the Waiohuli Trail, which crosses the road. This trail gives you a taste of the devasated forest, a cave adventure, as well as big panoramas. You begin with a steep climb for .75-mile to the junction with the Mamane

Polipoli trail

Trail—go right. Near this junction you'll find a small volcanic cone used by the ancients as a cave shelter. Over the next 2 miles you traverse native shrub, mainly the mamane trees. You then meet the Skyline Trail, above its first set of switchbacks on the ascent up the ridge to Red Hill. To return, go right, down to rejoin Waipoli Road. *Note:* You could begin this loop from the Skyline Trail, and descend the Mamane Trail.

The **Skyline Trail** takes you higher and higher, to the Haleakala summit. Begin by driving 4.25 miles in on Waipoli Road. Park about a mile past the junction with the road to Polipoli; about .5-mile past that junction is a turnout with a guardrail, after which the road bends left through forest and reaches an open saddle—where it becomes red-dirt switchbacks that thwart passenger vehicles. Views open dramatically when you reach the top of the switchbacks. Continue climbing to your left—a right hand junction takes you into a scrub-filled ancient crater on Kahua Road. After about .75-mile, Red Hill will be visible up and to your left. The trail continues straight up the ridge, much of the hike rises above vegetation, as the road becomes cinders.

For the **Polipoli Springs-Redwood Trail loop**, veer right from Waipoli Road 3.25 miles after the end of pavement, and drive down about .6-mile to the picnic area at Polipoli Springs. From the parking area, double back 100 feet on the road and go left down a short path that leads to the Polipoli Cabin. Hang a right at a signed trail when you reach the cabin. The soft-earth trail swerves down, at first through the partial wreckage of cypress and a few sugi pine, and then among redwoods. After a little less than a mile, at a shelter, go left on the Tie Trail. You'll drop 500 feet farther through redwoods and then ash trees. If you're quiet you might surprise a wild pig or two. After .5-mile the Tie Trail joins the Haleakala Ridge Trail, where you go left. At this altitude, sunlight often mixes with waning fog to produce glowing beams. You'll get ocean peeks at Kahoolawe, as the trail climbs during the next mile. At a junction above a big climb, go left on Polipoli Trail—where the Haleakala Ridge Trail continues right to join the road and Skyline Trail. The **shelter cave** is about .5-mile farther up the Polipoli Trail, just off the trail at a signed junction. The wide-mouthed cave, in bedrock, is in a depression in the forest. The Polipoli Trail contours through tattered eucalyptus and pine before reaching the picnic area parking.

At **Ali'i Kula Lavender Garden**, paths meander through about 9 acres of lavender (about 40 species) on open slopes of Kula at 4,000 feet. Culinary lunches and teatime garden tours are available by reservation, but you are free to poke about on your own. Stop by for a scone on the view deck at the Studio Gift Shop, and look inside for dozens of locally made lavender-inspired items—foodstuffs, beauty products, logo wear, sachets, oils, and candles. The gardens are the brainchild of the late Ali'i Chang, a personality on Maui. Oprah Winfrey owns a home nearby. Show up in the morning (hours are from 9 to 4) and you'll be treated to a view of paragliders descending from Haleakala and landing just outside the entrance to the garden.

Nearly 40 years old, the family-run, **Kula Botanical Gardens** was Maui's first and will be just the ticket for traveling families. It's groomed paths meander 8 acres featuring a koi pond, love birds, carved statuary, and African cranes, as well as 2,000 species of flowering plants and tropical trees—all of it set at a pleasant slope that affords a bird's-eye view of the ocean and West Maui hanging out there like some far-off land. Admission is about $7.50 for adults; hours are 9 to 4 daily.

Kula Botanical Garden, Ali`i Lavender Garden

Around the mountain from the Kula Forest Reserve is **Tedeschi Winery**, which sits amid **Ulupalakua Ranch**. Tedeschi's staff provide historical tours (normally at 10:30, 1:30, and 3) along with the vineyard's libation. Tasting room hours are 9 to 5 daily.

Talk Story: Tedeschi Vineyards, featuring sparkling wines made from pineapple, has been around since 1974, taking over the historic buildings of the James Makee estate. The Hawaiian royal family, including King David Kalakaua, and famous writers, such as Robert Louis Stevenson, frequented the grand estate. Makee planted numerous varieties of trees, now giants, and flowers in abundance. The Ulupalakua Ranch is still a working operation, and you're likely to see some of the paniolos down the street at the local store. *More Stuff:* Above the highway near the vineyards is the nonprofit **D. T. Fleming Arboretum**, Hawaii's oldest. Views are fabulous, as is the plantlife and grounds of this Maui treasure. Call for free tours; see page 235.

---

48. GREAT TAHITI   HIKE

WHAT'S BEST: Ruins tell the story of migrations from Tahiti 1,000 years ago—to hikers willing to endure sticker brush, beating sun, and high winds on an unmarked trail.

PARKING: Take Hwy. 37 (the Haleakala Hwy.) up the mountain and keep right as route becomes the Kula Hwy. After mm20, route changes again, to Hwy. 31. Continue past cinder quarry at mm21.5. At mm22.6, park on left at a shoulder; a 'government property' sign and gate will be barely visible to the left, up and off the road. *Note:* After mm19, as you come down the squiggly highway, note the two Lualailua Hills, lying ahead above the highway. At the saddle between the hills, a contour line of a road goes to the left, toward the upper part of the hill. This is the route to the ruins.

HIKE: Kahikinui ruins-Menehune footprints (3.5 mi., 300 ft.)

Talk Story: Kahikinui—or Great Tahiti—was one of Hawaii's earliest settlements, with a population nearing 2,000 scattered about these arid upslopes. Although fishing was primary for the village, freshwater was brackish at the coast and many structures were located near 1,500 feet to trap spring water with small dams. In Hawaiian, Kahiki also means "horizon," and the village was set in a location to observe the cinder cone which they named Hokukano, after the star, Hokupukano, which guided the ancient mariners on their 2,500-mile voyage to the Tahitian homelands. The cone is on the ocean side of the highway at mm17.5.

The Menehune footprints are the Holy Grail for archeological enthusiasts. A mystery even to the earliest Polynesians, the footprints are etched into a smooth lava shelf about 35 feet in diameter—some 30 prints measuring from 4- to 10-inches in length. They are thought to be a type of petroglyph left by the legendary Menehune, the diminutive precursors to the Tahitians. The prints are difficult to find, and hard to make out—good luck. *Be Aware:* Prepare for wind and sun on this off-trail excursion. Wear long pants if you have them. Footing is difficult, due to lava and brush. Also, respect the boundaries of the homesteads in the area.

For the **Kahikinui ruins-Menehune footprints** hike, head up from the roadway and through the gate that seems to be an entrance to nowhere. But you'll be able to follow a rocky path upward, and, after about 10 minutes, turn left at a right-angle on an old road. The road levels and leads through the saddle between the Lualailua Hills, which means "dual tranquility." Benign grasses and weeds will slap your shins as you make your way across the saddle. From the saddle head up to your right, picking your way under some trees just large enough to throw shade. Contour around, ascending a little to stay above the top of a gulch.

From the other side of the gulch—a homestead will be down to the left—you should pick up the trail which contours around the uppermost hill. The trail meets a road, which leads through a rickety, wire gate. Although ruins dot this area, you will find a major site to your left. Walk the smooth lava a few hundred feet and go left out to a promontory marked by a kiawe tree. Here lies the sprawling remains of a Kahikinui village site, that was once covered with a wooden superstructure and thatched roofing. *Be Aware:* Use caution to leave the site undisturbed. The footprints lie some 500 yards up the slope from this site, and about 300 yards from the base of the hill. Listen for the hushed voices on the wind from the villagers of the past; perhaps they will guide you to just the right spot. Keep an eye out, too, for lava tubes.

Pahihi Gulch

King's Trail ruins

49. MANAWAINUI GULCH   HIKE

WHAT'S BEST: Explore the fishing shrines on the lost portion of the King's Trail, or take a short but gnarly hike down to heiaus set at a cove in a canyon.

PARKING: Take Hwy. 37 (the Haleakala Hwy.) up the mountain and keep right as route becomes the Kula Hwy. After mm20, route changes again, to Hwy. 31. At the bottom of the long descent, at mm27.5, pull off at a large turnout on the right.

HIKE: Manawainui Gulch heiaus (.75-mi, 300 ft.); King's Trail (1.5 mi. or more, 200 ft.)

From the turnout, walk to the edge and take a gander down the black canyon that is **Manawainui Gulch**, where confused seas meet storm-washed boulders, the alluvium of Haleakala. To reach sea level, walk down the highway to where the guardrail joins the modern concrete bridge. (This steel rail was wiped out by a rockslide in 2007, closing the road for months; chain-link netting was drapped on the cliff faces to reduce the rock hazard.) Step over the guardrail—there is no trail—and traverse down toward the bridge. At the bottom, cross the drainage and cut back toward the ocean on the brush-covered bench. Going will be slow. Near the bottom, veer right off the bench, across the boulders to the rough shoreline. There you will find a medium-sized burial platform, built of black rock, and, just behind it, a smaller one built of coral stones.

To explore the **King's Trail**, walk down from the parking overlook and veer right and down. You won't see a trail or markers on this end of the ancient trail that begins some 6 miles away in La Perouse Bay. You'll see the first fishing shrine about .25-mile from the parking area, beyond the first shallow gully. Along the lava coast, you are likely to see modern fishermen, who drive down, somehow, and use ladders to get out to their favorite casting spots on sharp reefs that stick out into the waves. Prepared hikers can continue, making a true adventure of this little-used route. More ruins, a blowhole, and tide pools are in the offing.

50.   HUAKINI BAY   HIKE

WHAT'S BEST: A natural sea arch and a red-rock canyon impart a sense of Haleakala's geologic transformation happening in real time.

PARKING: Take Hwy. 37 (the Haleakala-Kula Hwy.) and keep right on the Kula Hwy. After mm20, the route changes to Hwy. 31. Continue to Manawainui Gulch, near mm27.5. *Note:* Further directions from this point are in hiking descriptions below.

HIKE: Natural Arch (up to .5-mi); Pahihi Gulch (2.75 mi., 200 ft.)

Talk Story: Along several miles of the highway, some half-dozen gulches are gouged into the 9,000-foot high wall that is the southern face of Haleakala. The great shield volcano was once about 5,000 feet higher, as over the eons much of its mass has eroded down gulches and fanned out to form this rugged coastline.

To see the **Natural Arch** before walking toward it, walk toward the ocean at the Manawainui turnout, as per TH48, and look down the coast to the sloping arch. To

Natural Arch

*Road to Kaupo trailhead, Nuʻu petroglyph, Koa Heiau ruins,
St. Joseph Church, Nuʻu highway, Halekiʻi Bay fisherman*

approach the arch from the coast, get in the car again and proceed to the bottom of the next gulch at Waiopai Bridge, another modern feat, at mm28.6. From the black-rock beach, go to your right along the rocky coast to get sort of near the arch. Battered by the sea, it forms an opening some 150 feet in length and about 50 feet high.

Pahihi Gulch is accessible from Huakini Bay, where the highway crosses a wide wash at sea level, near mm29.5. A massive boulder field rings the bay. This gulch is a canyon in the making, as it will continue to deepen over the millennia. Park at a shoulder on the left, just as you reach the bay. A hunter's trail leads through the greenery on the left side of the gulch's wide mouth—above the gravel bed that is the low point of wash, but not next to the cliff either. Stay left, heading toward a slide of yellowish rock. When you reach the slide, keep left of a large stand of kiawe trees.

Another gulch, Pukai, joins from the right. About .75-mile into the hike, you'll lose sight of the highway, as the gulch narrows pass to the left of a stand-alone hillock in the middle of the gulch. At this point, look left to see a cave below the cliff; hikers with partners and flashlights may want to explore with caution.

Almost a mile into the hike, you'll pass behind the stand-alone hillock, and will be surrounded on four sides by steep, unstable cliffs. Hunters use this area on weekends, and you're likely to find snares made of wire and hear falling rock caused by pigs and goats up high. Birdsong practically echoes in this natural atrium. From here the gulch narrows and curves, and you'll have to pick your way across its rocky bottom, deep-grass, and treed banks. Eventually, it becomes too steep and crumbly to safely walk. *Be Aware:* This is not a hike to take alone. Do not attempt during rains, and avoid falling rock by staying away from cliffs.

51. NU'U BAY   HIKE, SNORKEL

WHAT'S BEST: Petroglyphs, a birder's marsh, ruins, Haleakala views, and a snorkeling cove at an old landing: This won't be Maui's secluded secret much longer: In 2008, 4,300 acres of Nu'u Ranch were added Haleakala National Park.

PARKING: Take Hwy. 37 (the Haleakala Hwy.) and keep right on the Kula Hwy. After mm20, the route changes to Hwy. 31. Continue to where the road reaches sea level and pass mm30. *Note:* Further directions follow in hike descriptions.

HIKE: **Nu'u Bay to: Petroglyphs (.25-mi.), and Nu'u Landing-Kaupo Ranch Wildlife Marsh loop (1.75 mi.); Pu'u Maneoneo (.25-mi.)**

At mm30 the highway dips into an oasis of kiawe trees at **Nu'u Bay**, site of an ancient fishing village. From here, the new section of the national park extends inland through ohia-koa forest remnants to the crater rim, bordering with the Kahikinui Forest Reserve.

A first road leads in to the right very near mm30, and a second road is .5-mile afterward, where the road dips across a spillway. For the **petroglyphs** and the **loop hike**, look for a gate at mm30.7. After a very short distance down the road, curve to your right along a cliff less than 20 feet high. Footing is poor, with tall weeds covering rocks. Petroglyphs will be plainly visible in places, etched into the rocks. Closer inspections will reveal reddish pictographs, drawings on the surface. Anthropologists speculate as to the origins of these recordings. Follow the cliff as it loops out to the boulder beach to find a heiau sitting on a low bluff. *Be Aware:* Take care not to disturb this site.

Nu'u Landing is the low lava point you will see at the far east end of the beach. From the shore is one of the most scenic vistas on Maui: Look inland as the fissured walls of Haleakala and the Kaupo Gap rise some 8,000 feet.

To reach the landing, it's easier to cut inland and take a sandy road along the edge of the trees. At its end, you have to climb up 15 feet. An old concrete ramp leads into the water, the point of departure for cattle raised nearby in the old days. Take the trail past the landing. You'll come to a right-forking trail that leads down to rugged Nonou Bay. You can also stay left on a trail that leads over sharp lava to Apole Point, and to tiny Waiu Bay, which is on the opposite side of the point from Nu'u.

Once you've explored the point, backtrack on a road that leads from the base of the landing to the highway. The remains of Koa Heiau, a sprawling site, will be on your right, and an ancient salt pond will be on the left. Also on your left, just before the highway, is the tiny **Kaupo Ranch Wildlife Marsh**, a pond fringed by grasses which you can see through the trees. Once you reach the highway, near mm31, walk to the left down the road. After about .1-mile, look closely on your left for a chain-link gate in the fence that leads directly to the pond. If you're quiet, you are likely to see waterfowl and shorebirds taking a break at this tiny wetland on a rocky coast.

For the vistas from **Pu'u Maneoneo**, get back in the car and get the camera ready. After mm31 the road rises inland to a grassy bluff, as the terrain transitions from the arid "dismal coast" to the ranchlands of Kaupo. To the right as the road tops out are a few turnouts and short paths that lead to vantage points. The towering heights of Haleakala will be a crowd pleaser, but don't forget to take a gander up and down the coast. Put a gold star on the map marking this place.

SNORKEL: Experienced snorkelers can find excellent snorkeling and relatively safe waters at **Nu'u Landing**, at times even during the winter. Use the gate near mm31. Entry is near the landing. An even better spot is small **Nonou Bay,** which is to the right over rocks and down, not far beyond the grass patch at the landing. The walk down to the water is a hands-on affair, but the bay is more protected. This is a deep-water snorkeling area not for beginners—but a highly underrated spot when conditions are right. *Be Aware:* Don't attempt if the swell is high and test the water for currents.

WHAT'S BEST: Hike high or savor the coast, but don't just drive by beautiful, weather-beaten Kaupo.

PARKING: Take Hwy. 37 (the Haleakala Hwy.) and keep right as the route becomes the Kula Hwy. After mm20, the route changes to Hwy. 31. Continue as Hwy. 31 drops to coast and climbs again, reaching Kaupo Store at mm34.6. *Note:* Further directions follow in the hike descriptions.

HIKE: Kaupo Trail to: Haleakala National Park Boundary (7 mi., 2,700 ft.), or Kaupo Gap rim (13.75 mi., 5,500 ft.); Huialoha Church-coast (up to 1 mi.)

The front porch at funky Kaupo Store may well be the center of the universe. You'll have to rest a spell with a cold drink, watch the world go by, and draw your own conclusion. It is open 24 hours a day, except when it's not, a tradition that dates from 1925. (The long road closure in 2008 was hard on the store.) To hike the **Kaupo Trail**, drive not far past the store and turn left, before the sign noting that the national park is 8 miles ahead, and before the road drops down to a one-lane bridge. Drive in 1.4 miles on this one-lane, grassy road lined by low rock walls. The signed trailhead parking is on your left.

Road from Kaupo to Kipahulu, Kaupo

Huialoha Church, near Halekii Bay, Kahoolawe from Kaupo Road, Kaupo Store

Walk up the road .1-mile and go left down a left-bearing fork. You'll then see the trail on the right, heading up a grassy gully. For both the **Haleakala Park Boundary** and **Kaupo Gap** rim hikes, follow post markers, set a hundred feet or less apart to mark the trail when the grass gets taller. This trail is all about up. Views are with you from the get go, and they only become better. But many people like this trail for its native koa and ohia forests, which attract flocks of woodland birds.

Ascending on long switchbacks, you reach the park boundary at an elevation of nearly 4,000 feet, with the steep and jungly Manawainui Valley down to the right. The frozen wave of ancient lava that poured over the Kaupo Gap is to your left. At nearly 7,000 feet, the Kaupo Trail joins the Sliding Sands Trail that comes from the top of Haleakala. From here you are .25-mile from Paliku Cabin, to the right, and about 9 miles from the visitors center, to the left. For trekkers who can't get enough, the Kaupo Trail is Maui's best wilderness experience.

The **Huialoha Church** is a crown jewel, where nature has conspired to craft perfection. To get there, proceed past Kaupo Store and the one-lane bridge. After about .3-mile (at mm35.3) turn right on a rutted dirt road that drops down for .25-mile. (Due to vandalism, this road may be chained and closed to cars; permission to enter may be required.) The church, built in 1859, is set on acres of open grass, accented by coco palms and next to small Haleki'i Bay. You can also walk to the right as you face the water, on a boulder beach path that actually extends for miles to Waiuha Bay.

More Stuff: Three great heiaus in this region date from Chief Kekaulike's rule in 1730. The Loaloa Heiau is upstream to your left just after crossing the bridge beyond Kaupo Store; the Haleo Kane Heiau is to the right off the road to the Kaupo trailhead, where the road makes its right-angle to the left; and the Popoiwi Heiau is high on a hill off-road to the left, after crossing a second stream past Kaupo Store.

A place of worship of more recent lineage—St. Joseph Church, built in 1862—is right on the bumpy road before getting to the Kaupo Store; open grounds and a view of Kaupo Gap combine for a pleasant rest stop. *Note:* The highway continuing toward Hana sometimes closes due to falling rocks. Though very narrow in places and bumpy, the road is okay for passenger cars under dry conditions.

SNORKEL: Haleki'i Bay, at Huialoha Church, is among the best snorkeling spots along coast from Kipahulu to La Perouse, which isn't saying too much since most of the coast is totally unsafe. In the winter months, the seas can be flat and the entry okay. You enter deep water, with lots of rocks poking up just offshore, big enough to be called the Mokulau Islands. Net fishermen like this bay, as do scuba divers. *Be Aware:* If you see a big, fat, hairy guy sleeping on one of the few patches of sand, keep away: It's probably a Hawaiian monk seal, an endangered species for which discretion and the law prescribe a 100-foot buffer zone. Currents here can be strong.

Outer Islands

Molokai from Maui, leaving Lanai

Father Damien statue, St. Joseph's Church, Molokai

Molokini snorkeler, Hulopoe Beach Park on Lanai,
Royal Grove on Molokai, Lanai Ferry, chapel at Lodge at Koele

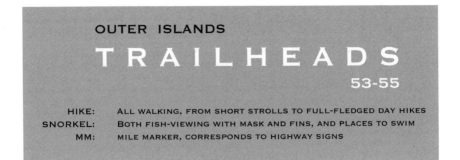

OUTER ISLANDS

T R A I L H E A D S
53-55

HIKE: ALL WALKING, FROM SHORT STROLLS TO FULL-FLEDGED DAY HIKES
SNORKEL: BOTH FISH-VIEWING WITH MASK AND FINS, AND PLACES TO SWIM
MM: MILE MARKER, CORRESPONDS TO HIGHWAY SIGNS

*Take a vacation within a vacation with a day trip to the
three islands that beckon from Maui's western shores.
Molokini is a half-day snorkeling experience. Although
you could spend an entire vacation, or lifetime for that
matter, on Lanai or Molokai, a day on either will
seem like a week's getaway.*

53. MOLOKINI   SNORKEL

WHAT'S BEST: A marine sanctuary awaits only a few miles off the coast, with waters
so clear you'll think you're flying instead of swimming.

TRANSPORTATION: A number of vessels make the short trip to Molokini. Some
of the best are those of the Maui Dive Shop, which has some half-dozen stores. They
offer smaller boats that seat a dozen or fewer passengers, two trained divers who give
hands-on help to beginners, and departures from the Kihei Boat Ramp—much closer
than some other outfitters, which leave from Lahaina and Ma'alaea. When making a
booking, ask your outfitter about these factors, since some of the boats are cattle cars.
Also get a reading on the weather, since Molokini's crescent shape opens toward the
trade winds, which bring big swells during the winter months. Inquire about cancellation policies. See *Resource Links* for telephone numbers.

Molokini Island came to be in dramatic fashion, when newly formed Haleakala
needed to let off steam. Molten lava pushed up from below, super-heating porous
rock of the earth's crust until the steam trapped within the rock burst in a gigantic,
circular explosion. When the dust and ash settled— viola!—it hardened and later
eroded from a circle to form a crescent. The fish have come, and Molokini is now
one of the world's best spots to snorkel. The island is called a tuft cone, the only one
formed in this manner on Maui. Aside from being a Marine Life Conservation District, Molokini is also a seabird sanctuary, but only our feathered friends are allowed
to alight on its 70-foot high ridge.

During the winter, waters usually are calmest inside the crescent during morning hours, and the early birds make the 20-minute trip from Kihei starting at 7 a.m. To enjoy warmer sun, take a later departure. Snorkeling boats have their mooring spots inside the crescent, in waters about 30-feet deep near the shore—with better visibility than the air in some cities.

On peak days, hundreds of fish lovers will be flopping about, prompting stories about oil slicks caused by sun block and lotions. Regardless, there's plenty of room inside the bowl (the outer edge of Molokini's bowl is submerged). On the convex side of the crescent is a world-famous scuba dive, a wall of several hundred feet. Specialized outfitters take tank divers to this side of the sanctuary.

Molokini

Onboard showers, anchored catamaran, Maui Dive Shop's Captain Rae and Michelle, Kihei Boat Ramp

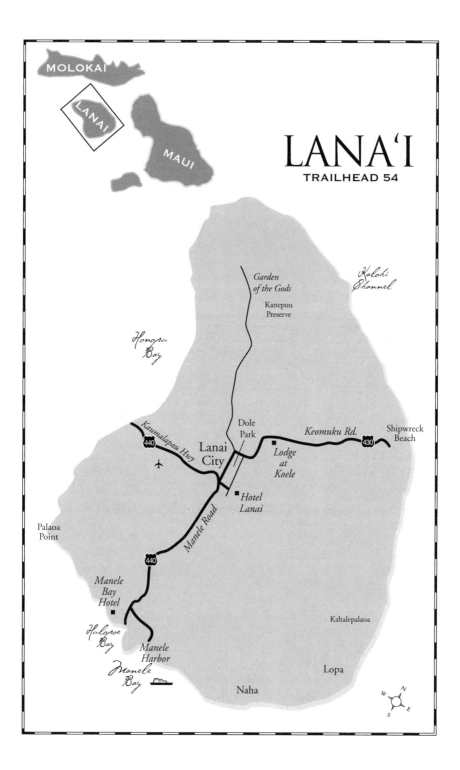

LANA‘I

TRAILHEAD 54

MOLOKAI

LANAI

MAUI

Kalohi Channel

Garden of the Gods

Kanepuu Preserve

Honopu Bay

Dole Park

Keomuku Rd. **430** Shipwreck Beach

440 Kaumalapau Hwy

Lanai City

Lodge at Koele

Hotel Lanai

Palaoa Point

Manele Road

440

Manele Bay Hotel

Kahalepalaoa

Hulopoe Bay

Manele Harbor

Manele Bay

Lopa

Naha

N
W E
S

WHAT'S BEST: Snorkel with spinner dolphin and walk coastal tide pools. Visit two world-class resorts, one on the beach and another high in the pines. Then take a stroll around a sleepy former pineapple town that is nothing but Old Hawaii. A day trip to Lanai is a vacation within a vacation. Rent a Jeep, or see it on foot using the shuttle bus.

TRANSPORTATION: *By Sea:* Lanai Expeditions has ferries departing early from both Lahaina and Ma'alea Bay (a real time-saver if you're not staying in West Maui). Call 1-800-695-2624, or 661-3756. Advance booking is required; tickets are about $50, round-trip. *By Land:* A shuttle bus is available at the Lanai harbor and makes stops included in the day trip; tickets are $10. Expeditions can arrange Jeep rentals and guided tours, and Dollar rents Jeeps in Lanai City (you have to buy a ticket on the shuttle bus anyway). First-time visitors will be happy with the shuttle bus tour. Repeat visitors may want to rent a car, but the experience may not justify the expense. Advice for Jeep drivers follows the day-trip schedule. Either way, you'll want to take a knapsack with lunch and water, and personal items. If you plan to snorkel, bring your gear.

PARKING: *Lahaina:* Turn toward the ocean off Hwy. 30, on Shaw St., and park at the lot at the corner of Front Street, or continue on Front to Prison St. Parking fees may be charged. *Ma'alea Harbor:* Located off Hwy. 30, north of Kihei, just west of the junction with Hwy. 31. Use the signed lot to the left at the entrance, or drive onto the breakwater. Parking is free.

SCHEDULE FOR A DAY TRIP TO LANAI

SAIL THE LANAI EXPEDITION FERRY: 6:45 A.M., LAHAINA HARBOR; 7 A.M. MA'ALEA HARBOR. The ride takes 45 to 60 minutes. During winter and spring, the cruise doubles as a whale-watching adventure, as the big mammals frolic in Auau Channel. You'll enjoy sunrise during the trip. *Note:* Check for current ferry schedules.

DEPART FERRY AT MANELE BAY, LANAI, 7:45 A.M. As you look at Lanai from Maui, the Manele Bay harbor is to the left, just out of sight. The ferry rounds the cliff and pulls into a small marina with a dock just big enough to make the landing. New (2008) restrooms, walkways, and covered waiting area have spritzed the place up. Board the shuttle bus for the short trip to the Four Seasons Resort at Manele, where you buy tickets. (You can walk the .25-mile to Hulopoe Bay; go up the road and take your first left. You'll reach the lawn of the beach park and see the resort up to the right.)

VISIT FOUR SEASONS MANELE. The resort, whose tiled roofs are slung low over Hulopoe Bay, manages to be grand without being ostentatious. It consistently ranks at the top of tropical travelers' best-places lists among all the world's destinations—six-foot vases, hardwood finish work, floral upholstery, museum quality paintings, and chandeliers the size of playsets hanging in front of towering windows that frame the bay. (Check the shuttle bus schedule before leaving the resort.)

WALK TO HULOPOE BAY BEACH PARK, TIDAL POOLS, SHARK COVE, 8:15 A.M. TO 9:30 A.M. Walk past the resort pool on a path to Hulopoe Beach Park. Encircling the park's lawn are tables and campsites, interspersed among ironwoods and palm trees—offering some of Hawaii's best beach camping; call the Four Seasons Manele or Maui County Parks for details.

To walk to the tide pools, go left (facing the ocean) at the beach and pick up a trail. In a few minutes, you'll see stairs leading down to a long shelf of pools that extend seaward to the point. These aquariums of nature, at low tide, will let you look in on marine life. Shark Cove is beyond the stairs and to the left, a sandy nook rimmed by 12-foot high, red cliffs. You need to use hands to climb down. The cliffs slope up as you encircle Shark Cove, rising to the 200-foot high head that separates Manele and Hulopoe bays. From the top you're above Pu'upehe Cove and Sweetheart Rock, a.k.a. Pu'upehe, the lava stack that is just offshore. Legend tells of poor Pehe, who drowned while hiding in a cave below, and was taken to the top and laid to rest by her distraught lover, Makakehau. This tale dates from around 900 AD, when the region was a Hawaiian village.

SNORKEL HULOPOE BAY, 9:30 A.M. TO 10:30 A.M. The spinner dolphin often congregate a few hundred feet offshore at the end of the beach that is closest to the hotel. A stream also enters the bay here, so waters can get murky after heavy rains. Attendants at the beach's snorkel shack can give you a dolphin report. Be sure to view the dolphins passively, letting them come to you, rather than pursuing. At the other end of the beach, snorkeling is also good offshore from the tide pools, perhaps better, although the dolphins aren't as frequent. Since 1976, when the marine conservation district was established, it's been against the rules to feed the fish when snorkeling.

Four Seasons Manele

CATCH SHUTTLE BUS TO LANAI CITY, MIDMORNING. Make sure you get on the right bus at the Four Seasons; others go to the golf course and airport. The 8-mile ride to Lanai City takes about 15 minutes, climbing 1,700 feet from the bay— halfway to Lanai's highest elevation—and crossing arid grasslands.

STROLL LANAI CITY AND HOTEL LANAI AND HAVE LUNCH, NOON TO EARLY AFTERNOON. The Hotel Lanai, built during the pineapple heyday of 1923, has a mountain-cabin feel, a single-story wood-frame under the shade of Norfolk pines. The hotel's rotisserie dining room draws visitors from the island's chi-chi hotels, and it's open for lunch. Uphill from the hotel is a golf course with pleasant walking paths.

Across the street is Dole Park, a several-acre lawn planted with Lanai City's trademark Norfolk pines (the ones with curly boughs are the less-common Cook Pine). Sanford Dole, the canned-fruit king, once owned Lanai and not coincidentally was Hawaii's first governor after the Hawaiian Kingdom was annexed by the United States. The town shops, along with quiet residential area, encircle the park. The best thing is to walk the perimeter, wandering to quiet back streets, which are laid out in a grid, as you may be directed by your fancy and the town's humorous signs. You can't get more folksy than Lanai City. To your right, on 7th street, is Tanigawa's, the choice for island-style plate lunches. Or try the Blue Ginger Café, for its pizza and burgers. Across Dole Park, on 8th Street, Richards Shopping Center has been selling groceries and gifts since 1946. Another old-fashioned general store, the International Food and Clothing Center, is

Shark Cove, Hotel Lanai, Lanai City

Hulopoe Beach Park, Koele Lodge

down 8th Street—behind the Pine Isle Market. Next door to the market is Pele's Garden, a health food store and juice bar. Schools and churches are at the opposite end of Dole Park from Hotel Lanai; you get a seaward view from behind them. Many of Lanai City's 2,800 residents have been living in these quiet cottages for 50 years, and to talk to them is a living history lesson.

Catch Bus at Hotel Lanai and visit the Four Seasons Lodge at Koele, 2 p.m. to 3:30 p.m. The lodge is about .5-mile from Hotel Lanai, walking distance if the bus schedule doesn't cooperate with yours. Head up Lanai Avenue, pass 3rd Street, and go right where it becomes Keomuku Highway. This place is hard to anticipate. Stately Norfolks line the entrance of the Four Seasons Lodge at Koele, which resides on green slopes like a colonial plantation manor, a ridge of native forest rising above it. It does not evoke Hawaii to the uninitiated, but this site was the center for the Lanai Ranch cattle operations from 1874 to 1951. Inside the elegant 102-room hotel—which is of recent construction—are two-story fireplaces and truss beams.

Behind the lodge is a 40-acre arboretum, most of it a rolling lawn with large pond, several gazebos, and a glass conservatory full of blossoming orchids. Royal palms, towering kukuis, African tulips, and a number of other trees and flowering shrubbery line a path that encircles the grounds. A few structures remain from the ranching days.

CATCH SHUTTLE BUS TO MANELE BAY FOR RETURN FERRY If you have time and energy, you can walk out to the right of the harbor's breakwater, toward Pail Leino Haunui, and to watch for the white ship to round the point. The timing is right for a sunset cruise into into Maui, a wondrous sight as you approach from the sea. (Unless the schedule has change, a Lahaina-bound ferry departs at 4:30 p.m., and the one headed to Ma'alea leaves at 5:30 p.m.)

JEEP TOURS: Rental is pricey, at about $139 a day, but if you rent one you'll want to take the dirt road north through the Garden of the Gods to Polihua Beach. (Turn left just north of Koele Lodge, between the stables and tennis courts.) After five rutted miles, you'll pass the dryland forests of the Kanepu'u Nature Preserve, with strolling choices for bird-watchers. Soon after comes the mile-long rise of red-dirt strewn with boulders, the Garden of the Gods, a pretty sight though it doesn't quite measure up to its name. The real treat comes after the road snakes down steeply over 4 miles to reach Polihua Beach. Backed by kiawe forest, the deep and two-mile-long run of sand faces open sea—a real out-there experience.

Polihua Beach, Garden of the Gods

Shipwreck Beach is another highlight for Jeepsters. Going north from Koele Lodge, Keomuku Road, or Highway 430, swerves northeast and down about 7 miles to the beaches on the east shore. Go left at the bottom (the road right, often very muddy, passes the spread-out, ramshackle structures of Keomuku Village).

The Shipwreck road becomes sandy, so you may want to walk the last bit. Offshore to the west is the steel-skeleton hull of a liberty ship that the Navy tried to sink after World War II. Across the channel is a big look at Molokai. You can walk your brains out on Shipwreck; to the left is beach-and-bluff route of several miles that reaches Polihau Beach.

Shipwreck Beach, Keomuku Road

The premier hike/drive/bike on Lanai is the Munro Trail, which follows the 3,700-foot ridgeline from above the Lodge at Koele. At mm1 north of the lodge, turn right toward the cemetery. After .25-mile you'll reach the trailhead, which is passable via Jeep in only the driest of weather and chancey at that. Better to get out of the wheels and walk, or rent a bike in Lanai City. Mountain biking is a growth industry on Lanai. In addtion to the Munro Trail, three trails take off north from the road to Garden of the Gods.: Kuamo'o, Kahue, and Lapaiki. Best track forks left after the garden, the Kaena Trail, which drops to the northwest and then forks several times on a rugged route down to the coast. Be prepared if trying this adventure.

Hulopoe Beach, Lanai City

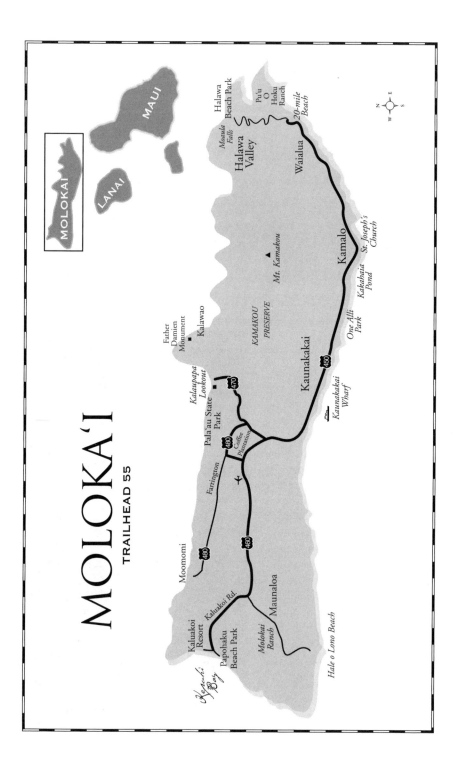

MOLOKAʻI

TRAILHEAD 55

Molokai southeast coast

WHAT'S BEST: To know what Maui was like in 1950, take a trip to Molokai tomorrow—quiet towns, serrated green ridges, ancient fishponds, open pastures, and expansive white sand beaches. Select from one of three driving tours, or stay overnight to do them all.

TRANSPORTATION: *By Boat passage:* Charter boats visit Molokai, but your best bet is an Island Marine Ferry, which departs Monday, Wednesday, Friday, and Saturday for day trips from Lahaina. Call for current times and ticket prices. Boat travel is recommended because you'll see the island's offshore waters and sight plenty of whales during the early spring migrations. *Note:* Island Marine also offers car rentals and guided tours, in addition to simple round-trip tickets. *By Air:* Several airlines make the short hop to Hoʻolehua Airport. *Helicopter:* Blue Hawaiian has a day-trip to take it all in from on high. See *Resource Links* for all phone numbers.

PARKING AT LAHAINA: On the south end of town, turn toward the ocean off Hwy. 30, on Shaw St., and park at the lot at the corner of Shaw and Front streets. You'll have to walk a few blocks, but this free lot should have no time restrictions.

CAR RENTAL ON MOLOKAI: You'll need your own wheels or a tour taxi to see Molokai. See *Resource Links* for car rentals. If you are taking the ferry, be sure to discuss transportation to and from the airport to pick up your rental car and drop it off. See if your car can be made available at the ferry dock in Kaunakakai.

The airport is a 15-minute drive from the harbor. Island Kine Rentals is located near the harbor in Kaunakakai, and they have a shuttle bus that makes the short drive to

One Aliʻi Beach Park

their office. Their cars may not be as spiffy, but they are convenient and this is definitely a local-style family business, operating out of a home, with a dog likely to be sleeping on the sofa while auntie is in the corner watching TV. If you use Island Kine, or any of the other rental agencies, try to get the paperwork done over the phone when you make reservations to expedite things on the day of arrival.

THREE MOLOKAI DRIVING TOURS

All three tours assume a morning ferry passage with a return trip that same afternoon, making you feel like you've watched an epic movie on fast forward. Of course, you can stay overnight which will allow time to do it all. *Notes:* All tours include a visit to the Kalaupapa Overlook of Father Damien's leper colony, and a walk through Kaunakakai Town. All tours assume a ferry departure back to Maui at 2:30 p.m. Check for most recent ferry schedule. Pack snacks and a few bottles of water before embarking on your drive. Your tour choices:

EAST MOLOKAI TOUR: Begins with mountainous side of the island that has green escarpments, ancient fishponds and heiaus, and churches. Continues to road's end at the rain forest of Halawa Valley and Moaula Falls. Ends with Kalaupapa Overlook and Kaunakakai Town.

WEST MOLOKAI TOUR: Begins with Kalaupapa Overlook, and then continues on the arid west slopes to a coffee plantation, cowboy country, and the long white-sand beaches on the far coast. Ends with Kaunakakai Town.

ALL-ISLAND TOUR: Includes all of the above, with the exception of certain portions that will be noted in the tour descriptions. Excludes Halawa Valley. This is a scouting tour for visitors who might be considering spending an entire vacation on Molokai. You might be the only people in a hurry on the island if embarking on this whirlwind.

FOR ALL TOURS: BOARD ISLAND MARINE FERRY, LAHAINA HARBOR 6:30 A.M. You'll catch sunrise in the Pailolo Channel, which can be choppy when the trade winds are up, but the ride is usually bumpier on the return voyage. The open top deck of the *Princess*, which doubles as a whale-watching dinner cruiser, allows for an experiential voyage. Waters get calmer about two-thirds of the way on the 100-minute journey, when the ferry gets in the lee of Molokai.

Kaunakakai Wharf is midway on the southern coast of Molokai, which is about 38 miles long. Like Maui, Molokai is really two former islands that are joined now by an isthmus. Unlike Maui, the mountainous, green side is the higher, with Kamakou Peak rising to 4,961 feet, while the red-dirt and grasslands of the west reach an elevation of less than 1,400 feet. Fewer than 7,000 people live on Molokai, most of them in Kaunakakai.

St Joseph's Church, Ualapue Fishpond, Kamakou ridges

BEGIN EAST MOLOKAI AND ALL-ISLAND TOURS, KAUNAKAKAI, 9 A.M. (FOR WEST MOLOKAI TOUR, SKIP TO "BEGIN WEST MOLOKAI" PARAGRAPH BELOW.)

Head east out of town on Highway 450, the Kamehameha V Highway. A 28-mile barrier coral reef, one of the longest outside of Australia's, extends offshore along the highway. Although shallow waters limit snorkeling opportunities, the reef provided ideal conditions for a series of fishponds that were constructed by the first Polynesian voyagers. The Kalokoeli Pond is offshore the Molokai Beach Cottages before mm2. Just after mm3 are the One Ali'i Beach Parks, two of them, pleasantly decorated with coco palms and fronted by three fish ponds along a mile of coast—Ali'i, Kaoini, and Kanoa. Look for semi-circles of stone that extend into the water.

At mm5, the green relief rises inland, near Kawela. In the late 1700s, this is where Kamehameha the Great's seaborne warriors conquered Molokai on the way to his final battle for Oahu. Near mm6, look inland to the east, as Kamakou, the tallest peak in the island, comes into view. Look also on the right, amid big kiawe trees and coco palms, for Kakahaia Beach Park, which is a National Wildlife Refuge that includes fishpond ruins. Over the next several miles, the straight highway hugs the coast, passing five more ancient fishponds. *More Stuff:* To hike the 2,700-acre Kamakou Preserve, contact The Nature Conservancy on Molokai.

At mm10, as you enter a reduced speed zone and the highway curves left inland, turn right at spur road to visit Kamalo Harbor—you'll see the water from the road. The old wharf here symbolizes several centuries of inter-island commerce, since this was the best natural harbor on the coast. In recent times, the barrier reef was excavated to construct the wharf at Kaunakakai. After making the turns through the Kamalo settlement, you'll come to St. Joseph's Church, which was built by Father Damien de Veuster in 1876—the Catholic priest had arrived three years earlier from Maui. A statue of the priest and a small cemetery grace the grounds.

The highway swerves inland for the next several miles, as you pass several intriguing roads that lead toward the east ridge of Kamakou. At mm14 are the portrait quality grounds of Our Lady of Seven Sorrows Church, Father Damien's first effort, dating from 1874. Across the street is Ulapu'e Fish Pond, on the National Register of His-

Windsurfing off Pauwalu, Wailalua Pavilion, Malo'o

toric Places. The next mile or two is the site of one of the larger settlements of ancient Molokai. Past the bridge at mm15, look for a sign and gate noting the Ili'iliopae Heiau, more than 30,000 square feet, that lies inland less than .5-mile on a trail that transects the island.

By mm17, as the road nears the shore, you'll see breakers that note the waning of the barrier reef. West Maui lies a few miles across the channel. Pockets of sandy beach appear past mm18, and the jagged ridges inland give way to open green slopes, with a pleasing assortment of trees. At mm20 you get to east Molokai's best beach, Murphy Beach Park, a.k.a. 20-Mile Beach, your opportunity to snorkel or take a dip. The park's fishpond and swerving strip of palmy sand are a prime beach walk, with views of Maui and the tiny seabird sanctuary island offshore to the north—Kanaha Rock and Moku Ho'oniki. Camping is available at the Waialua Pavilion, where Kamehameha V spent his formative years.

NOTE: ROAD NARROWS AFTER MM20. FOR ALL-ISLAND TOUR, TURN AROUND AND MAKE THE 40-MINUTE DRIVE BACK TO KAUNAKAKAI. TO CONTINUE ALL-ISLAND TEXT, SKIP TO "BEGIN WEST MOLOKAI TOUR" PARAGRAPH.

EAST MOLOKAI TOUR CONTINUED. Sleepy Molokai becomes more so, as Highway 450 narrows after Murphy's Beach. Some areas are definite one-laners. You'll curve inland and climb to a viewpoint at Puhakuloa Point, below which the tiers of waves attract local surfers by the six-pack. This is known locally as Tooth Rock, or Rocky Point. The highway leaves the coast, at Sandy Beach, and climbs into the grassy hills and ironwood forests near mm22.

You'll navigate the toe of east Molokai, reaching an elevation of about 600 feet through the lands of Pu'u o Hoku Ranch. You want horse pics, you got 'em. You'll pass ranch headquarters and a road on the right to Kalanikaula Sacred Kukui Grove, named for Molokai's famous kahuna. Then, near mm26, where the road hairpins left, is a fabulous overlook of Halawa Valley and Bay. Inland to the left is 500-foot Hipuapua Falls and the top part of 250-foot cascade of Moaula Falls. To the north and west is Molokai's roadless north shore, where sea cliffs reach 3,000 feet.

The parklike road then makes a symphonic descent to the Halawa Beach Park, which features two, small sandy beaches, one on either side of the stream—straight at road's end. Snorkeling, body surfing, and board surfing are possibilities. A trail leads inland to both falls, which descend from forks of the stream. This valley was one of Hawaii's earliest settlements, dating from as early as 600 AD, and many archeological sites are yet to be discovered. Two tidal waves in the mid-1900s did damage, to both ruins and plant life. TURN AROUND AND DRIVE BACK TO KAUNAKAKAI. SEE NEXT PARAGRAPH TO CONTINUE TOUR.

Kalaupapa Peninsula

BEGIN WEST MOLOKAI TOUR (AND TO CONTINUE ALL-ISLAND AND EAST MOLOKAI TOUR) GO WEST FROM KAUNAKAKAI ON HIGHWAY 460, THE MAUNALOA HIGHWAY.

Just past mm1 is Kioea Beach Park, which has no beach to speak of but is notable for its Kapuaiwa Royal Coconut Grove, planted for Kamehameha V in the 1860s. It's the only accessible royal grove remaining in Hawaii. Heads up for falling coconuts if walking beneath the trees.

AFTER MM4 TURN RIGHT ON HIGHWAY 470, THE KALAE HIGHWAY. The road sweeps over the isthmus, greening up with Norfolk pines, ironwoods, and koa trees. Just before mm4, on the left by a golf course, is the Molokai Museum and Cultural Center, alongside the Meyer Sugar Mill site. Near mm5 you'll reach the north side of the island, where, just past the Molokai Stables, the Kukuiohapu'u Trail switchbacks down to the Kalaupapa Peninsula, a National Historical Park. This is the site of the leper colony overseen by Father Damien in the late 1800s. *More Stuff:* The 3-mile, 1,600-foot hike down is by permit only. Put this on your lifetime to-do list, and call Damien Tours or Molokai Stables.

After the trailhead, the road enters 34-acre Pala'au State Park, passing a picnic pavilion and campground, and comes to a dead end. A short trail to the right of the parking area leads through cypress and eucalyptus about .25-mile to the Kalaupapa Lookout. The squat peninsula far below was formed by a relatively recent wave of lava that created a 2.5-mile nub pointing due north. On the tip you'll see the lighthouse, built in 1909. The Kauhako Crater near the base of the peninsula is now a lake. After absorbing the view, head back to the parking lot and, if you have time, go left on another .25-mile trail that leads to Phallic Rock. Few will be able to resist the hike, although those expecting a towering monolith will be disappointed. Partially sculpted by human hands, the rock is an ancient Hawaiian fertility symbol that even today is the locale for the occasional tete-a-tete.

FOR EAST MOLOKAI TOUR, SKIP TO "RETURN TO KAUNAKAKAI" PARA-GRAPH, AND DRIVE THERE. CONTINUE WEST MOLOKAI AND ALL-ISLAND TOURS BELOW.

BACKTRACK ON HIGHWAY 470 AND, AFTER THE GOLF COURSE, TURN RIGHT ON HIGHWAY 480, WHICH IS FARRINGTON AVENUE.

Note: Both tours from here are similar, but All-Island Tour people need to manage time, bearing in mind it takes about 30 minutes to drive back to the harbor from west shore beaches. The West Molokai Tour people can take more time at each stop. At the Farrington junction are the coffee plantation groves, where Coffees of Hawaii offers complimentary pick-me-ups, as well as wagon tours. Coffee has supplanted cane as a cash crop. The Cook House, housed in an old sugar shack, is an institution.

CONTINUE ON HIGHWAY 480. PASS MM2, AND TURN LEFT AS HIGHWAY 480 BECOMES PU'UPE'ELUA AVENUE. THEN TURN RIGHT, HEADING WEST AT HIGHWAY 460. You'll pass the small airport and head out on a red-dirt straightaway. Just before mm13, you'll be able to see Oahu to the northwest, alight on the sea.

Kepuhi Beach, Papohaku Beach and Park

AT MM15, TURN RIGHT ON KALUAKOI ROAD, TOWARD THE RESORT. You'll descend on a grassland road, sparsely lined with ironwoods. After 3 miles, turn right toward the Kaluakoi Villas, and follow the resort's road to its end, near the gift shop. A path leads from the modest, but tasteful condo complex to Kepuhi Beach, which has grass terraces shaded by coco palms and sandy patches interrupted by black-rock reefs—places for good snorkeling. A path leads to the right, past a lava point, to the north end of the beach that is favored by surfers. To the left, a road and path skirts a golf course site, past Pu'u o Kaiaka, to Papohaku Beach Park; see next paragraph for driving instructions. Coast hikers will have room to roam both north and south.

BACKTRACK FROM THE RESORT AND TURN RIGHT ON KALUAKOI ROAD. CONTINUE FOR 1 MILE AND TURN RIGHT INTO PAPOHAKU BEACH PARK. This place is a beach camper's fantasy. Large native trees and coco palms decorate its sprawling lawn, which opens up to Papohaku Beach—some 3 miles of open sand, the longest in Maui County. Snorkeling and bodysurfing features are included. *More Stuff:* The road continues for several more miles, passing a short trail to Po'olau Beach on the way. At road's end are several miles of road and trail, fronted by a half-dozen beaches, that end at Molokai's southwest tip.

FOR ALL-ISLAND TOUR, DRIVE BACK TO KAUNAKAKAI; SKIP TO "RETURN TO KAUNAKAKAI" PARAGRAPH. FOR WEST MOLOKAI TOUR, CONTINUE BELOW.

Kaunakakai

Backtrack on Kaluakoi Road—watch out for deer—and turn right at the top of the grade toward Maunaloa. West Molokai's only town, once a camp for pineapple workers, is less than two miles away. Its lazy asphalt track is stained red and and bordered by Norfolk pines and native Hawaiian trees. It was once the home of Molokai Ranch which allowed visitors the opportunity to experience authentic ranch life. The ranch ceased all operations in 2008.

Wind is frequent in Maunaloa, and near the Big Wind Kite Factory, you'll often see colorful creations dancing in the sky. Although not a tropical-vacation-looking town, Maunaloa in ancient times is thought to be the birthplace of hula, the most Hawaiian of dances that enacts history and legend. *More Stuff:* The road continues down to the coast—you can see breakers from town—to Hale o Lono Harbor, which is the start of the yearly outrigger race to Maui. Other dirt roads fan out over southwest Molokai.

RETURN TO KAUNAKAKAI – ALL TOURS

Save time for a stroll around Kaunakakai. The grocery, mercantile, and gift shops along the main street, Ala Malama Avenue, are a throwback to a simpler time. These are not tourist shops. Then stroll out toward Kaunakakai Wharf. Before reaching the water, you'll pass the gardens at Malama Cultural Park. At the water is Wharf Beach, not a great swimming area, but in the afternoon you should see one of the local canoe clubs putting in.

At the end of the wharf, opposite the ferry docking area, is a cruising sailboat harbor. Take a look back at Molokai and get a mental imprint to take away with you. Your memory of the place will have a way of catching up to the experience a day or two (or a year or two) after your ship has returned to Lahaina.

Kaunakakai Harbor

Free Advice & Opinion

DISCLAIMER

Think of this book as you would any other piece of outdoor gear. It will help you do what you want to do, but its depends upon you to supply responsible judgment and common sense. The publisher and authors are not responsible for injury, damage, or legal violations that may occur when someone is using this guidebook. Please contact public agencies to familiarize yourself with the most current rules and regulations. Posted signs and changes in trail status determined by public agencies supersede any recommendations in this book. Be careful, have fun.

HIKING

Never walk downhill with your hands in your pockets … A cell phone is safety insurance on remote trails … You see fewer cell phones in Maui because people here see their friends in person … Stay out of stream valleys in the rain … If stranded by a flooding stream, sit and wait it out before crossing … Don't cross if water is above your crotch … Flash-flood threat is greatest on the northeast coast and Hana Highway … You often can hear a rumbling flood coming, along with the smell of fresh earth … If the stream rises a little, get to high ground … Backtrack when you get lost … Never try to walk cross-country in Hawaii … Watch your watch: Note when you leave the car, and allow time for your return before sunset, plus an hour insurance time … Ancient roads don't contour, they undulate … Always bring water … Wear bright clothes, other than green colored … Parents: never take your eyes off the kids …

Hunter's are out on weekends and holidays … All beaches are public places to the high-tide line … If you're feet are burning on the surface of hot sand, dig down a few inches … On woodland trails, don't take your eyes off the ground for more than two steps … If you hike in Maui, you will slip … Hiking poles are a third leg … Lawyers' Paradox: Paths with the least amount of danger have the most warning signs … And vice versa … In sunny conditions, try to hike before 10 a.m. and after 2 p.m. … Never climb or walk under cliffs and outcroppings; Hawaiian rocks are unstable … Going down steep hills, you want to fall on your butt, not forward … Wild pigs of 200-pounds or more have right-of-way on trails …

Do not remove or disturb rocks at a heiau or other archeological site; these places are still being discovered and preserved … Same goes for plants; Hawaii is home to the largest reserves of endangered species … Hike with a buddy … Stay on trails … If you get caught out at night, sit down and wait for morning; don't hike at night … Always hike with a prepared knapsack; see *Calabash* … Carry water on all hikes, and drink when you're not thirsty … Haleakala is high; plan to be short of breath and adjust your pace for the altitude … Bring warm clothing … Both hypothermia and heat exhaustion are possible during the same day on Haleakala …

Never turn your back on the ocean at tide pools and beach walks … You need a permit to camp on beaches, or anywhere else, on Maui … Erosion is a big problem here; don't cut switchbacks on trails … If you must hike alone, always let someone know where you're going … Assess how long a hike will take before you leave; see *How to Use This Book* … Forests on Maui are too deep to walk through … Edges of cliffs might appear solid, when they are only a mat of grasses … In groups, don't lose sight of the person behind you … Stay calm if lost or in trouble.

KAYAKING

Kayaking is the easiest way to snorkel the Kinau preserve … Kayaks with no rudders or freeboards are no good in the wind … Always call and get weather and marine reports … Ask local outfitters for trip advice … File this under unnecessary advice: stay at least 100 yards from a whale … Wind shifts and sudden choppy water can mean a storm is brewing … Keep your center of gravity low … Lash your paddle to the boat … Wear

a life jacket … Don't go out alone … Maintain your balance: a canoe or kayak won't tip by itself … Make your outbound voyage into the wind, to have the wind with you on the return … Sunscreen your neck … Don't trap sea turtles between boats.

SNORKELING

Rubber booties help with rocky entries … Swim fins are not made for walking forward, except by professional clowns … To enter the water, back in; or, put on your mask, dive in, and put on the flippers while you're bobbing around … Most snorkeling tours take you to places you can get to from shore … Most fish will be around the rocky points between sandy coves … Or in coral beds … Walking on coral reef crushes living things … Only monk seals are allowed to be naked on Hawaiian beaches … Lifeguards generally will place hazard signs on beaches, but don't rely on it … Wave action means more rip currents and danger from shore breaks … Stay away from wave action in rocky areas … Check depth of the water first before diving …

Don't touch a Portuguese man-of-war, a jellyfish with tentacles … MSG helps on man-of-war stings …To test for rip current, lie face-down in the water and observe if you are being carried away … If caught in a rip current, don't swim against it … Swim perpendicular to the current to break free … Lifeguards will be at most county beaches, but not at state beaches … Always swim with a buddy … Good surfing conditions are poor snorkeling conditions … Some people snorekeling waters are clearest in the morning … Don't feed the fish; it disturbs the ecological balance of the reef … Presence of other swimmers does not mean conditions are safe … Avoid a sunburn by wearing a T-shirt or rash guard …

Calm water means safer swimming … But watch for boat traffic … Touching a finger to the top of your head is a diver's sign to say you're OK … Incoming waves mean water needs to go back out to sea through a channels; channels can be observed as blue underwater canals, or choppy places where the waves aren't breaking … Sticking your finger or hand in a hole in the reef is a bad idea … Shark attacks are rare, but to make them even more rare, stay out of murky waters near streams, and don't swim at dusk or before dawn … Don't touch sea turtles … Sea urchins will sting if you touch them … Watch the water for several minutes before entering to assess possible hazards … Try to enter at sandy areas … If in doubt, don't go out.

HEALTH

Haole Rot, or sun-splotched skin, is cured by Selsun Blue shampoo … Pump or treat stream water before drinking … Green coconuts are full of water; smash the stem end on a rock … Coconut water helps ailing kidneys . . . Wind evaporates sweat; don't forget to drink water when hiking in breezes … Beware of the white ooze when handling just-picked mangoes; it will burn your skin … Accidents happen; tragedies happen when you're not prepared for accidents …

Tropical sun is fierce; use waterproof sunscreen with SPF 15 or higher, containing zinc oxide and Parsol 1789 … Wear a wide-brim hat … Avoid streams and ponds when you have cuts or abrasions … Treat even small cuts with antibiotics … Leptospirosis, a bacteria in fresh water, causes flu-like symptoms … Dengue fever is, in rare cases, carried by mosquitoes; use repellant in jungle environments … Don't eat strange plants or fruits; some are poisonous … Drinking water helps prevent heat exhaustion … So does wearing loose-fitting clothes … Provide shade and elevate the feet if someone collapses … 1 to 2 liters per person per day, drink it for health and as a liquid safety precaution.

SURFING

Rules one through ten: beginners should hire an instructor ... Outfitters and instructors will happily give advice to novices ... Biggest summer surf: West shore beaches; Biggest Winter surf: east shore beaches ... Eddie would go ... Check *Best of* for beginners' beaches ... See *Resource Links* for instructors ... More waves to surf means Hawaiian surfers are less surly about wave space ... Hawaiians invented surfing; this is the place to learn ... A reasonably good athlete can stand up in one day with a long board on small waves.

DRIVING

Preventing road rage, local-style: park for a while and watch the sea ... Pull over for local traffic on the Hana Highway ... Aloha driving: go the speed limit and don't tailgate ... Broken glass at a parking spot is a sign of break ins ... Save your driving tours for weekdays ... Be in Paia by dawn to avoid the Hana Highway traffic ... Or leave later, and explore to Nahiku ... One rental car parked attracts others on scenic highways ... Driving in Maui traffic is okay, but getting across traffic is hard ... Always turn right ... See the *Driving Tour* at the start of each trailhead section for specifics of road conditions ...

Take valuables with you when leaving your car ... Check your insurance coverage (including that with your credit card) before leaving home ... Hang bead leis from your rearview mirror to make your car appear more local ... Vandals are only supposed to break into tourist cars ... Your rental car company may advise leaving your car unlocked ... Bring a package of baby wipes to freshen up after a hike or after eating a papaya while driving ... Four-wheel drive doesn't help with Maui's biggest hazard on remote roads: they are narrow ... Drive safely ... Drive Aloha.

Maui Calabash

LITERALLY, A CALABASH IS A GOURD USED AS A WATER
VESSEL. IN HAWAII, THE CALABASH IS A GROUP OF
FRIENDS, LIKE FAMILY, THOUGH NOT BLOOD RELATED.

TIMELINE

1,750,000 BC: West Maui volcano breaks the surface.

900,000 BC: Haleakala sees daylight.

200: First Polynesians voyage to Hawaii from the Marquesas.

800: Second wave of Polynesians, from Tahiti; round-trip migrations.

1300: Round-trip migrations cease; Hawaiians alone in the islands.

1500-EARLY 1600s: Reign of King Piʻilanai and his heirs. Major heiaus and the road around Maui (alaloa) constructed.

1736: End of reign of King Kekaulike.

1765: Beginning of reign of King Kahekili.

1776: Kahekili defeats invaders from Big Island at Battle of the Sand Hills.

1777: Queen Kaʻahumanu is born—Kamehameha's favorite wife and enlightened leader.

1778: British Captain James Cook sights Maui's windward coast, but doesn't land.

1787: French Captain Jean Francois La Perouse becomes the first known Westerner to set foot on Maui, at Makena. Calls it "dismal coast."

1790: Most recent lava flow on Maui, at Cape Kinau (although new charcoal dating suggests the eruption was 300 to 500 years ago). Native population of Hawaii 300,000. Kamehameha the Great defeats Maui's King Kahekili at Iao Valley. American ship *Eleanor*, under Captain Simon Metcalf, slaughters 100 Hawaiians in Olowalu Massacre.

1802: Kamehameha I declares Lahaina capital of Hawaiian kingdom.

1810: Hawaiian Islands united under single rule of Kamehameha the Great, after Kauai capitulates without a battle.

1819: Kamehameha the Great dies. Queen Kaʻahumanu topples old religion of sacrifices and kapus. First whaling ship arrives in Lahaina from Massachusetts.

1823: First New England missionaries arrive, Reverend Richards.

1824: Queen Kaʻahumanu bases code of laws on Ten Commandments. Kamehameha II dies while visiting England.

1825: Conflicts between lawless whalers and missionaries, who have support of the queen, as well as Kamehameha's heirs to the throne.

1826: Mexican ship brings mosquitoes to Maui.

1828: First sugar mill.

1831: Lahainaluna High School, the first west of the Great Divide, is established.

1832: Queen Ka'ahumanu dies.

1835: Missionary Dwight Baldwin arrives.

1842: Some 40 whaling ships visit Lahaina.

1852: Prison erected in Lahaina.

1860: Visiting whaling ships number 325.

1870: Henry P. Baldwin and Samuel Alexander, sons of missionaries, buy their first 12 acres to plant sugar. Their heirs become major land owners.

1850: Capital of Hawaii moved from Lahaina to Honolulu.

1852: First Chinese immigrants arrive to work sugar plantations.

1870: Native population of Hawaii 56,000; mortality due to Western diseases.

1885: First Japanese immigrant workers arrive.

1893: United States Marines enter Pearl Harbor, annex Hawaii as a U.S. Territory. James Dole appointed first governor.

1901: Dole organizes Hawaiian Pineapple Company. Buys Lanai in 1922.

1916: Haleakala made part of national park system; becomes park in 1961.

1926: First Hana Highway, for vehicles, completed.

1934: Inter-island air mail begun.

1936: Pan American Airlines crosses the Pacific. Haleakala Visitors Center built.

1941: Japanese attack Pearl Harbor.

1946: Hotel Hana Maui becomes the island's first resort; tidal wave kills 12 at Hana.

1959: Hawaii becomes the 50th state.

1961: Ka'anapali becomes Hawaii's first master-planned resort.

1969: Kipahulu added to Haleakala National Park.

1970: Maui population 46,000.

1980s: Makena becomes a state park. Haleakala designated as International Biosphere Reserve.

1993: Resolution by United States Congress apologizes to Hawaiians for the overthrow of the Hawaiian Kingdom.

1990s: Wal Mart, Home Depot, Costco.

2000: Maui population 135,000.

2002: Hawaiian Nation, other groups, strive to restore status of Hawaiian Kingdom.

2005: National travel magazine's readers vote Maui's beaches the best in the U.S.

2008: State closes Ahihi-Kinau Natural Area for two-year study.

2012: Kapalua Resorts arboretum and coastal trails a success.

Baby Beach, Lahaina

THE WORLD'S VACATION HOT SPOT

Only Hawaii can lay claim to being the world's vacation hot spot. Just offshore the Hawaiian Islands, under water that is two-miles deep, molten lava has been roiling up from the mantle of the earth for nearly 100-million years. Volcanic magma from this unique hot spot piles up and eventually bursts the surface, where, to make a long story short, the magic of rainwater, weather, and evolution transform the lava into tropical islands.

The hot spot has remained in the same place. Meanwhile, the earth's crust has been moving northwest, rotating over it like the shell of an egg rotating around its yolk. The rate of movement is about four inches per year. Once at the surface, the lava forms shield volcanoes that rise several miles high, which then move slowly northward on this geologic conveyor belt—only to have wind, waves, and rain slowly erode the peaks and submerge them once again into the sea.

Submerged volcanoes are called seamounts. The Emperor Seamounts that are now some 2,500 miles away off the western tip of Alaska's Aleutian Islands started out at the Hawaiian hot spot. Midway Island, about 1,300 miles distant in the middle of the Pacific, is actually the northwest terminus of the Hawaiian Archipelago, a chain of about 130 islands and sea-washed atolls that comprise the state.

The eight major islands normally associated with Hawaii are the highest mountain range in the world, if measured from their summits to the ocean floor. But they're getting shorter all the time, and they will inevitably be reclaimed by the tides. Kauai, the most-northwesterly among the major islands is several million years older than Maui and, since its birth, has moved about 300 miles and eroded some 5,000 feet in elevation. Maui's Haleakala, still an active volcano, towers 10,000 feet, but was once about 15,000 feet above sea level.

The good news is, new islands continue to emerge. Today, about 20 miles off the southeast coast of the Big Island, magma is boiling into seawater to form the volcano of Loihi, which will one day be the ninth among the primary islands. Time-shares are not yet available.

Volcanoes aren't the only forces of nature that has created Hawaiian real estate. Rising and falling sea levels, caused by waning and waxing ice ages, have created a riddle: What is now four islands, that used to be six islands, that used to be one island? Answer: Maui County. Today, the county consists of Maui, Kahoolawe, Lanai, and Molokai. Way back when, Maui was two islands, West Maui, which is about a million years older than East Maui, or Haleakala. Similarly, Molokai is comprised of two nearby volcanoes of different ages that used to be separated by water. In yet another geologic time, all these islands were combined as one—Maui-nui—when vastly larger polar ice caps resulted in a much lower sea level.

Today, with 728 square miles, Maui is second largest in the major Hawaiian chain—although the Big Island is five times larger. Maui has the most beaches and best swimming among the islands. Its sister islands, less than 10 miles away, provide always changing offshore views. The environs of East and West Maui are vastly different, making a visit like two islands in one. And Haleakala is almost like a third island—a lunar landscape high in the sky. Rain forests, deserts, waterfalls, wildlife ponds, tropical beaches—the list goes on and Maui has it all.

These tumultuous lands of Hawaii have moved about 300 feet north since the prehistoric migration of human beings arrived—the last place on earth to be settled—less than 2,000 years ago. The human race made its way across Asia, then island-hopped down through Indonesia to Fiji, New Zealand, and finally to Tahiti and the other Polynesian islands of the South Pacific. The first Hawaiian voyagers were the legendary Menehunes, the little people, who are thought to have sailed northward some 2,000 miles from the Marquesas. Petroglyphs, irrigation ditches, and fishponds supply archeological evidence to support the mythological origins of these first settlers.

Around 1000 AD, a second wave of Polynesians began to arrive on Hawaiian shores, this one primarily from Tahiti. The second wave is thought to have subjugated the Menehunes, whose numbers were relatively few. Navigating 100-foot long sailing canoes hand-hewn from logs, the Tahitians brought with them most of the plants commonly associated with Hawaii, such as coconut palms, breadfruit, bananas, taro and many others that were to form the cornerstones of their agrarian life.

For several centuries, back-and-forth migrations are thought to have taken place from Tahiti to the nine major Hawaiian Islands, two of which—Maui and Hawaii—were actively spitting lava. The history of these migrations has been preserved over the centuries through hula and chanting. The mythological exploits of gods and demigods, as told in the hula, have their origins is real acts by real people. For instance, the demigod Maui-tikitiki-a-Taranga—from whom the island derives its name—was probably an ancient explorer and warrior. Legends say he captured the sun at Haleakala thereby insuring a longer growing season for the people. This myth may have derived from the man's understanding of the solstice and its relation to crop production.

Around 1300 AD, the migrations from the South Pacific ceased. The Polynesians became Hawaiians, isolated from the rest of the world by several thousands of miles of blue Pacific in all directions—the most-isolated landmass on earth. Effectively, the Hawaiians were as independent as the people of earth are today, alone on a planet in the middle of an ocean of space. This isolation lasted for nearly 500 years, during which time Hawaiian civilization flourished. Learning to live in concert with the abundant land and sea became both religion and science.

Each village was located in an ahupua'a, a triangle-shaped parcel of land that included a seacoast and stream that extended over farmlands and had its origins in the interior woodlands. Expertise in farming, fishing, building, weaving—all crafts—was overseen by a kahuna, who passed knowledge to the next generation. All in nature was preserved and nurtured for future generations.

These several centuries were Hawaii's golden era, as each island prospered independently under ruling chiefs. On Maui during the 1500s, Chief Pi'ilani built huge heiaus and began a roadway system around the island that was furthered through the royal lineage of his sons. On all the islands the ruling chiefs, or ali'i, traced their genealogical heritage to common ancestors, and thus the bloodlines of the ancients, along with their knowledge, was handed from generation to generation.

By the time British Captain James Cook sighted *Mowee* in 1778, the Hawaiian population had grown to an estimated 300,000—and growth pains were evident. During the 100 years prior to Cook's sighting, the islands of Hawaii had been at war. The success of their way of life had brought about population increases that in turn created struggles over finite space and resources. On Maui, Chief Kekaulike and, later, Chief Kahekili, engaged in land and sea battles with the ruling chiefs of the Big Island. The Hana coast of Maui often changed hands between rulers of these two islands.

These skirmishes ended in 1790, when the Big Island's Kamehameha I, defeated the forces of Maui in the Iao Valley. After negotiating a truce with the chief of Kauai, Kamehameha the Great became the first king of Hawaii, ruler of all islands. As smart as he was big and ferocious, he used cannons from a captured American trading vessel to defeat his enemies on Maui once and for all.

Beginning in 1800, new forces converged on Maui, many of them, but not all, for the betterment of the common people. Educational and societal reforms were made by Kamehameha's heirs to the throne, and more significantly by the influence of Queen Ka'ahumanu and Queen Keopuolani. The reforms were aided by the influence of missionaries who arrived during this period, helping to develop the best school system west of the Rockies and a literacy rate superior to the average among Americans at that time.

Also arriving during the 1800s were merchant ships from all points on the compass. British and American ships called in droves, replenishing fresh water and food supplies of trading vessels bound for the Orient. Sandalwood became the island's first export, and forests were denuded. Whaling was huge well into the 1800s, with several hundred lawless vessels dropping anchor in Lahaina during the heyday.

But the real boom came with sugar, as America's sweet tooth was satisfied by Hawaiian cane. Vast tracts of land were altered to become cane fields. Some of the sons of missionary families, like Baldwin and Alexander, went on to become cane growers and rulers of state government.

Since the native population decreased to some 50,000 people, due to diseases brought by Europeans, laborers flocked here from throughout the world. Maui's ethnic diversity—Filipinos, Chinese, Japanese, Portuguese, and many others—is a result of labor demands needed to satisfy the sweet tooth.

Eventually, these business interests developed to the point where the United Sates, in 1898, annexed Hawaii as an U.S. Territory. Statehood came in August of 1959. In spite of its American heritage—forever established by the events of World War II—the islands remain distinctly Polynesian.

An effort to restore Hawaiian sovereignty is alive today, and many schools and organizations foster the language, dance, and way of life that developed over the centuries when this island nation was a world apart. Similarly, efforts are underway to re-establish public access to the majority of land that is now in the hands of a half-dozen corporations—and to safeguard from development Maui's natural beauty that was preserved by the ancients, and today is the basis for the island's tourist industry.

HALEAKALA MISCELLANY

Haleakala's oldest rocks are 910,000 years old … the oldest island in the Hawaiian Archipelago, Kure Atoll, is 28-million years ago … Historical maps and interviews suggest the last eruption was in 1790; new charcoal dating by volcanologist peg the date at 1450 to 1600; whichever, current seismic rumblings say it's still an active volcano … The summit is 10,023 feet … When you make the drive up, you pass through as many biological life zones (seven) as you would on a trip from Mexico to Alaska … Haleakala used to be about 15,000 feet: erosion … Measured from the ocean floor, Haleakala is 28,000 feet …

Haleakala crater is technically not a crater, but an eroded valley, pocked with cinder cones … The "crater" is 19 square miles … The National Park is 28, 665 acres … That's about one-tenth acre per visitor, if the yearly total all came on the same day … Rainfall: Summit, 40 inches; Headquarters, 53 inches; Kipahulu, 187 inches … Maximum wind recorded: 128 m.p.h. in 1990, but the wind indicator broke … Temperatures: Average, 53 degrees, High, 80 degrees, Low, 11 degrees … To walk all the trails you need to do 27 miles.

MAUI MAN

If you thought a map of Maui looks like the head and shoulders of a man lifting out of the water, you weren't being silly. Legend says (as recounted in Inez Ashdown's Ke Alaloa O Maui*) that the Goddess Pele agrees with you.*

"As you study the map of Maui you note that it resembles the head, neck and shoulders of a man. That is how Pele formed the brave land named for the demigod, Maui, whom she loved dearly. His head is West Maui, with Lahaina, Land-of-prophecies, as his mouth and Eke Crater as his ear. Kahakuloa, the Everlasting-master, is his forehead. Ma'alaea is his throat and Kahului is the nape of his neck. His broad shoulders are all of East Maui, with the Haleakala Crater as his heart."

WHALES, SHARKS, DOLPHINS, TURTLES AND OTHER CREATURES

WHALES

Dolphins, porpoises, and whales are all cetaceans—83 species of warm-blooded mammals ... Blue whales, at 100 feet, are the largest ... A whale's tongue can weigh as much as an elephant ... Humpbacks range from 40- to 60-feet in length, with females slightly larger, and can tip the scales at more than 80,000 pounds ... The oldest known humpback was 48 ... A swimming whale's tail goes up and down; fish tails go from side to side ... They can motor up to 20 mph, but cruise around 5 mph ... They can dive for about 15 minutes between breaths ... A month-long cruise gets humpbacks from summer feeding areas in Alaska to winter breeding areas in Hawaii and Mexico ... February and March are the best months to whale watch ...

Newborn calves weigh in at 3,000 pounds ... A whale birth has rarely been documented ... Neither has mating ... Gestation is 10 to 12 months ... Hawaiian population before commercial whaling, 1905: 15,000; by 1966: 1,000; Today, after endangered species status of 1970s: 7,000 ... Humpbacks do not have vocal cords, and how they produce their songs is unknown ... Songs are made up of phrases and last 6 to 18 minutes ... Feeding takes place in Alaska; they use reserves to migrate and do not feed in Hawaii ... They wean their calves here.

SHARKS

Hawaii has 40 species, ranging from the 8-inch pygmy to the 50-foot whale shark ... Maui has had 3 shark attacks over 12 years, including one fatality ... Cars pose a much greater risk to people than do sharks ... About eight species are seen near shore: reef blacktip, Galapagos, reef whitetip, scalloped hammerhead, blacktip, gray reef, sandbar, and tiger ... Tiger sharks are the biggest, reaching 18 feet, and the most dangerous ... Tigers range from island to island in Hawaii ... Sharks can hear and smell over a distance of 2 miles ... They can also detect prey by sensing electromagnetic fields ... Sharks only bite humans by mistake ... oops ...

To avoid sharks: Swim with a buddy ... Stay out of the water at dawn and dusk, when sharks feed near shore ... Don't bleed in the water, or enter with open cuts ... Stay out of murky water and away from streams ... Don't splash around or wear shiny jewelry ... Stay away from spear fishermen ... And, as if you need this one, do not provoke or harass a shark.

SEA TURTLES

Three species are native to Hawaii: green, hawksbill, and leatherback … Life-spans are unknown, but they start dating after age 25 … Turtles are featured in petroglyphs and Hawaiian mythology … Green turtles are the most common; vegetarians, weighing 200 pounds, they migrate hundreds of miles every several years to mate and nest in the French Frigate Shoals, which are in the northwestern part of the Hawaiian Archipelago … Hawksbills are endangered, with perhaps only 50 adult females left in Hawaii; one of the few nesting grounds is Ma'alaea Bay … Directed by starlight and moonlight, hawksbills nest on beaches; efforts are underway to modify coastal electrical lighting that has confused them, causing deaths … Leatherbacks can be 8-feet long and weigh up to a ton; you'll find them in deep offshore waters feeding on jellyfish.

HAWAIIAN SPINNER DOLPHIN

Spinners swim close to shore during the day … No one knows for sure why they corkscrew when leaping from the water … They go out at night to deeper water to feed on squid and small fish … Their diurnal migrations are opposite those of sharks, their main predator ... Life-span is around 20 years … Gestation period is 10 to 12 months … Calves stay with their mothers for 7 months after birth … Mothers give birth every 2 or 3 years … Marine debris and boats, along with shoreline development, pose the greatest threat to the spinners … Other dolphins is Hawaiian waters include, bottlenose and spotted … Some of the best places to see spinners are Lanai and Little Beach … Let them come to you, and don't chase after them … These are wild animals.

NENE

The Hawaiian goose, is the state bird … It's the rarest goose in the world … Do not feed them … Most likely sightings are at the Halemau'u Trail and Kolua Cabin, Haleakala … They'll come to you, don't go after them … Observe nene crossing signs when driving; they're for real.

Nene

MONK SEALS

One of only two native Hawaiian mammals … The other is the hoary bat; sorry people … Only 1,300 Hawaiian monk seals remain, and they are endangered … The Caribbean monk seal became extinct in 1952 … Most monk seals live in the northwest Hawaiian Archipelago … If you see a monk seal "hauled-out," it's a local; they live where they are born … Stay at least 100 feet from a beached seal … Old monk seals are 25 to 30 years … Pups are about 3 feet and 30 pounds at birth … Six weeks later, at 200 pounds, they're on their own … Sharks are their main predators—but marine debris and habitat destruction historically has been more deadly.

CORAL

Reefs may look like rocks, but coral is actually colonies of tiny animals that are related to sea anemones … They have cylindrical bodies called polyps that secrete stony cups of limestone around themselves … Corals have developed over 500 million years … Tender moment: That oily shimmer sometimes in the water is coral climaxing, as part of its reproductive process… Home for coral: between the 30th latitudes, in saltwater less than 300 feet deep … Coral comes in many shapes, like cauliflower, lobe, rice, mushroom, and finger … Called the rain forest of the sea, some old-growth coral is 200 years old … Thank coral for white-sand beaches … 80 per cent of reefs in the United States are in Hawaii … Don't touch the living coral.

ET CETERAS

There are no native Hawaiian reptiles or amphibians … Used to be 140 native Hawaiian birds; 70 are now extinct, 30 are endangered, and 12 are on the brink of extinction … Hawaii's landmass is .2% of the United States' total; 75% of the country's plant and bird extinctions have occurred here … One-quarter of the fish you see snorkeling are found only in Hawaii.

climate

Weather webcam: www.hawaiiweathertoday.com

Weather phone: *Maui, 808-866-944-5025*
                        Lanai, 808-565-6063
                        Molokai, 808-522-2477

RAINFALL (PER YEAR)

Kaupo coast 12"
Kihei 15"
Lahaina 17"
Kahului 21"
Kula 23"
Kapalua 31"
Haleakala 57"
Hana 83"
Iao Valley/West Maui Mountains 200"
Hanawi Reserve/East Rain Forests 350"

Mauka, or mountain, showers occur any time of the year, mostly on windward slopes and valleys. In ancient Maui, several dozen different types of rain were identified. Maui's latitude is 20° 50', north, which is south of the Tropic of Cancer. The climate is subtropical, with average humidity of 56 to 72 percent.

TEMPERATURES (TYPICAL, DEGREES FAHRENHEIT)

	Summer (hi/lo)	Winter (hi/lo)
Lahaina	87/77	80/70
Kahului	85/75	79/65
Kihei	89/79	82/72
Hana	84/74	78/64
Kula	82/64	66/45
Haleakala	65/45	52/29

*Ocean temperature is in the mid- to high-70s—
refreshing upon entry, but instantly comfortable.*

Keanae YMCA Camp

WINDS

Trade winds blow from the northeast, from 7- to 28-days per month, with the highest frequency coming in June. Kihei and Ka'anapali are the most sheltered from trade winds, and their accompanying storms. The windiest spots are Ma'alaea and Kahului, where the winds are funneled across the isthmus. The Kaupo coast and Hana get direct winds, but are not subject to accelerated winds caused by the funneling effect. Wind speeds average 12 mph, lightest during the winter, but gusts of 25-to-30 mph are common. Winds on Haleakala can reach hurricane force. Kona winds come from the southwest, most often in the winter. *The Hawaiians have some 40 different names for the winds on the various parts of the island.*

SURF

During the winter, surf is largest on the eastern shores, reaching more than 20 feet near Paia. The pattern shifts during the summer, when western shores of Kihei and Lahaina get their seasonally high surf—the Kona surf. North shores and the southern coast have active coastal surf year round. Maui has more than 80 accessible beaches, with more miles of swimming beach than any other island, including the Big Island which is five-times bigger. *When Hawaiians speak of the eight seas, they are referring to the channels that separate all the islands, which all have different characteristics.*

THE GREEN FLASH

In Hawaii, conditions are optimal for observing the green—or emerald—flash, the illusive burst of color that occurs at times just as the sun settles into the horizon. Scientists say green wavelengths of color separate from orange and red wavelengths, as they are bent, prismlike, around the curvature of the earth. Has to be on a hazeless, flat horizon. Whatever, the green flash is rare and fortuitous.

WHAT TO DO IN 'BAD' WEATHER

TOO WINDY ... GO TO:
> Valley Isle, TH11-TH14; or to Sunny South, TH1-TH7.

TO RAINY ...GO TO:
> Sunny South, TH1-TH6; or Valley Isle, TH10-TH12; or Haleakala, TH48 through TH52. Or see *Museums and Attractions in Resource Links.*

TOO HOT ... GO TO:
> Valley Isle, TH16-TH20; Windward Coast, TH21-TH24; Hana Highway, TH37 to TH41; or Haleakala, TH45-TH47

TOO MUGGY ... GO TO:
> Valley Isle, TH16-TH20; or Haleakala, TH45-TH47

TAKE ADVANTAGE OF CLEAR WEATHER, GO TO:
> Valley Isle, TH15-TH20; or Windward Coast, TH22-TH25; or Hana Highway, TH36-TH41; or Haleakala, TH46; or Outer Islands, TH53-TH55

PACKLIST

*Maui is a shopper's paradise. You may prefer to arrive with
just the basics and leave dressed head-to-toe Hawaiian style.
Shop Wailea, Kaanapali or Makawao for upscale resortwear
or load the cart at WalMart, the Lahina Cannery Mall or
Kaahumanu Center, where there's plenty of aloha wear
and inexpensive T-shirts to bring home to friends.*

ONE-WEEK VACATION

Shoes
> Slippers (a.k.a. zoris, go-aheads, thongs, slappers, flip-flops)
> Plane and hotel shoes (loafers, clean athletic shoes, or boat shoes)
> Hiking shoes (light weight hikers or cross-trainers)
> Surf shoe (optional, Teva or bootie-style)

Dress, or Khakis plus Aloha shirt for plane, hotels
Swimming suit
Two or three pair shorts
4 or 5 short sleeve tops, synthetic dri-fit
1 or 2 long sleeve tops (Haleakala hikers bring 2 for layering)
Gore-Tex shell, or equivalent, rain jacket
Fleece vest, lightweight (optional)
Sun hat
Sunglasses
Gloves (optional, for warmth on Haleakala, and to protect hands on lava hikes.)
Retractable hiking pole
Mask, fins, snorkel
Knapsack

> Antibiotic
> Band Aids
> Energy bars, emergency food
> Flashlight
> Handkerchief
> Mosquito repellant
> Small bottle hydrogen peroxide
> Sunscreen, lip balm
> Swiss Army knife
> Water bottles
> Water purification tablets or pump
> Whistle

FARMER'S MARKETS

Ka'ahumanu Shopping Center, Kahului
 Friday, 9:30 a.m. to 5 p.m., 877-3369
Kahului Shopping Center
 W 7:30 a.m. to 1 p.m., 573-1934
Keanae Open Market — 2nd Sat. every month
Honokowai Market, Kahana
 M, W, F, 7 a.m. to 11 a.m.
South Kihei Market (old Suda Store)
 M, W, F, 1:30 p.m. to 5:30 p.m.
Maui Swap Meet, Kahului, Pu'uhene Avenue
 Saturday, 7 a.m. to noon, 877-3100
Hana Farmers & Crafter's Market,
 Hasegawa Service Station
 Tu, W, Th, 10 a.m. to 4 p.m.

FREE HULA SHOWS

Whalers Village, Ka'anapali, 661-4567
 Mon., Tu, Wed., F, Sat, 7 p.m. to 8 p.m.
Lahaina Cannery Mall, 661-5304
 Sat and Sun, 1 p.m.(Keiki Hula);
 Tue and Th, 7 p.m. (Polynesian Dance)
Old Lahaina Center, 661-9913
 Tue., Fri., 11:30 a.m.
Ka'anapali Beach Hotel, 661-0011
 Nightly, 6:30 p.m. to 7:30 p.m.
Kapalua Shops, 669-3754
 Thu., 10 a.m. to 11 a.m.
Lahaina Center, 667-9216
 Wed., 2:30 p.m., Fri., 6 p.m.

LUAUS

Honuaula Luau, Marriott, 808-875-7710
Feast at Lele, 800-248-5828, 667-5353
Drums of Pacific, Hyatt, 808-667-4727
Old Lahaina Luau, 800-248-5828, 667-2998
Ka'anapali Sunset Luau at Black Rock,
 808-877-HULA

surfin' da Web

INFORMATIONAL LINKS:

www.co.maui.hi.us/ (county government)
www.gohawaii.com
www.lanai.com
www.hawaii.gov
www.hawaiiweathertoday.com (live cams)
www.hookele.com (cultural)
www.infomaui.com
www.mauidirect.com
www.kpoa.com (radio)
www.makena.com (golf)
www.maui.about.com
www.maui.net
www.maui.worldweb.com
www.mauiaccommodations.com
www.mauifishing.com
www.mauimapp.com
www.mauinews.com
www.molokai-hawaii.com
www.nps.gov/hale/ (Haleakala)
www.ohanapages.com
www.spotlighthawaii.com
www.tnc.org/hawaii (Nature Conservancy)
www.visitmaui.com
www.visitmolokai.com
www.hawaii-forest.com
www.windsurfari.com
www.trailblazertravelbooks.com
www.hawaiitrails.org
www.hawaiistate.hi.us/dlnr
www.hi.sierraclub.org
www.thisweek.com
www.bestplaceshawaii.com
www.hawaii-nation.org/
www.alternative-hawaii.com
www.maui-golf.com/
www.pacificislandbooks.com
www.surfinggoatdairy.com
www.muleride.com
www.hawaiianbeachrentals.com

LINK CALABASH

www.trailblazerhawaii.com
www.surfingmavericks.com/xx105
www.mauiwedding.net
www.mauimenusonline.com
www.madeinmaui.com
www.hotelmolokai.com
www.mauinokaoi.net
www.mauihi.com
www.mauioceancenter.com
www.muleride.com (Molokai)
www.bluehawaiian.com
www.lanairesorts.com
www.hawaiianair.com
www.maui.cc.com
www.lanaionline.com
www.mavsurfer.com/frank_quirarte/gallery
www.hotellanai.com
www.aloha-hawaii.com
www.pacificwhale.org
www.banana.ifa.hawaii.edu
www.extremesportsmaui.com
www.actionsportsmaui.com
www.mauioceancenter.com
www.mauiprincess.com

Trailblazer KIDS

The Hawaiian word keiki (KAY-key) means both 'child' and also the green shoot of a new banana plant. Bananas are plants, not trees, and each year a new generation must be nurtured to maturity, just like children.

In Hawaii, children are reared not only by the family, but also by the ohana—the extended family of 'aunties' and 'uncles' that make up the community. In recent years on Maui, this ohana-based rearing has been reinforced by new, 'immerging' schools, which further not only the Hawaiian language, but also traditional crafts and customs. Activities are listed in order of trailhead numbers.

ALL-STAR ATTRACTIONS

Maui Ocean Center, TH9, page 47
The best aquarium in Hawaii—a world-class attraction.

Hawaii Nature Center-Iao Needle, TH25, page 92
The state park, county gardens, and the center's hands-on museum combine for Maui's best tropical experience.

Hana Highway, Driving Tour, page 111
A rain forest thrill ride with multiple sideshows. Paia town for picnic food.

Pi'ilanihale Heiau-Kahanu Gardens, TH39, page 128
The greatness of ancient Hawaii lives on.

Haleakala National Park, TH46, page 156
Take a trip to a desert island two miles in the sky.

Molokini Island, TH53, page 177
A former cone volcano is now a natural marine aquarium, just few miles offshore

Lanai, TH54, page 181
Ride the ferry from Lahaina and take a vacation within a vacation.

KEIKI POOLS

Ahihi Cove, TH2, page 32
Schools of snorkelers gather since it's right on the road.

Ulua Beach, TH6, page 40
Sits in the middle of other pretty Wailea Resorts beaches.

Charley Young Beach Park, TH7, page 41
Coco palm terraces make this slightly more attractive than other Kamaole beaches.

Koieie Loko Ia Fishpond, TH8, page 44
Ancient, restored fishpond is next to the humpback whale center.

Olowalu Beach, TH12, page 61
Tour boats anchor offshore; flat-sand entry is easy.

Pu'unoa (Baby) Beach, TH13, page 65
Where Lahaina's moms & dads go. Sweet.

Honolua Marine Preserve, TH16, page 72
Fabulously fishy coral. Storm runoff can muddy the waters.

Baby Baldwin Beach, TH30, page 101
A tropical swimming pool with a sand grandstand.

Pools of Oheo, TH44, page 137
This national park can be a zoo during prime conditions.

NATURE WALKS

Wetlands Boardwalk, TH9, page 45
Bet the kids run down the long ramp.
Dragon's Teeth, TH15, page 69
Waves explode on a weirdly jagged reef. (Watch out.)

Nakalele Blowhole, TH17, page 74
A short adventure walk to a saltwater geyser. (Stay back.)
Ohai Loop Trail, TH18, page 76
Mellow coastal bluff trail on a wild coast.
Swinging Bridges, TH23, page 89
Indiana Jones-type jungle adventure for hearty kids. (Not during rains.)
Tropical Gardens of Maui, TH25, page 92
The bridge over the stream adds to the green adventure (admission is charged).
Twin Falls, TH35, page 119
Easy wide path up a garden, alongside white water.
Garden of Eden, TH36, page 122
Kids will love the big parrots at this "Jurassic" park. (Admission charged.)
Keanae Arboretum, TH37, page 124
An inviting path into a park with massive trees.
Pipiwai Trail, TH44, page 137
Waterfalls, bridges, and a bamboo forest are just the ticket for active families.

Sliding Sands Trail, TH46, page 159
Haleakala's signature hike. Don't forget the sunscreen and water.

A DAY AT THE BEACH
All the ingredients to log some towel time: normally safe swimming and wave play, with sand and a shoreline that will look good in the family album.

Big Beach, TH3, page 34
Maluaka Beach, TH4, page 35
Po'olenalena Beach, TH5, page 36
Keawakapu Beach, TH6, page 40
Pu'unoa (Baby) Beach, TH13, page 65
Kahekili Beach Park, TH14, page 67
Kapalua Beach, TH15, page 69
Baldwin Beach Park, TH31, page 102
Hamoa Beach, TH42, page 135

LITTLE WALKS TO BIG PLACES

McGregor Point vistas, TH11, page 56
Whale watch at sunset.
Lahaina Seawall, TH13, page 64
See seagoing Lahaina from land.

Lipoa Point, TH16, page 72
Look down on surfers, or go farther to a seascape.

Kahakuloa Head, TH20, page 78
A seaside perch to watch whales and birds.

Kukuipuka Heiau, TH22, page 87
Up steps to an airborne view.

Kahuna Point, TH34, page 109
Hidden down a rural road; home to Halehaku Heiau.

Fagan's Cross, TH41, page 132
A mini-workout to the best view of Hana.

White Hill, Red Hill, TH47, page 158
Get as high as possible on Haleakala.

Skyline Trail, TH47, page 162
Even the trailhead parking lot is high in the sky.

Huialoha Church, TH52, page 173
Grassy banks, wave or rock skipping along the little beach. Away from it all.

BEST PICNIC PARKS

Polo Beach, TH6, page 40
Nice shaded tables at the gateway to Wailea resort beaches.

Kamaole III Beach Park, TH7, page 41 *Get a plate lunch across the street and spend the day—plenty of locals do.*

Waipuilani Park, TH8, page 44
Tucked away in north Kihei, grassy expanse with lonely beach.

Haycraft Beach Park, TH9, page 47
A little secret down the street from Maui Ocean Center.

Olowalu Landing, TH12, page 60
No facilities, but this quiet spot has many pluses.

Launiupoko Beach Park, TH12, page 61
Pull off the road to tables under palms. Classic.

DT Fleming Beach Park, TH15, page 69
Locals and surfers gather. Don't count on swimming.

Waihe'e Beach Park, TH24, page 90
A forested beachside beauty that is off the tourist radar.

Kaumahina Wayside, TH37, page 123
This view park on the way to Hana was spruced up in 2005.

Waianapanapa State Park, TH40, page 130
Lots to do along Hana's most-scenic coastline. Spooky cave exploring.

Kipahulu Point Park, TH44, page 140

This is where world-traveler Charles Lindbergh wanted to end his days.
Rice Park, Driving Tour, Page 150
Great view from Kula. Easy pull off.
Polipoli Springs, TH47, page 162
A pleasing high-forest getaway that won't seem like Maui.

FAMILY FREEBIES

Hawaiian Islands Humpback Whale Sanctuary, TH8, page 44
Also snorkel in the saltwater pond and visit little Vancouver Monument.

Lahaina Town, TH13, page 62
A seagoing tourist town with both glitz and history. Let 'em run under the big banyan tree. See the hula show daily at Lahaina Cannery Mall.
For the Birds, Ka'anapali, TH14, page 66, 808-661-1234
The luscious grounds of the Hyatt Regency are home to penguins, flamingos, swans, parrots, and a pair of Indonesian cranes. Stop by and say Aloha.

Maui Swap Meet, TH28, page 97
Everybody can find a personal souvenir and a tempting snack.
Kanaha Beach Park, TH29, page 98
Take a ringside seat for the windsurfing and kiteboarding spectacle.
Waianapanapa State Park, TH40, page 130
Picnic, hike, swim–either in the ocean or a fresh pond.

HAWAIIAN HISTORY ADVENTURES

King's Trail, TH1, page 29
Prepare for an adventure; best example of an ancient Hawaiian highway.
Koieie Loko Ia Fishpond, TH8, page 44
Swim around in a pool made centuries ago.
Olowalu Petroglyphs, TH12, page 58
Maui's best ancient rock pictures, and among Hawaii's best.
Kepaniwai Heritage Gardens, TH25, page 92
See the different countries that combine to make Hawaii at this garden park.
Historical Buildings Tour, TH27, page 95
The Baldwin House Museum still reflects its former residents. Picnic under the trees.
Keanae Village-Wailua, TH37, page 122
Agrarian Old Hawaii is on display. Not tourist towns. Fresh buttery banana bread for sale.
Pi'ilanihale Heiau, TH39, page 129
A temple rising from the jungle.
Nu'uanu Landing-petroglyphs, TH51, page 170
Some of Maui's first arrivals left their mark.

Tedeschi Winery, TH47, page 164
King Kalakua loved the parklike grounds, high in cowboy country. Cool off those sunburns.
Nuʻuanu Landing-petroglyphs, TH51, page 170
Some of Maui's first arrivals left their mark.

A BAG OF TRICKS

Atlantis Submarine Ride, Lahaina, 800-548-6262
Yes, a real under water journey in the fish-filled coral waters.
Ulalena show at the Maui Theater, Lahaina, 661-9913
Hula and chanting—the old song and dance— tell the history of Hawaii.
Lahaina-Kaʻanapali Railroad (Sugar Cane Train), 661-0089
A 12-mile, narrated ride on vintage open-air cars may be the fastest thing over the land during heavy traffic periods. One 400-foot long trestle crosses high over a stream valley.
Rooftop Golf, Kaʻanapali, 661-2000
Atop the Embassy Suites resort is a putt-putt course with a birdie view.

Zoo Maui, Kula, 878-2189
More than 100 creatures reside in the mountain air, including the Hawaiian nene and an African giraffe. Open Saturdays and by appointment.
Hawaii Experience Domed Theater, Lahaina, 661-7111, 661-8314
Pick a rainy or lazy day and see Hawaii from underneath a three-story tall dome—Maui's Haleakala, Kauaʻi's Waimea Canyon, humpback whales and other wildlife.

Resource Links

PUBLIC AGENCIES
COUNTY OF MAUI
Department of Parks & Recreation, 270-7230, 270-7383
Aquatics Division, 270-6137
Beach Parks, camping, 270-7389
Recreation Program, 270-7979
Office of Economic Development, 270-7710

STATE OF HAWAII
Department of Land and Natural Resources, 984-8110
Aquatic Resources Division, 243-5294
Boating and Ocean Recreation, 243-5824, 587-1882
Enforcement, 984-8110
Kanaha Pond, Forestry and Wildlife Division, 984-8100
Historic Preservation Division, 243-5169
Land Division, 984-8103
Natural Area Reserves, 873-3506
Parks, Camping, 984-8109
Na Ala Hele Trails, 873-3508 or 3509
Waianapanapa Park caretaker, 248-4843
Volunteer Services, 586-7200

FEDERAL
Haleakala National Park, 572-4400, 572-4459
Kipahulu District, 248-7375
Weather, 877-5111
Road Closures 986-1200
Kealia Pond Wildlife Refuge, 875-1582

TRANSPORTATION
See Getting Around Maui *in the front of this book for more travel information.*

AIR FROM THE MAINLAND
American, 800-433-7300, 244-5522
Hawaiian, 871-6132, 800-367-5320
Delta, 800-325-1999
Northwest, 800-225-2525
Alaska, 800-252-7522
United, 800-241-6522

MOLOKAI AND LANAI

Commercial Flyer, 888-266-3597
go! Airlines, 888-435-9462
Molokai Air Shuttle, 567-6847
Hawaiian Air, 567-6510
Island Air, 567-6115
Pacific Wings, 567-6814

CAR RENTALS

Alamo, 800-327-9633, 871-6235
Avis, 800-321-3712, 871-7575
Budget, 800-527-7000, 871-8811
Dollar, 800-800-4000, 877-2731
Hertz, 800-654-3011, 877-5167
Aloha Cars-R-Us, 800-655-7989
Aloha Rent a Car, 877-452-5642
BioBeetle, 877-8736121
Maui Cruisers, 249-2319

LANAI

Dollar, 565-7227
Adventure Lanai EcoCentre, 565-7373

MOLOKAI

Island Kine Auto Rental, 1-866-527-7368, 553-5242
Budget, 567-6877, 871-8811
Dollar, 567-6156

PUBLIC BUSES, Maui Bus, 270-7511, or Robert's Hawaii, 871-4838

BIKE RENTALS, 874-0068, 661-9005, 877-7744

FERRIES

Also ask for car rentals and tours.

Expeditions (Lanai), 800-695-2624, 661-3756
Maui Princess Cruises, 877-500-6284
Molokai-Maui Ferry, 866-307-6524

WEST MAUI EXPRESS (SHOPPER SHUTTLE)

Connects all of West Maui, 877-7308
AIRPORT SHUTTLE, 875-8070, 661-6667, 800-977-2605
TAXIS, 244-7278, 874-8294, 665-0003

VISITOR INFORMATION
Also contact Public Organizations.

Maui Visitors Bureau, 800-525-6284, 244-3530
Maui Chamber of Commerce, 871-7711
County Office of Economic Development, 270-7710
Activity Owners Association of Hawaii, 800-398-9698
Destination Lanai, 800-947-4774, 565-7600
Molokai Visitors Association, 800-800-6367, 553-3876
Weather forecast, 877-5111, 877-3477
Lanai, 565-6033; Molokai, 552-2477

SUPPLEMENTAL MAPS
Free maps are available in shopping centers, on the plane, and from the visitors bureau. Trailblazer's maps and directions are enough for you to get around the island, but a street map and detailed, all-purpose map is a good idea. (A GPS and USGS topo maps, while informational, are not useful for hiking. The hardest part here is finding the trailhead. After that, rough, dense topography requires that you stay on trail and turn back if you lose the trail. On coastal walks, you just need to know where the ocean is.)

Map of Maui, the Valley Isle, University of Hawaii Press. Full Color Topographic,
2840 Kolowalu Street, Honolulu, HI, 96822. *Best all-purpose map. Indexes place names and shows unpaved roads.*
Maui Recreation Map, Department of Land and Natural Resources, 984-8100.
Available free. Shows hunter's forest reserves, state hiking trails.
The Ready Mapbook of Maui County, Odyssey Publishing, 888-729-1074,
935-0092. *Best street map. In book form.*
Maui County Bicycle Map, Maui Visitors Bureau, 244-3530
Maui County Shoreline Access Guide, County Parks Department, 270-7389
Map of the Neighbor Islands, Hawaii, Maui & Kauai, Compass Maps,
800-441-6277 *Fold-up street map. Needs update, includes neighbor islands.*
Nelles Maui, Molokai, Lanai;. Nellesl.verlagt-online.de *German company. Good all-purpose map, available in bookstores. Has street details.*

NEWSPAPERS AND NEWSLETTERS
Maui News (daily), 800-827-0347, 244-3981
Centerpiece Magazine, 242-2787
Haleakala Times, 579-8020
Ho'omalu O Ka Wa'a (Hana Cultural Center) 248-8622
Ka Waiola (Maui Tomorrow), 877-2462
Keepers of the Coast (Surfrider Foundation), 243-0858
Lahaina News (weekly), 667-7866

newspapers and newsletters, cont'd—
Maui's Gold Coast Magazine, 572-5523
Maui Magazine, 661-1155
Maui Outdoor News, Maui Scene (dining, entertainment), 242-6350
Maui Times (bi-monthly), 661-3786
Maui Weekly, 875-1700
Voice of Haleakala, 572-4400
Lanai Times, (monthly), 565-6538
The Dispatch (Molokai), 552-2781
Molokai Advertiser-News, 558-8253

MUSEUMS & ATTRACTIONS
Alexander & Baldwin Sugar Museum, 871-8058
Bailey House Museum, 244-3326
Baldwin Museum and Courthouse, 661-3262
Hale Paʻahao prison, 667-1985
Hana Cultural Center, 248-8622
Hawaii Experience Domed Theater, 661-7111
Hawaii Nature Center, Iao Valley, 244-6500
Hui Noeau Visual Arts Center (Baldwin Estate), 572-6560
Humpback Whale National Marine Sanctuary, 800-831-4888
Keawalaʻi Congregational Church, 879-5557
Marriott Luau, 661-6887
Maui Ocean Center, 270-7000
Maui Swap Meet, 877-3100, 242-0240
Maui Tropical Plantation 244-7643
Molokai Museum and Cultural Center, 567-6436
Piʻilanihale Heiau, 248-8912
Lahaina Kaʻanapali Railroad (Sugar Cane Train), 661-0089
Tedeschi Winery, 878-1266, 878-6058
Ulalena Show at Maui Theater, 661-9913
Whale Museum, 661-5992
Wo Hing Museum, 661-4020

GARDENS
Aliʻi Kula Lavender, 878-3004, 878-8090
Garden of Eden, 572-9899
Kahanu National Tropical Botanical Garden, 248-8912
Kula Botanical Garden, 878-1715
Maui Nui Botanical Garden, 249-2798
Tropical Gardens of Maui 244-3085

PRESERVATION AND CULTURAL GROUPS

Call ahead of your visit to arrange to volunteer.
Coastal Lands Conservation, 538-6616
Community Work Day Program, 877-2524
Fishpond Ohana Restoration, 879-7926
Friends of Kukuipuka, 242-4931
Friends of Moku'ula, 661-3659
Hana Cultural Center, 248-8622
Hawaiian Islands Humpback Whale
        National Marine Sanctuary, 800-831-4888, 879-2818
Hawaiian Nation, 242-6840
Hawaiian Natural History Association, 985-6051
Hui Noeau Visual Arts Center, 572-6560
Malama Kahakai (coastal preservation), 579-9802
Maui Arts & Cultural Center, 242-2787
Maui Coastal Land Trust, 244-5263
Maui Cultural Lands (Malama Honokowai), 572-8085
Maui Historical Society, 244-3326
Maui Museums Association, 871-8058
Pacific Whale Foundation, 800-942-5311, 249-8811
Project Kaeo, projectkaeo.blogspot.com
Protect Kaho'olawe Ohana, 573-7819
Sierra Club, 579-9802, 573-3454; hikes, 573-4147
Surfrider Foundation, 800-743-7873, 243-0858
Lanai, The Nature Conservancy 565-7430

RECREATIONAL OUTFITTERS, TOURS

BICYCLE
Cruiser Phil's, 893-2332
Maui Mountain Cruisers, 800-232-6248
Haleakala Bike Company, 888-922-2453, 575-9575
Maui Downhill, 800-535-2453, 871-2155
Mountain Riders Bike Tours, 800-706-7700, 242-973
South Maui Bicycles, 874-0068; West Maui Cycles, 661-9005

ZIPLINES
Skyline Eco-Adventures, 878-8400

SPORT FISHING
Lucky Strike Charters, 800-474-4606
Hawaii Division of Aquatic Resources, 243-5294
Maui Fishing Charters, 877-661-0338

HELICOPTERS

A number of reliable companies fly Maui's skies, but you won't find a safer, more luxurious, or more adventurous ride than on Blue Hawaiian Helicopters. Aboard the quiet Eco-Star, you can cruise from Molokai to the Big Island, from Haleakala to the lush valleys Hana Highway in between. 1-800-745-2583, 871-8444

HIKES

Sierra Club, 573-4147, 538-6616 *Contact for schedule of hikes.*
D. T. Fleming Arboretum, 572-1097 *Free tours Ulupalakua.*
East Maui Irrigation (EMI) waiver, 579-9516
  Waivers for Hana Highway area for Sierra Club and Mauna Ala hikes
Hawaii Nature Center, Iao Valley, 244-6500
Hike Maui, 879-5270, 866-324-6284 *These guys are pros.*
Kapalua Resort Center, 665-4386, 665-5454 (shuttle)
  Free coastal & mountain trials on resort land. Free shuttle.
Kipahulu Ohana, 248-8558 *Cultural, botanical walks near Pools of Oheo*
Mauna Ala Hiking Club, Box 329, Pu'uene, HI 96784, 875-8171
  Join for $5 ($7 with card) and get EMI waiver to hike Hana Highway
The Nature Conservancy, 572-7849 *Waikomo Ridge*
Olowalu Culural Preserve, 633-0378 *Volunteer in historic valley.*
Waihee Valley Plantation, 244-2120; Wailuku Water Co., 244-7051
  Looks like the Swinging Bridges hikes are closed for now.

HORSES

Molokai Mule Ride, 800-567-7550
Ironwood Ranch, Kapalua, 669-4991
Piiholo Ranch, 357-5544
Makena Stables, 879-0244
Mendes Ranch, Kahakuloa, 871-5222
Pony Express Tours, Kula, 667-2200

KAYAKS, CANOES

Hana Maui Sea Sports (also snorkel, surf), 248-7711, 264-9566
Makena Kayak, 879-8426
Maui Ultra Dive (also surf), Kihei, 875-4004
South Pacific Kayaks, Kihei, 800-776-2326, 875-4848

SURFING

You get a bang for your buck hiring a surfing guide.
Girls Gone Surfing, 800-280-0103
Goofy Foot, Lahaina, 244-9283, 229-6737
Honolua Surf, 891-8229, 661-8848
Surf Dog Maui, 250-7873

surfing, cont'd—

      Outrageous Adventures, Lahaina, 1-877-339-1400, 669-1400

      Second Wind, 800-936-7787

      Soul Surfing Maui, 870-7873

SNORKEL AND SCUBA

Ask about boat size and cancellation policy.

      Maui Dive Shop, 879-1775; Kihei, 879-3388, 879-1533;

            Kahana, 661-6166, 669-3800; Ka'anapali, 661-5117;

            Lahaina, 661-5388; Ma'alaea, 244-5514

      B&B Scuba, 875-2861

      Quicksilver, 662-0075

      Boss Frogs, Kihei (ask for other locations) 875-4477 x16

      Ed Robinson's Diving (scuba), 800-635-1273, 879-3584

      Ehukai Catamaran, Lanai (also whale watch), 871-0626

      Extended Horizons (scuba), 667-0611

      Hawaiian Rafting Adventures, 661-7333

      Lahaina Divers (scuba), 800-998-3483, 667-7496

      Maui Undersea Adventures, 874-2276

      Mike Severns Diving (scuba), 879-6596

      Snorkel Bob, 879-7449, 661-4421

      Trilogy, 888-874-5649

WINDSURFING/KITEBOARDING/STAND UP PADDLE

      Action Sports Maui, 871-5857

      Hawaiian Sailboarding Techniques (HST), 871-5423

      Hi-Tech Surf Sports, 871-7766

      Proflight Paragliding (Haleakala), 874-5433

      Second Wind, 877-7467

WHALE WATCHING, CRUISES

Also see Best Of section for places to view whales from land.
The ferries to Molokai and Lanai double as whale-watching excursions.

      Expeditions, Lahaina, 661-3756

      Maui-Lahaina Princess,

            Island Marine Institute 800-275-6969, 661-8397

      Pacific Whale Foundation, 800-942-5311, 249-8811

      Blue Water Rafting, 879-7238

      Explorer, Lahaina, 661-5550

      Gemini, Lahaina, 669-0508

      Pride of Maui (also snorkel), 242-0955

      Teralani, Ka'anapali, 661-0365

      Ultimate Whale Watch, 667-5678

GOLF

Makena Golf Course, 891-4000
Kapalua Golf, 888-227-6054
Dunes at Maui Lani, 873-7911, ext. 2
Waiehu Municipal Golf Course, 244-5934

MOLOKAI

Damien Tours, Kalaupapa, 567-6171
Halawa Falls Cultural Hike, 553-4355
Historical Hike West Molokai, 800-274-9303
Kalaupapa National Historical Park, 567-6802
Molokai Mule Ride, Kalaupapa, 800-567-7550, 567-6088
The Nature Conservancy 553-5236
Molokai Ranch Hawaii, 877-726-4656, 552-2741
Pu'u O Hoku Ranch, 558-8109
Molokai Bicycle, 553-3931
Snorkeling with Bill Kapuni, 553-9867

LANAI

The Nature Conservancy, 565-7430
Adventure Lanai Ecocentre, 565-7373
Luaiwa Petroglyphs, 565-7600
Munro Trail, 565-7600

Where to stay

Calling is a good way to find out which places have aloha. Inquire about amenities and location specifics, and be sure to ask if you are getting the lowest rate. Almost all listings are oceanfront or ocean view. Prices vary by region, as noted below. Some luxury resort hotels are more than $400 per night; economy-minded travelers should be able to find a place for about $75 per night. Some condominiums have monthly rates. Camping and rustic cabins are available for much less. For island-wide bed & breakfast referrals, try Hawaii Bed & Breakfast, 800-262-9912.

All area codes are 808 unless toll-free numbers are noted.
(H) = Hotel, resort, (C) = Condos (B) = Bed & Breakfast, cottages, (A) = Rental agency

SUNNY SOUTH (MAKENA, WAILEA, KIHEI, NORTH KIHEI)

Best swimming beaches and sunny weather. Arid surroundings. Wailea is a high-end resort strip. Kihei has mid-range condos and resorts, most across the road from beach parks. North Kihei's beaches aren't as popular, and the area is quieter and often more economically priced.

MAKENA
Makena Landing (B) 879-6286
Maui Prince Hotel (H) 800-321-6248, 874-1111

WAILEA
Four Seasons (H) 874-8000
Grand Wailea Resort (H) 800-888-6100
Outrigger Wailea Resort (H) 1-800-688-7444, 874-7981
Polo Beach Club, Wailea Eluua Village (C) 879-1595

KIHEI
Condominium Rentals Hawaii (A)
    800-367-5242
Hale Pau Hana (C) 800-367-6036
Kihei Beach Resort (C) 800-367-6034
Kihei Maui Vacations (A) 800-541-6284
Kihei Surfside (C) 800-367-5240
Mana Kai Maui (C) 879-1561

Maui Kamaole (C) 800-367-5242,
    874-5151
Maui Parkshore (C) 879-1600
Maui Vista (H) 879-7966
Royal Mauian Resort (H) 879-1263
What a Wonderful World (B)
    879-9103

NORTH KIHEI
Aston Maui Lu (H) 800-321-2558
Kauhale Makai, (C) 879-8888
Kealia Resort (H) 879-0952
Kihei Holiday (C) 879-9228

Koa Resort (C) 800-541-3060,
Luana Kai Resort (H) 879-1268
Maui Schooner (H) 879-5247
Waipuilani (C) 879-1458

VALLEY ISLE (Lahaina, Ka'anapali, Kahana, Kapalua)

Excellent swimming beaches. Tropical greenery inland. Lahaina is a quaint but active tourist town, with moderate to high room rates. Ka'anapali is a high-end resort strip. Kahana has mid- to high-end condos and resorts, packed together but with back-door ocean settings. Kapalua has higher-end resorts and nice cove beaches. Weather is sunniest in Lahaina-Ka'anapali.

Lahaina

Aloha Lani Inn (B) 572-5642
Lahaina Inn (H) 800-669-3444
Lahaina Roads, Pu'upana (C) 800-669-6284
Lahaina Shores Resort (H) 800-642-6284, 661-4835
Makai Inn (B) 661-0410
Aina Nalu Resort (C) 800-462-6262
Pioneer Inn (H) 800-457-5457
Plantation Inn (H) 667-9225

Ka'anapali

Aston-Maui Ka'anapali Villas (C) 800-922-7866
Hyatt Regency (H) 800-233-1234, 661-1234
Ka'anapali Beach Hotel (H) 800-262-8450
Sheraton Maui (H) 800-782-9488
Westin Maui (H) 888-625-4949, 667-2525

Kahana-Kapalua

Hale Kai (C) 800-446-7307
Hale Napili (C) 669-6184
Honokeana (C) 800-237-4948
Kahana Sunset (C) 800-669-1488
Kahana Village (C) 800-824-3065
Mauian Hotel on Napili (H)
    800-367-5034
Napili Bay (C) 888-661-7200
Napili Sunset (C) 800-447-9229
Napili Surf Beach Resort (C)
    800-541-0638
Polynesian Shores (C)
    800-433-6284
Ritz-Carlton (H) 800-262-8440

WINDWARD COAST (Ma'alaea, Wailuku, Kahului, Paia)

Yes, it can be windy. Kahului and Wailuku are working towns, with some resorts on the bay; rates are low to moderate. Ma'alaea is a long beach; rates are moderate. All windward coast listings are centrally located, most convenient for trailblazers who plan to spend days exploring. Paia has mostly B&Bs in quiet settings, with moderate rates. Weather is not the sunniest, but beaches are good. Also there's quick access to the Hana Highway and Haleakala.

MA'ALAEA

Kanai A Nalu (C) 244-3911
Ma'alaea Bay Rentals (A) 800-367-6084
Ma'alaea Surf (C) 800-423-7953
Noni Lani Cottages (C) 800-733-2688

KAHULUI-WAILUKU

Banana Bungalow Hostel (B) 244-5090
Maui Seaside Hotel (H) 800-560-5552
Northshore Inn (H) 242-8999
Old Wailuku Inn (H) 244-5897

PAIA

Ho'okipa Bayview Cottage (B) 800-258-6770
Inn at Mama's Fish House (H) 800-860-4852
Kua Cove Plantation (B) 579-8988
Maui Vacation Properties (A) 800-782-6105
Spyglass House, Beach House (B) 800-475-6695

KULA

Cool country settings are away from beaches and resorts.

Country Garden Cottage (B) 878-2858
Haikuleana (B) 575-2890
Hawaiian Islands B&B (B) 800-258-7895
Kula Lodge (H) 800-233-1535, 878-1535

Kula Lynn Farm (B) 878-6320
Malu Manu (B) 888-878-6161
Peace of Maui (B) 888-475-5045
Silver Cloud Ranch (B) 800-532-1111

HANA

A beautiful non-resort area, away from the rest of Maui. For quiet, outdoor adventures. Not as sunny. Rates range from economy to pricey.

Ala'Aina (B) 877-216-1733
Ekena Bed & Breakfast (B) 248-7047
Hamoa Bay Bungalows (B) 248-7884
Hana Ali'i Holidays (A) 800-548-0478
Hana Paradise Cottages 248-7746
Hana Oceanfront Cottages (C) 877-
Hotel Traavasa Hana (H) 855-868-7282
Kulani's Hideaway (B) 248-8234

Luana Spa Retreat, 248-8855
Tradewinds Cottage (B) 248-8980
Tree Houses of Hana (B) 248-7241

LANAI

Hotel Lanai, 800-795-7211, 565-7211 (moderately priced)
Jasmine House, Dreams Come True (B) 566-6961
Lanai City House (B) 565-6071
Four Seasons at Manele Bay, Lodge at Koele (H), 800-321-4666, 565-7300
Yellow House on the Corner (B) 565-7779

MOLOKAI

Hotel Molokai (H) 553-5347
Kahale Mala (B) 553-9001
Kaluakoi Villas (C) 800-525-1470, 800-367-5004, 552-2721
Kamalo Plantation (B) 558-8236
Molokai Friendly Isle Realty (A) 800-600-4158
Molokai Lodge (camp and lodge) 877-726-4656, 660-2710
Pu'umana-Pauwalu Beachfront Cottages (B) 800-673-0520
Sheraton Molokai-Kaupoa Villas (H) 877-726-4656, 660-2725

CAMPING & RUSTIC CABINS

County of Maui Beach Parks, 270-7389

Beach camping won't be a wilderness experience. Kanaha is good.
The county parks on Lanai and Molokai are excellent.

Molokai	Lanai
County of Maui, 553-3204	Hulopoe Beach Park, 565-3978
Hawaiian Homelands, 567-6104	
Molokai Ranch (private), 877-726-4656	

State Parks and Cabins, 984-8109; Molokai, 558-8150

Waianapanapa, Polipoli, Pala'au, Waialua

Waianapanapa has excellent beach cabins, although rustic, near Hana. Polipoli is a high-elevation cabin, forest location. Pala'au and Waialua are great places on Molokai.

Haleakala National Park, cabins, tents, and backpacking, 572-4400

Hosmer Grove and Oheo campgrounds;
Holua, Kapalaoa, Paliku cabins

Hosmer is high-elevation tent camping. Oheo is excellent beachside camping. The cabins are rustic and set in dramatic locations. Prepare for cold weather .

YMCA Camp Keanae, 248-8355;

Rustic cabins, dorms and tent sites available. Memorably beautiful ocean bluff location.

Where to eat

Cuisine may range from burgers to gourmet, and prices from cheap to swank, but these eateries are all island-style winners. Give them a call before you go to see if they meet your tastes. Not all serve dinner. (A special mahalo to Sue Kanegai for her tasteful tips.)

(C) Cheap or take-out (under $10)   (M) Moderate, family ($10-$20)   (P) Pricey, special occasion (over $20)

All area codes are 808.

WAILEA-KIHEI

Annie's Deli & Catering, Kihei (C) 875-0128
Da Kitchen, Kihei (C) 875-7782
Five Palms Beach Grill (M) 879-2607
Hapa's Brewhaus, Kihei (M) 879-9001
Hawaiian Moons Natural Foods (C) 875-4356
Joe's Bar & Grill, Wailea (M) 667-6636
SeaWatch, Wailea (M) 875-8080
Sushi Go!, Kihei (C) 875-8744
Tommy Bahama Café, Wailea (P) 875-9983

MA'ALAEA-LAHAINA-KAPALUA

Aloha Mixed Plate, Lahaina (C) 661-3322
Canoes, Lahaina (P) 661-0937
Cool Cat Cafe, Lahaina, (C) 667-0908
Erik's Seafood Grotto, Kahana (P) 669-4806
Gerard's, Lahaina (P) 661-8939
Honolua Store, Kapalua (C) 669-6128
Kimo's, Lahaina (P) 661-4811
Lahaina Coolers (M) 661-7082
Leodas Kitchen and Pie Shop, Olowalu (M) 667-2855
Ma'alaea Waterfront (P) 244-9028
Mama'a Ribs & Rotisserie, Kahana (C) 665-6262
Mango Grill & Bar, Lahaina (M) 667-1929
Plantation House, Kapalua (P) 669-6299
Roy's Kahana Bar & Grill (P) 669-6999

WAILUKU-KAHALUI

Ichiban Restaurant (C) 871-6977
Maui Bake Shop & Deli, Wailuku (C) 242-0064
Maui Mixed Plate, Kahului (C) 877-0706
Maui Tropical Plantaion (C) 244-7643
Mike's Restaurant, Wailuku (C)244-7888
Saigon Café, Wailuku (M) 243-9560
Sam Sato's, Wailuku (M) 244-7124
Tasty Crust Restaurant, (C) 244-0845

PAIA-KULA

Cafe Des Amis, Paia (M) 579-6323
Cafe Mambo & Picnics, Paia (C-M) 579-8021
Fresh Mint Vietnamese Vegetarian (M) 579-9144
Hali'imaile General Store (P) 572-2666
Komoda Store & Bakery, Makawao (C) 572-7261
Kula Lodge (P) 878-1535
Makawao Steak House (P) 572-8711
Mama's Fish House, Kuau (P) 579-8488
Mana Foods, Paia (C-M) 579-8078
Paia Fish Market (M) 579-8030
Pukulani Superette (C) 572-7616

ROAD TO HANA

Aunty Sandy's Banana Bread,
    Keanae, 248-8031
Pauwela Café (C) 575-9242

LANAI

Blue Ginger Café (M) 565-6363
Hotel Lanai (P) 565-4700
Pele's Garden (M) 565-9629
Tanigawa's (C) 565-6537

Tutu's Snack Shop (C) 248-8224
Travaasa Hana (P) 248-8211
Laulima Farms, Kipahulu (C)
    248-8669

MOLOKAI

Big Daddy's (M) 553-5841
Hotel Molokai (P) 553-5347
Kamuela's Cookhouse
    (M) 567-9655
The Neighborhood Store (C) 558-8498

STORES, GIFTS, ART, CRAFTS

Calasa Service, Kula, 878-1818
The Coffee Store, Kahului, 800-327-9661, 871-6860
David Waren Gallery, Makawao, 572-1288
Ed Lane, Kihei, 875-0828
Fabric Mart (Hawaiian galore), Kahului, 871-5770
Gallery Maui (Deborah Zaleski), Makawao, 572-8092
Gecko Trading Co. Botique, Makawao, 572-0249
Hasegawa General Store, Hana, 248-8231, 248-7079
Hot Island Glass, Makawao, 572-4527
Island Soap and Candleworks, Wailuku, 986-8383
Kaupo Store, 248-8054
Kula Marketplace, 878-2125
Lahaina Arts Society, 661-0111
Lahaina Cannery Mall, 661-5304
Made in Maui Association, 871-7711
Malia and Sons (wood carving), 757-0202
Maui Crafts Guild, Paia, 579-9697
Maui Creations, Kahului, 873-7955
Maui Grown Market (Rent-a-Dog), 579-9345
Maui Hands, Paia, 579-9245; Makawao, 572-5194
Pacific Green, Makawao, 573-2727
Ululani's By the Bay, Kahakuloa, 244-7151
Upcountry Harvest, Kula, 800-575-6470, 878-2824
Whalers Village, Ka'anapali, 661-4567

HAWAIIANOLOGISTS

Hawaiian quilts: Wailani Johanson, 661-0325
Steel guitar: Henry Allen, 669-6189
Hula: Kumu, 553-8348, Tommy and Noa Akima, 242-2927,
      Nina Maxwell, 572-8038
Leis: Gordean Bailey, 878-3828
Carving: Sam Kaai, 572-0076
Hawaiian language: Kiope Raymond, 878-3564
Lauhala weaving: Pohaku Kaho'ohanohano, 572-5626

LANAI

Heart of Lanai Gallery, 565-6678
International Food & Clothing, 565-6433
Petroglyphs of the Square, 565-6587
Richard's, 565-6047

MOLOKAI

Big Wind Kite Factory, 552-2364
Kamakana Fine Arts, 553-8520

HAWAIIAN GLOSSARY

The Hawaiian language was first written by missionaries in the 1820s, who transcribed phonetically. *Hawaiian Grammar*, which is now out of print, was published by Lorrin Andrews in 1854. Only 12 letters were needed—A, E, I, O, U, plus the consonants, H, K, L, M, N, P, and W. Note that there is no B. and S. in Hawaiian.

Hawaiian can be thought of as a dialect of the Polynesian language; others include Samoan, Tahitian, Marquesan, and Maori. The original home of the Polynesians was India, and after a long period of migrations they reached the South Pacific, as their language transformed with their travels. Today, an increasing number of schools in Hawaii are centered around teaching the language, as well as the crafts, dance, and legends. Vowels may follow each other, but consonants stand alone. A "W" is sometimes pronounced as a "V," when in the middle of a word. Words always end in a vowel. The funny apostrophe (ʻ) between some vowels is called an okina. It creates a glottal stop in the word; for instance, in "ahupuaʻa," the ending is pronounced "ah-ah." Among all words, stress is usually placed on the second to the last syllable, unless the word only has two syllables, in which case the last is stressed.

SELECTED WORDS

aʻa – sharp, broken lava

ahupuaʻa – a division of land around
    which a village lived; watershed

aina – land, country

ahi - fire

akaaka – to laugh

akua – God, deity

ale – an ocean wave

aliʻi – chief or chiefess descended from
    original chiefs or nobles

aloha – hello or goodbye, welcome or
    farewell, love and best wishes

aumakua – a class of ancient gods;

hale – house

haleakala – house of the sun

hana – work

haole – foreigner, sometimes Caucasian

hau – breeze, dew; a king of tree

heiau – temple, church, worship ground

hoaloha – a friend

hoku – a star

holua – a sled, or sliding place

honi – to touch, taste, kiss

honu – a turtle

hoʻokipa – to entertain, to lodge

huhu – angry, offended

hui – group, meeting

hukilau – group net fishing

hula – dance that enacts the stories
    that become myths

Iao needle – Jupiter appearing as the
    moving star

ike – to see, know

iki – small, little

imu – pit or oven used for roasting

ipo – sweetheart, darling

kaʻa – cart or car

kaʻanapali – rolling precipice

kahului – gathering together

kahuna – teacher, expert, priest

kai – the sea

kamaʻaina – native born, or
    longtime   resident

kamaole - childless

kanaka – the people

Na Ala Hele — trails for walking

kane – man
kapalua – two borders
kapu – forbidden, no trespassing
kaupo – night landing
keanae – the mullet
keawakapu – the sacred harbor
keiki – child, or young banana plant
kihei – a man's garment, cloak
kipahulu – sojourn at forest fringe
kokua – help
kopa'a – sugar
kukui – a type of tree; lamp or torch
kula – country, field
lahaina – cruel sun
lanai – deck, porch, patio
laulau – fish, pork, sweet potatoes and
    taro leaves in steamed pouch
lei – garland of flowers, vines, or beads
    worn around the neck
lolo – dumb
lomi lomi – a traditional massage
lono – report or news;
    one of the great gods
luau – feast
mahalo – thank you
mahina – lunar month
makai – toward the sea
makahiki – fall celebration of return of
    peace and fertility; a year
makena - abundance
malama – solar month; light
mana – spiritual power
mauka – toward the mountain, inland
mauna – mountain
Mele Kalikimaka – Merry Christmas
menehune – dwarf person; legendary
    first settlers
moana – ocean
molokini – many ties
moku – island
Na Ala Hele -- "trails for walking"
nalu – surf breaking on the beach
nani – pretty, beautiful

nene – Hawaiian goose
niu - coconut
ohana – family
ohia – mountain apple
oluolu – please
olowalu – many hills
o'ne – sand
opala - rubbish
pahoehoe – smooth, undulating lava
paia - noisy
pali – cliff
paniolo – Hawaiian cowboy
pele – the goddess of volcanoes
peleleu – a large, double canoe
poi – pasty food made from taro
pono – good, blessed;
    in balance with nature
puka – a hole
pu'u – hill or cinder cone
pupu – snack or hors d'oeuvres
tutu – grandmother
ula - red
ulu – the breadfruit tree
ulupalakua – ripe breadfruit ridge
wahine – woman
waianapanapa – glistening water
wai – fresh water
waihe'e – slippery water
wailea – water of lea,
    goddess of canoe makers
wailuku – water of breaking waves
wiki – fast, quickly

Index

FOR PUBLISHER-DIRECT SAVINGS TO INDIVIDUALS AND GROUPS,
AND FOR BOOK-TRADE ORDERS, PLEASE CONTACT:

DIAMOND VALLEY COMPANY

89 LOWER MANZANITA DRIVE, MARKLEEVILLE, CA 96120

Phone-fax 530-694-2740
www.trailblazertravelbooks.com
wwwtrailblazerhawaii.com
e-mail: trailblazertravelbooks@gmail.com

All titles are also available at bookstores and websites, as well as in e-Book form
Please contact the publisher with comments, corrections, and suggestions.

Diamond Valley Company's
TRAILBLAZER TRAVEL BOOK SERIES

ALPINE SIERRA TRAILBLAZER
Where to Hike, Ski, Bike, Fish, Drive
From Tahoe to Yosemite
ISBN 0-9786371-0-0
ISBN 978-0-9786371-0-1
"A must-have guide. The best and most attractive guidebook for the Sierra. With you every step of the way."—Tahoe Action

GOLDEN GATE TRAILBLAZER
Where to Hike, Walk, Bike
In San Francisco and Marin
ISBN e-Book 978-0-9829919-7-8
ISBN 978-0-9670072-7-4
"Makes you want to strap on your boots and go!"—Sunset Magazine

KAUAI TRAILBLAZER
Where to Hike, Snorkel, Bike, Paddle, Surf
ISBN e-Book 978-0-9829918-0-9
ISBN 978-0-9786371-4-9
"Number one, world-wide among adventure guides."—Barnesandnoble.com

MAUI TRAILBLAZER
Where to Hike, Snorkel, Surf, Drive
ISBN e-Book 978-0-9829919-2-3
ISBN 978-0-9670072-4-3
"The best of them all."—Maui Weekly

HAWAII THE BIG ISLAND TRAILBLAZER
Where to Hike, Snorkel, Surf, Bike, Drive
ISBN e-Book 978-0-09829919-3-0
ISBN 978-0-9670072-5-0
"Top three world-wide among adventure guides."—Barnesandnoble.com

OAHU TRAILBLAZER
Where to Hike, Snorkel, Surf
From Honolulu to the North Shore
ISBN e-Book 978-9829919-1-6
ISBN 978-0-9786371-2-5
"Marvelously flexible. A well-marked trail of tropical adventures."
—San Francisco Chronicle

NO WORRIES HAWAII
A Vactation Planning Guide for
Kauai, Oahu, Maui, and the Big Island
ISBN e-Book 978-0-9829919-4-7
ISBN 978-0-9670072-9-8
"Really a travel planning guide without peer."
—Guide to Travel Guides

NO WORRIES PARIS
A Photographic Walking Guide
ISBN e-Book 978-0-9829919-5-4
ISBN 978-0-9786371-5-6

"Trailblazers are deserving of ongoing praise. You are guaranteed a unique experience that is high quality and perfect for independent travelers."—Midwest Book Review

"Trailblazers are the essential books to pack when planning a trip to Hawaii."—About.com

"Long story told short—there are no guidebooks for Hawaii that begin to compare to the Trailblazer books."—Maui Weekly

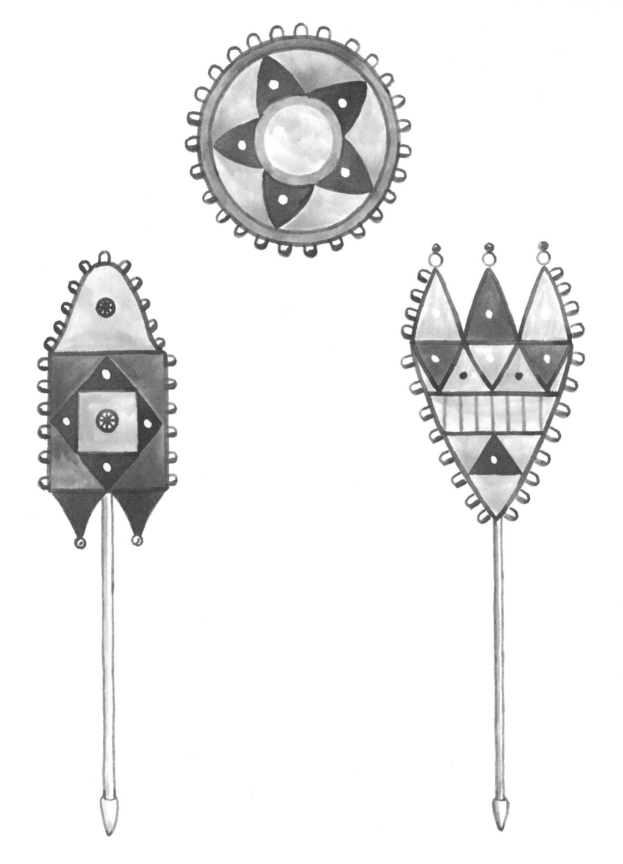

index

acknowledgments

The author would like to thank all those who made the writing of this book possible: Gabi Tubbs for her vision, Jane O'Shea for her warm support and guidance, Vanessa Courtier for her sense of style, Kate Simunek for her delightful illustrations, Linda Burgess for her inspired photography, Sarah Widdicombe and Patsy North for their sensitive and meticulous editing, and Kathy Seely for her unfailing help.

Particular thanks to the needlewomen in my family: Rosemary Bennett, Elsa Wheatcroft and Elizabeth Hook who inspired and taught me the pleasure of making and stitching; to my two small daughters, Hester and Beatrix, for their enthusiasm and to my husband Rob, for his encouragement.

The author and publisher would like to thank the textile artists who designed and made the projects and without whom the book would have remained unwritten: Marie Wahed (Bags of Style), Helen Ashworth (Crib Quilt and Summer, Winter Bedspread), Diana Mott-Thornton (Pleated & Pressed Pillows and Evening Wrap), Karen Howse (Decorated Box), Rosalind Brown (Silk Lampshade), Helen Banzhaf (Book Cover), Claire Sowden (Button Collection), Linda Miller (Lying on a Rug), Sarah Denison (Pieced Tablecloth), Janice Gilmore (Pins with Panache), Louise Brownlow (Dancing Doll), and Kate Peacock (Table Settings).

Special thanks to Judy Barry, Senior Lecturer, Embroidery Course, Department of Textiles and Fashion, Manchester Metropolitan University and Course Tutor, Department of Textiles and Fashion, Royal College of Art, for her invaluable advice and technical expertise. Many thanks to Madeira for their help and selection of threads.

The publisher thanks Ian Muggeridge for D.T.P. assistance, and Sally Harding for her invaluable editorial assistance.

112